To Xa

from Xol-

Chustmas. 1943

THE STORY OF
TWENTIETH-CENTURY
EXPLORATION

HEAVY GOING AMONG GREENLAND'S ICY MOUNTAINS
By courtesy of Martin Lindsay, Esq.

Fr.

THE STORY OF
TWENTIETH-CENTURY
EXPLORATION

BY

CHARLES E. KEY F.R.G.S.

With Sixteen Half-tone Illustrations
and Twelve Maps

GEORGE G. HARRAP & CO. LTD.
LONDON   TORONTO   BOMBAY   SYDNEY

First published July 1937
by GEORGE G. HARRAP & CO. LTD.
182 *High Holborn, London, W.C.*1

Reprinted May 1939

MADE IN GREAT BRITAIN. PRINTED AT THE PITMAN PRESS, BATH

PREFACE

Whither, O splendid ship, thy white sails crowding,
Leaning across the bosom of the urgent West,
That fearest nor sea rising, nor sky clouding,
Whither away, fair rover, and what thy quest?

ROBERT BRIDGES

THE lure of the unexplored has a universal magnetic attraction. Over the brow of the hill the imaginative traveller always hopes for a vision of delight, for the crock of gold at the rainbow's end. The Kirghiz believe that on the top of the 'Father of the Ice-mountains' (Mustaghata) is a mysterious city called Yanaidar. Here is an entrancing Garden of Eden, where death, cold, darkness, old age, and ugliness are unknown. Such delights, however, are not for ordinary mortals. The way is barred by fearsome chasms and blinding ice-fields. The Bedouin of the Sahara tell tales of the Oasis of the Sirens—a Jack-o'-lantern pleasance, which lures the wanderer into the sands and then vanishes. In other days men sought the Golden Fleece, the Gardens of the Hesperides, the Mountains of the Moon, or the Lost Atlantis. Now men seek coal-mines in the Arctic or try to reach the North Pole by submarine. Some, with vaunting ambition, delve down to the fathomless depths of the ocean, or soar into the stratosphere and dream of the day when excursions to the moon or into stellar space will be practicable. The lure of the unexplored will be as potent a thousand years from now as it was when old Pytheas set off from Massilia to discover Britain for the Greeks.

The twentieth century has been a great epoch in the story of exploration. Many journeys have been accomplished which, not so long ago, were thought to be impossible. The story is not finished yet. It may be strange, but it is true, that we have better maps of some parts of the moon than we have of certain 'blank' portions of the Polar regions. There are at the present time as many expeditions to the unknown lands as there have ever been.

5

This book is not intended for the student who requires detailed information. It does not even tell the whole story of what has been discovered during the present century—to do that would require many volumes. The maps are merely sketch-maps intended to enlighten and help the general reader who has little detailed knowledge of the uttermost regions of the earth. The book does pretend, however, to give a general account of what, in the opinion of the author, are the most important or significant expeditions of the century. Exigencies of space and the necessity for selection in a wide field can alone excuse the omission of the work achieved by Rasmussen, Dainelli, Skrine, Wegener, Long-staff, and some of the recent explorers of Arabia, the Sahara, Ellesmere Land, and so on.

The compilation of the book has involved reference to many volumes, articles, and maps, and I must express my thanks to the librarian of the Royal Geographical Society for his much valued assistance.

I am also indebted to Messrs John Murray for permission to quote extracts from Captain Scott's *Diary*, and to the following for the information or illustrations they have supplied:

P. A. Clayton, Esq., Colonel P. T. Etherton, Miss Rosita Forbes, Dr G. Noel Humphreys, Martin Lindsay, Esq., The Mount Everest Committee, J. M. Scott, Esq., and F. S. Smythe, Esq.

CONTENTS

CHAPTER   PAGE

I. EXPLORING THE AMAZON   13

The mystery of Colonel Fawcett—The search for Colonel Fawcett—The River of Doubt—Hamilton Rice in snake-infested forests.

II. THROUGH THE WASTES OF ASIA AND TIBET   42

The adventures of Sven Hedin—Aurel Stein and the ruins of desert Cathay—Rawling on the Great Plateau—The Gartok expedition—Freya Stark in the wilds of Persia—In search of Ophir—Philby in Arabia.

III. THE CONQUEST OF THE NORTH POLE   84

Peary's journey to the Pole—The Amundsen-Ellsworth expedition—The adventures of Nobile and Amundsen—Byrd's flight to the Pole—The Papanin Expedition.

IV. AMONG THE HEAD-HUNTERS OF NEW GUINEA   103

The adventures of Staniforth Smith—Captain Rawling discovers the pigmies—The cannibals of the Central Highlands.

V. ACROSS THE HEART OF AUSTRALIA   122

The recent explorations of Michael Terry.

VI. THE HOME OF THE BLIZZARD   128

Scott's first expedition—The discovery of the Magnetic Pole—Mawson in the Antarctic—Jean Charcot and the *Pourquoi Pas?* The Voyage of the *Endurance*.

VII. THE ROOF OF THE WORLD   152

The conquest of Mount Kamet—The story of Nanda Devi.

VIII. NEW LIGHT ON THE DARK CONTINENT   170

The mountains of the moon—Rosita Forbes and the secret of the Sahara—The adventures of Hassanein Bey—In search of Zerzura.

IX. THE CONQUEST OF THE SOUTH POLE   192

Amundsen's journey to the Pole—The tragedy of Captain Scott—Admiral Byrd and the 'Little America' expedition—Lincoln Ellsworth's trans-Antarctic flight.

X. GREENLAND'S ICY MOUNTAINS   220

Marooned on the ice-cap—Amundsen in the north-east passage—The story of Gino Watkins.

CHAPTER   PAGE
XI. ADVENTURES IN NORTHERNMOST AMERICA   238
Wilkins's Arctic flights—The conquest of the north-west passage
—Stefansson's Arctic explorations.

XII. THE SUMMIT OF THE EARTH   263
The early Everest expeditions—The Everest flight—The 1936
expedition.

INDEX   281

ILLUSTRATIONS

Heavy Going among Greenland's Icy Mountains
Frontispiece

	PAGE
Nomad Family of Western Tibet	58
Lhatse Fort and Monastery	64
Tapiro Pigmies	112
Charcot's Polar Ship, the "Pourquoi Pas?"	138
The "Endurance" crushed by Ice	142
On the Summit of Mount Kamet	154
Air-photograph of Mount Stanley, Ruwenzori	174
Rosita Forbes Asleep on a Camel	178
The "Terra Nova" Ice-bound	200
At the South Pole	204
Little America	216
Watkins hunting in his Kayak	234
Stefansson repairing a Broken Sled	256
Ice-pinnacles on Rongbuk Glacier	264
Approaching Everest and Makalu from the South	274

MAPS

PAGE

MODERN EXPLORATIONS IN THE AMAZON BASIN   39

THE HEART OF ASIA, SHOWING THE REGIONS EXPLORED
BY HEDIN AND STEIN   43

RECENT JOURNEYS ACROSS THE ARABIAN DESERTS   81

THE CONQUEST OF THE NORTH POLE AND RECENT
JOURNEYS IN GREENLAND   99

THE MODERN MAP OF NEW GUINEA   120

SHACKLETON'S EXPEDITION, 1914–1917   149

THE APPROACHES TO NANDA DEVI   157

JOURNEYS IN SEARCH OF THE SECRETS OF THE SAHARA   187

THE CONQUEST OF THE SOUTH POLE   211

SOUTH GREENLAND, SHOWING THE JOURNEYS OF WATKINS,
SCOTT, AND LINDSAY   236

THE EXPLORATORY JOURNEYS OF STEFANSSON, 1914–1918   261

SKETCH-PLAN SHOWING THE ROUTE FOLLOWED BY THE
EVEREST EXPEDITIONS OF 1924 AND 1933   279

CHAPTER I

EXPLORING THE AMAZON

The perplex'd paths of this drear wood,
The nodding horror of whose shady brows
Threats the forlorn and wand'ring passenger.

MILTON

THE MYSTERY OF COLONEL FAWCETT

FEW legends about the unknown parts of the earth have enjoyed such longevity as the myth of El Dorado. Ever since the time of Pizarro the forests to the east of the Andes have been a favourite hunting-ground for the 'City of Gold,' or, as it was called, the 'Grand Paititi.' Some hundreds of the Spanish Conquistadores threw away their lives in the quest, and it is recorded that in the sixteenth century a certain priest called Chavez actually visited the city and gazed in wonder on its treasuries of gold, silver, and amber. It was this gilded will-o'-the-wisp which lured Colonel Fawcett to his fate. Fawcett knew that in the region called the Caupolican there are areas of thousands of square miles into which no white man has ever entered. Most of the main rivers have been explored, but nothing is known of the country a hundred yards away from the banks.

Fawcett was a man of great courage and imagination, and the possibility that somewhere in the Amazon basin there existed a 'lost world' or a forgotten race of white Indians attracted him again and again into the heart of the matted forests and pestiferous swamps. He had heard strange tales. Colonel Rondon had found beautifully carved stones and polished jade frogs where no jade is known to exist, intricately worked charms far beyond the artistic capabilities of the untutored Indians, and strange rock-carvings, some of which, representing the Sun-god, were over six feet high and graved to a depth of more than an inch.

Exploration to the east of the Andes has been rendered especially dangerous owing to the hostility of the natives.

13

On the fringes of civilization they have been sacrificed to the God of Rubber, their villages have been burnt, and their plantations destroyed. The result has been a war of stealthy reprisals. When a savage meets a white man on the great green plateau, his first impulse is to transfix him with one of his terrible seven-foot arrows. Starvation is the second serious danger which threatens the explorer, for game is nowhere plentiful. The myriads of rivers, swamps, and lagoons are haunted by that monster of the night, the anaconda. Poisonous snakes are as common as rats in a disused warehouse. Then, too, there are legions of noisome insects: piums, which attack in thousands and cover the victim with tiny blood-blisters; mosquitoes so small that they will penetrate any net; moths and flies that lay their eggs under the skin, which becomes infested with maggots; jiggers, which penetrate beneath the toe-nails; and ticks, which burrow and die under the skin. But worst of all are the ants. One virulent species inhabits the *palos santos*, or sacred trees, and the natives sometimes bind their captives to these trees and leave them to a horrid death. Near the Abuna river there are complete groves of sacred trees which are impassable by man or beast. Another kind of tree, found on the higher ground, exudes a poisonous liquor which causes painful swellings. One of Fawcett's Indians suffered in this way.

Fawcett was engaged for some years in helping to determine the boundaries of Bolivia, Peru, and Brazil. Everywhere he heard tales of a strange people—the remnants of the civilized Incas. When he visited the Royal Geographical Society in 1910 he said:

> There have been rumours in the interior of South America of the existence of a strange tribe. The evidence is necessarily weak. Yet I have met half a dozen men who swear to a glimpse of white Indians with red hair. Such communication as there has been in certain parts with the wild Indians asserts the existence of such a race with blue eyes. Plenty of people have heard of them in the interior. They even have a name—the Morcegos, or bats—the people who travel and hunt by night and hide by day. Some of my informants I have known well, and I believe there may be some foundation for the story. . . .

There may be many curious things hidden in the forests of the Amazon basin. There are rumours of old ruins and strange animals—of tracks huge and unrecognized. Fables gather, of course, around unexplored places, but we must not forget that the African pigmy and the okapi were for long discredited.[1]

In 1906, as a result of a revolution, a new frontier-line had to be arranged between Bolivia and Brazil. The geographical details of the proposed frontier were very imperfectly known, and it was in connexion with the work of delimitation that Fawcett went to the frontier of Bolivia in 1906. On the Abuna river, which has the reputation of being the most unhealthy in the Amazonas, Fawcett killed a large anaconda. These huge water-snakes normally hunt at night-time and have a characteristic odour which betrays their horrid presence. This particular specimen was coiled round a trunk with its tail in the water. Fawcett said that it measured forty-eight feet out of the water, and he estimated that there were another seventeen feet immersed. The serpent was so big that it was useless to attempt to carry it away or even to skin it. Moreover, the native porters were anxious to leave the vicinity because they believed that the anaconda's mate would seek vengeance. A little later Fawcett was told that near Corumba a snake which measured no less than eighty-five feet had been killed.

Fawcett's work for the Boundary Commission took him to the little-known Rio Verde. He took with him two Indians, an Argentine waiter, a silversmith from Paraguay, and a Spanish baker—a motley crowd, but the only *peons* he could find who would dare to accompany him into the wilds. The object of the expedition was to ascend the stream to its source, and they hoped to be able to sail a long way. But on the second day they had to abandon their small boats owing to the constant rapids. By the end of the next day the *peons* were so exhausted with the arduous scrambling that all the food-supplies had to be dumped, and they pushed on through dense undergrowth carrying hammocks, rifles, and equipment on their backs.

Fawcett had reckoned on a plentiful supply of fish, but

[1] *Geographical Journal*, Vol. xxxv, May, 1910.

before long the water became bitter and strongly impreg-
nated with iron. Now there were few fish and no game.
The next three weeks were a nightmare. For food they
depended largely on palm-tops. They were eaten alive
by insects, drenched by violent storms, and scratched and
torn as they crawled half a mile a day through dense cane
and thorny undergrowth. The perpetual damp rotted their
boots. When at length open country near the source of the
river was reached, Fawcett abandoned the idea of returning
by the same route, and decided to strike across country to
the town of Matto Grosso.

Although there were now fewer trees, their difficulties
were not ended. Palms were scarce, and they had to rely
for food on hard, tasteless nuts called *chunta*. The whole
party grew deaf for want of food, and the *peons*, praying for
death, had to be beaten to make them continue. Although
the plateau had seemed level, there were sudden deep gorges
to be circumvented, and beneath the coarse, matted grass
were innumerable jagged boulders. One assistant was badly
bitten by a tucandera, which is a very poisonous black ant
about an inch long.

When it seemed probable that they were doomed to die
of starvation, Fawcett was lucky enough to shoot a deer—
the only animal they had seen in the hills. A few days later,
when the party had reached a forest, three black monkeys
walked into camp. Within ten minutes the *peons* had de-
voured them, fur and all. They also found some honey,
which made some of them drunk while others had convul-
sions. After a week of hacking through the forest, the
emaciated party stumbled into Matto Grosso and promptly
made themselves sick on coarse sugar, for which they had
developed an extraordinary craving. The course of the Rio
Verde had been mapped, but it cost the lives of five of the
peons, who died soon afterwards.

In June, 1910, Fawcett began his explorations in the
Caupolican region, through which runs the border-line of
Peru and Bolivia. The entire country is peopled by savages,
the warlike Guarayos being especially hostile. It had been
agreed that a tributary called the Heath should be part of

the frontier, but this stream had never been explored farther than a few miles above its junction with the Madre de Dios. Bodies of Peruvian soldiers numbering as many as a hundred had previously attempted this Herculean labour, but more often than not only a handful had returned; the Guarayos have a nasty habit of poisoning water-supplies and picking off stragglers one by one.

On this occasion Fawcett was accompanied by three English soldiers who had served with him in the artillery, a doctor, and two other white men. They left La Paz in June, crossed Lake Titicaca, and then followed the Inca Mining-company's road across the Cordilleras. At first Fawcett thought it would be possible to cut across country from a place called Astillero to the river Heath and set off with eight well-loaded mules. At the same time he arranged for a depôt to be set up at the mouth of the Heath. But his mules stuck fast in treacherous bogs, and after ten days of tree-cutting the party had advanced only fifteen miles. As supplies were running short, Fawcett returned to Astillero, abandoned his mules, and set off for the mouth of the Heath by boat.

From this point he started with three small canoes and plenty of provisions. Progress was rapid at first, for the Heath soon developed into a broad though tortuous river. There were occasional rapids and concealed snags, but the men poled the canoes steadily along beneath the shade of the thickly forested banks.

Then with dramatic suddenness they came face to face with death. As they were rounding a turn in the river, Fawcett and his companions saw a native village of newly made palm-huts. It occupied a strategic position on a jutting sand-bank where the river narrowed. They heard an uproar of barking dogs and yelling savages and saw that beneath a red earth cliff on the opposite bank fifteen large canoes were beached. Fawcett landed beside them, and the savages had disappeared as if by magic; but this was only the calm before the storm. As the second canoe came to the mooring-place, an arrow pierced its side. This was the signal for a regular fusillade, but by a miracle none of the explorers was hit.

Probably the whole expedition was saved because Fawcett had given explicit instructions that there was to be no firing unless as a last resource. Todd, one of the ex-soldiers, struck up a tune on the accordion, putting his faith apparently in the old maxim that "music hath charms to soothe the savage breast." For some time, however, the shower of missiles continued, and the sand-bank began to look like a young plantation of six-foot arrows. These weapons had long barbed points of heavy wood and shafts of light cane in which the feathers were set spirally.

After about an hour of long-range bombardment, a party of savages began to collect in the rear of the explorers. Fawcett now made a bold move. Armed only with a small book which contained a brief vocabulary of Guarayo words, he advanced to the river's edge and addressed a few guttural words to the unseen attackers. At last two natives showed themselves and indicated by signs that they wished Fawcett to take one of the canoes and come across the river. Accompanied by one of his men, Fawcett launched a dug-out and poled it across. On the farther bank they were met by thirty savages, who took them to their chief. Fawcett presented his hat to the chief's son and, thanks to the few Guarayo words which he could command, managed to get on friendly terms. Two of the Indians came across to the sand-bank, collected their arrows, and not only assisted in making a camp, but also brought presents of bananas, fish-necklaces, and parrots.

On the following morning Fawcett went with some of the savages to a lagoon in the forest. Here he was amazed to see a number of fish of all kinds floating about on the surface, alive but quite incapable of moving. They had been para-lysed by the juice of the manuna-tree—a milky fluid which is poured on the surface of the ponds. Sometimes this same juice is used for the purpose of suicide, since many of the old men and women are driven to this desperate act from the constant shortage of food-supplies.

The encounter with the Guarayos had one other fortunate result. Messages were sent up-river, and the explorers were not molested again, although as they journeyed along the river they frequently saw plantations and other signs of native populations. After days of hauling heavy canoes through rapids, they entered hilly country covered with rank vegetation and rotten, moss-bearded trees, where they met a tribe called the Chunchos. The men-folk wore shirts of bark, and the women nothing. At first these Indians were hostile, but they became friendly after receiving liberal presents of knives and sugar. Above this point the Heath became a series of torrential streams which hurled themselves through rugged gorges. The party now had to carry every-thing on their backs and clamber over slippery boulders or along ledges of greasy slate. On the banks the undergrowth was so thick that they dared not leave the river-bed. Here there were no fish and no game, and apart from the usual insect-pests, constant rains made fire-making an impossi-bility, and four of the men were bitten by vampire-bats on the same night.

The weird stories about the vampire-bat have aroused a good deal of incredulity, but Fawcett gives the following account of its habits:

> The soft whirring of its wings over the head prior to biting has a curiously soporific effect. One feels absolutely nothing. I awoke one morning to find the upper end of my hammock saturated with blood. There are no recognizable ill-effects, but in some parts of the civilized Caupolican it is impossible to keep cattle, and in the upper Tambopata the Indian rubber-pickers suffer from a species of anaemia attributed to the repeated attacks of this pest.[1]

Finally the source of the Heath was located, and Fawcett made his way across country back to La Paz.

Owing to the intervention of the Great War, Fawcett was unable to return to his quest until 1920. The expedition of that year failed owing to the breakdown of his com-panions, but he remained convinced that he would one day succeed. "There are strange beasts," he wrote, "and weird insects for the naturalist, and reason, at any rate, for not condemning as a myth the existence of the mysterious white

---

[1] *Geographical Journal*, vol. xxxvii, p. 377.

Indian. There are rumours of forest-pigmies and old ruins. Nearer civilization there are lost mines."

In 1924 he left England again—this time with the financial assistance of the Royal Geographical Society. In March, 1925, accompanied by his son, Jack, and another Englishman, Raleigh Rimell, he arrived at a place called Cuyaba. From this stepping-off point he reported:

> All our equipment is here undamaged, and the instruments are in good order. I do not think it is at all probable that we can get any information back from in or beyond the region of these primitive people (who have the unpleasant habit of carrying their victims threaded on bamboos or slung to them by the tendons of arms and feet, feeding on them in a state of decomposition) but I shall attempt to get it out through the agency of Indians, if I can. . . . Science will, I hope, be greatly benefited, geography can scarcely fail to gain a good deal, and I am confident that we shall find the key to much lost history.

They left Cuyaba on April 20 and reached Bakairi Post in the state of Matto Grosso on May 15. Rimell was suffering from a poisoned foot. On May 20 Colonel Fawcett sent a report from Dead-horse Camp to the North American Newspaper Alliance:

> From Fort Bakairi, whence I sent my previous dispatches, our journey has been no bed of roses. We have cut our way through miles of *cerraba*, a forest of low, dry scrub; we have crossed innumerable small streams by swimming and fording; we have climbed rocky hills of forbidding aspect; we have been eaten by bugs. . . . Our two guides go back from here. They are more and more nervous as we push further into the Indian country.

Fawcett was now near the head-waters of the Xingu, and he proposed to strike eastward. A year passed by; the little party had disappeared into the blue, and no reports came in. This gave rise to no anxiety, however, because they had said that they might spend two years in the forests if they found anything of importance. Two years passed; still there was no news. It was now feared that some evil had befallen them. The Royal Geographical Society offered to help any volunteer who would endeavour to obtain news of Colonel Fawcett.

All kinds of rumours began to circulate. A certain Mr Courteville reported that he had met an old man on the Cuyaba road who might be Fawcett. The story was embellished, and it was asserted that not only had the search for the fabled city failed, but that the explorer had settled down as a farmer. The story on investigation proved to be full of inconsistencies. Eventually, in 1928, Commander Dyott, who had already travelled far and wide in the Amazon basin, raised a relief-expedition. He was accompanied by two wireless-experts and two photographers, and he proposed to maintain contact by means of wireless.

THE SEARCH FOR COLONEL FAWCETT

In May Dyott's party left Cuyaba in motor-trucks for the rim of the highlands, about twenty-eight miles away. Before long they had to transfer their stores from cars to mules and bullocks, and so they tramped on, assisted by eight *camaradas*. Four days' rough journey brought them to the Bakairi of Fawcett's report. It was merely a few ramshackle huts enclosed with barbed-wire fences to keep out Indians. Here they took on additional supplies of rice and *farinha* (dried grain) and also engaged five Bakari Indians as guides. Owing to the shortage of pasture—it was the dry season—they had to move in four sections.

By a stroke of good luck they chanced to fall in with a Bakari Indian, called Bernadino, who had been one of Fawcett's guides. Bernadino led the way across country towards the Kuluseu, one of the head-waters of the Xingu. Apparently after leaving Dead-horse Camp, Fawcett had sailed down this stream with two canoes. The country here was open, hard, and rocky, with belts of forest along the sides of the larger streams. For some hundreds of miles the only inhabitants were hostile Indians. Here and there the search-party found signs that the trail had been blazed, and eventually they had no difficulty in locating Dead-horse Camp.

Dyott was now faced with an arduous passage across the

21

great Central Plateau of Brazil. In many places he saw isolated sheer-sided hills such as those described in the 'lost world' legend. He saw escarpments crowned by eminences worn by wind and rain into peculiar shapes which at a distance might be mistaken for houses, towers, or even ruined cities. He also noticed that the slanting rays of the sun reflected from some of the polished rocks might well have given rise to the stories of flashing lights seen in the windows of ancient stone buildings.

Six days after leaving Bakairi they reached the banks of the Kuluseu. According to Bernadino, Fawcett had embarked his party on two canoes and had sailed downstream to the *malocas* of the Anauqua Indians. A *maloca* is a kind of communal hut, and sometimes a whole village with some hundreds of inhabitants contains only a few *malocas*. Dyott launched his canvas canoes and for the next four weeks fought his way downstream, covering a distance of sixty miles as the crow flies. This slow progress was mainly due to the fact that the Kuluseu twisted and turned like a writhing snake, and also because constant watch had to be kept lest the canvas boats should be ripped open on the innumerable sprags and submerged logs. On some of the bends there were intricate tangles of sticks, which bristled like hedgehogs, and elsewhere huge trees had fallen astride the stream, forming a barricade of branches and roots which had to be hacked away before they could advance. There were comparatively free patches, but they were short, and they inevitably heralded a series of rapids with ugly rows of jagged black rocks. Once they found a camping-ground and saw a 'Y' cut on a tree. This sign, according to Bernadino, indicated one of Fawcett's camping-grounds.

Soon afterwards they reached the land of the Anauquas and encountered the Indians. The savages were completely naked. The men carried bows five or six feet long, and all of them began to hang about the camp, peering into boxes, fingering the materials of the white men's clothes, and asking by unmistakable gestures to be given garments. Dyott soon ascertained that Fawcett had spent three nights at this spot. He had camped in a small clearing, and one of the Y-shaped

22

stakes used for holding a cooking-pot over a camp-fire still remained in position. Thence Fawcett had travelled to the *malocas* of this very tribe. Dyott decided to do likewise. He was accompanied by two white companions and about twenty Indians, and after two hours' walk through the jungle, reached a group of huts built round a clearing. The roofs of the *malocas* were thatched with palm-leaves, and they extended so low that they almost touched the ground. Each hut had two doors, one of which opened on to the clearing, and the other led to the jungle outside.

Aloique, the chief of the Indians, lived at the far end of the village. He was a short, stocky fellow with coarse black hair cut short like a mop and small, shifty eyes. At his command a large palm-leaf mat was unrolled in the centre of the clearing, and a palaver began. One of Dyott's Indians could speak a few words of the Anauqua language, but the explorer found that he could manage quite well by using signs. In the midst of the performance Aloique's wife squirmed her way into the group. She was carrying her infant son, and about his neck hung several ornaments. At the end of one string dangled a small oval brass plate, bearing the inscription: "W. S. Silver and Company, King William House, Eastcheap, London." Here indeed was a clue! Messrs Silver and Company had supplied Fawcett with ten air-tight cases which had similar metal plates attached to them. A few minutes later Dyott stumbled upon another clue, this time in the chief's *maloca*. It was a small metal trunk.

Dyott realized that he must proceed warily. He learned that Aloique and five other Indians had accompanied Fawcett for a day's march east of the Kuluene river carrying stores. Dyott asked if the same men would take him to this place. There was a general refusal. Each man repeated the word "Suyá" and hit the back of his head with the edge of his flattened palm to indicate that in the region beyond the Kuluene lived the warlike Suyás, who have a habit of approaching strangers under the cloak of friendliness and then at the first opportunity hitting them over the backs of their heads.

23

It was now time to be returning to the camp on the river, and Dyott requested Aloique and a few other Indians to come with him and discuss the matter further. To his surprise the whole tribe followed at his heels, foisting handfuls of dusty *farinha* on him, with the hope that counter-presents of knives and so on might be forthcoming. In order to avoid these unwelcome attentions, Dyott ordered the main body to sail down the Kuluseu to the point where it joins the Kuluene. There they were to establish a base-camp while Dyott continued his investigations among the Anauquas.

This rearrangement involved the opening of several boxes, and the curiosity and covetousness of the savages were fully aroused. Dyott spent that night lying full length, grasping a rifle, a revolver, two *machetes*, fourteen knives, and an assortment of hardware, and pretending to sleep. The Indians not only refused to go away, but during the night they made more than one effort at stealthy burglary. When dawn came, the *camaradas* loaded up the stores in the canoes and left for the base-camp, leaving Dyott and two companions with the Indians. Dyott returned to the village with Aloique, and that evening he was treated to a ceremonial dance and was promised that on the next day some men would accompany the *caraiba* (white man) to the Kuluene river. Aloique now informed the explorer that the tin box had been given to him by Fawcett. As far as Dyott could interpret his signs, Aloique said that he and another Indian had accompanied Fawcett for one day's march east of the Kuluene, and that from there on the *caraibas* had advanced alone. One of the white men was limping. Aloique ended his pantomimic recital by indicating that Fawcett had died of thirst in the dry *pique* area beyond.

When Dyott asked Aloique if he would take him to this last camp the Indian scowled evilly and said, "Suyás, Suyás, bad people, no good." At this point the conversation was interrupted, and the ceremonial dance began. Two Indians dressed in feather ornaments suddenly appeared at the door of the *maloca* and began to make weird noises on large wooden horns, waving the instruments up and down and stamping their feet in unison. This ceremony was repeated

24

in all the huts. Later the men formed into two lines, and the women in two rows at right-angles, and all the dancers began to sway and stamp in time to the music.

Dyott spent that night in a *maloca* where no less than eighty Indians were housed. All of the inmates were related, but each family-group swung their hammocks in one part, and each of these groups had a fire to itself. On the next morning Dyott set off for the Kuluene, accompanied by Aloique and some other Indians. The trail appeared to lead into the heart of a tremendous swamp and ended abruptly on a solitary patch of dry land. Several rickety canoes were produced as if by magic, and on they went, threading the narrow channels of deep water. Twenty minutes later they reached dry ground again, but after two hours further marching they were once again in a swamp. Canoes were conjured up out of the tall grass, and they paddled off down a labyrinth of narrow channels above which waved the delicate fronds of palm-trees. Suddenly the narrow channel opened out into a vast lake. On they sailed for an hour and a half, and then they reached a belt of dense forest beyond which lay a swampy plain.

Here, in an open space, where there were the remains of several *malocas*, Aloique pointed out another camping-site. Dyott searched round and found another clue in the shape of a powder-flask. Another day's march through a dry wilderness of withered trees brought them to yet another camp. Soon afterwards they came upon a village of the Kalapalos Indians, where they were well received, although the women were particularly inquisitive and even rolled up Dyott's sleeves to see for themselves whether the skin white extended beyond the hands. Three of the older women went so far as to bring along their unmarried daughters and plainly offered them in marriage. Dyott was now faced with the difficulty of finding some presents for his new hosts, since he had already parted with all his knives and fish-hooks. Fortunately he remembered that he had brought in his pack a quantity of cheap jewellery, and the glittering pins and ear-rings soon put the Kalapalos in such a good humour that they promised to guide him to the Kuluene.

Some of these Indians wore fine ornaments cut out of hard diorite, and one women had a pottery doll suggestive of the ancient Inca arts.

The chief said that the three tall *caraibas* had been killed beyond the Kuluene. "Kalapalos follow," he said. "One day we see smoke from camp-fire. Two day we see smoke from camp-fire. Three day we see smoke. Four day we see smoke. Five day no smoke. *Caraibas* killed by Indians—Anauqua Indians bad people." He also declared that the offending Indians had left a chaplet of black and yellow feathers dangling from a string across the trail—a common warning-sign not to pass beyond for fear of death. This was something of a revelation. Dyott began to suspect that the shifty Aloique knew more about the end of Fawcett than he had admitted, but the Anauqua still insisted on his ignorance. His tales were like the shifting sands; he now declared that the Suyás had killed Fawcett.

On the next day Dyott arrived at the Kuluene and once again noticed the mysterious Y-shaped blaze-marks. On the farther bank, where there was another camp-site, Aloique staged a pantomimic show in which he indicated that the white men had marched five days eastward and then had been clubbed by the Suyás. Dyott, however, was now fully convinced that the Indian was the real culprit and before long was to have further proof of his murderous character.

On the next day Dyott began his journey down the Kuluene, planning to return if he could persuade some Indians to join him on that five days' march eastward. Aloique promised to come if he were given presents of a rifle and a shirt. On the following day the little flotilla (they were accompanied by some of the Kalapalos) encountered a number of canoes of the Wicuru tribe. These newcomers were very hopeful of extracting presents. Dyott gave them a few trifles, but they would not be fobbed off, and joined in the procession. Late in the afternoon, at a place where a neck of land jutted out and narrowed the stream, they came upon the rest of the Wicurus. Dyott noticed that many of the members of this tribe had very light skins.

Beneath ligatures, which they wore on arms and legs, the skin was almost white. They were certainly the nearest approach to white Indians that I have ever seen, and sufficiently light to give rise to some of the extraordinary stories Fawcett related about white Indians in these parts.

Since it was obviously dangerous to tarry in such a dangerous spot, Dyott beckoned to the Wicurus to follow and promised presents when he reached the base-camp. The Anauquas and Kalapalos spurted along, followed by many of the Wicurus who had crowded into their canoes.

So the lengthy flotilla reached the junction of the Kuluseu and the Kuluene. The base-camp had been well chosen on a sandy spit, but it had attracted a rare crowd of 'fortune-hunters.' The sand-bar swarmed with Indians, and *Putzinga* (gifts) was the word on every lip. That evening one of Dyott's Indians, who understood Anauqua, came in with some startling news. He had overheard Aloique plotting with his companions to go with Dyott east of the Kuluene and there kill him and decamp with all his possessions. Dyott proceeded to call his bluff, and announced that his whole party would go with Aloique to Fawcett's last camp. But when the morning came, Aloique and his Anauquas had vanished—probably because they feared that Dyott was about to avenge the death of Fawcett on their own guilty heads.

This new turn of events meant that there was little hope of finding Fawcett's grave. Indeed, it now became clear that any return up-river would be attended with grave perils. The remaining Indians became aggressive. They pushed their way into the enclosure and helped themselves to such things as they could lay hands on. The white men found it necessary to display rifles and revolvers as a deterrent. At midday yet another fleet of highly excited savages arrived. When it became evident that presents were not to be distributed immediately, they began to scowl with anger and impatience.

Dyott saved the situation by calling all the natives together for a pow-wow. He lay down on the sands as if exhausted and closed his eyes. For a few seconds he snored. Then,

opening his eyes again, he pointed to the east, saying "*Iti*"—
which means 'sun.' He then got up briskly, opened a box,
and went through the motions of handing out knives to the
multitude. He repeated his dumb-show until all the Indians
understood that in the morning when the sun rose he would
give them all presents. So the meeting broke up amicably,
and after a good deal of talking, the savages retired to their
hammocks a hundred yards away.

Then came a patient vigil before the zero-hour. At midnight the white men rose, and in absolute silence the canoes
were made ready. An hour's hard work, and the canoes slid
gently into the moonlit waters. They dared not use their
paddles until they had drifted along for half an hour. Then
they dug the blades deep into the water and sped away for
dear life. For fourteen hours they toiled like galley-slaves,
and by that time they were on the Xingu. A week later
they reached the first signs of civilization—a rubber-
gatherer's hut on the lower Xingu. Dyott had failed in his
efforts to find Colonel Fawcett, but he had discovered
enough to show what his probable fate had been. Moreover,
he had done much to shed light on the stories of walled
cities, white Indians, and strange peoples. The Grand
Paititi may well be only a fable, but it is certain that the
Amazon basin still has many secrets to yield to scientists
imbued with the necessary spirit of adventure.

Dyott's discoveries, however, were not the final episode
of this strange, eventful story. During the last few years
several people have come forward with tales of encounters
in Matto Grosso with white men, one of whom might have
been Colonel Fawcett. In 1932 two expeditions went out
to try to solve the problem. Mr Stephen Rattin heard of a
white captive in the hands of Indians along a tributary of
the São Manoel; but in the next year Rattin himself disappeared when seeking to reach this captive. In the same
year Peter Fleming failed in an attempt to reach Fawcett's
last camp.

In July, 1933, a Signor Pessione was told a strange story
on an estate near Cuyaba. An Indian woman stated that
while her son was still at the breast, there arrived at her

village three white men and some Indians descending the Kuluene in a large canoe. Her description of the white men tallied fairly well with the Fawcett party. She said that she had seen them frequently—the last time apparently about a year before. Not only were the white men well, but they had learned to speak the Indian language. The elder man was the chief of the tribe, and the younger man had married a native chief's daughter and had a fair-haired, blue-eyed son. The white men could not escape, because they were surrounded by hostile Suyás, and even the tribe they were with would kill them if they attempted to escape. It was established that the Indian woman had belonged to the Anauqua tribe, and since her son was now about ten years old, her date for the arrival of the white men was about correct.

During the following year (1934) an American missionary made a canoe-trip down the Kuluene and came to a village of the Kuikuru Indians.

His report states:

> Later the old chief brought to us a young boy, who is perhaps the most famous boy in the whole Xingu region. When the above-mentioned Colonel Fawcett and his son entered this region some years ago they lived among the Kuikuru Indians for quite some time, and the son had two children, a boy and a girl, by an Indian woman. The girl died, and it was the boy whom the chief brought to see us. . . . His skin was decidedly white, his hair was light in colour, and his eyes were blue.

This story and the account of the Indian woman certainly seem to show that two white men had lived with the Indians in this district a few years before 1934.

The American missionary also heard of an explorer called Winton Jones who had met some Indians who knew Fawcett Winton Jones ultimately fell into the hands of the Inaurita Indians and sent a message for help to the Brazilian Government. Later it was found that Jones had been deserted by his Indian guides and had then been poisoned by the Kalapalos. The American missionary was told that the unfortunate Jones had recovered and was making his way down the Xingu, but since then no news had been received of him.

The Fawcett mystery has aroused such a great deal of publicity that it is probable that rumours will continue, but it is almost certain that such a long period of silence means that the expedition was annihilated by the Indians.

THE RIVER OF DOUBT

The Amazon is in many ways the most remarkable river in the world. Approximately one-tenth of the flowing waters of the earth meander between its forest-clad banks. Two thousand miles from the mouth the bed is still deep enough to permit ocean-going steamers, and its gigantic basin is in area almost the size of Europe. Here, too, are the most extensive forests, or selvas, in the world, whose riotous luxuriance is only rivalled by the forests of the Congo and Malaysia. Here, in the impenetrable fastnesses, imaginative novelists still conceive Montezuman civilizations and the lost fantastic worlds of the geological past. Even sober naturalists and practical explorers have speculated about the weird possibilities behind those twining green curtains which fringe lagoons choked with masses of lilies and water-hyacinths. Colonel Fawcett fondly believed that he might find a lost race of white natives; Theodore Roosevelt found strange carvings on the rocky banks of the River of Doubt; and Doctor Moreno found in a cave farther south the fresh fragments of skin of the mylodon, of 'extinct tigers,' and of the 'extinct' type of horse called the onohipidium.

When the twentieth century dawned, the Amazon forests still concealed a number of their major secrets. Vast tributary-streams, possibly a thousand miles long, were suspected to exist, but no one had sailed down them. Between those confluents already known there existed, and still exist, many spaces left vaguely blank on the map. Here and there adventurous 'rubber men' had advanced a few miles along subsidiary streams, but further progress was usually barred by dangerous rapids and hostile Indians. In previous ages the work of exploration had been left largely to Europeans, but now the Brazilian Government has taken up the task with considerable success. For many years the Brazilian Colonel Rondon explored the western highlands of Brazil, chiefly as a pioneer for telegraph-lines and railroads. During that time he travelled over fourteen thousand miles in a territory for the most part unexplored previously.

Sometimes his men were stricken with beri-beri, a disease caused by lack of vitamins; sometimes they suffered from hunger or fever; but the work went on. When Rondon reached the Gy-Parana in 1909, a third of his party were so weak that they could hardly crawl. Their clothes had been torn to tatters, and for months they had existed on wild fruits, nuts, and what little game they could shoot. Then they met a starving stranger who had been lost in the forest for four months, and whose diet had consisted of brazil-nuts and insect-grubs. A new canoe was built, and the expedition started down stream with eleven fever-patients plus the famished wanderer. Even so, the forms of military discipline were maintained. When the ragged bugler sounded the call, every one sprang to attention to hear the orders of the day. When they did eventually reach a rubber-camp, three of the party were literally naked.

When Colonel Rondon heard that Theodore Roosevelt was about to begin a zoological expedition to the Amazon he suggested that they should join forces and explore the River of Doubt, the head-waters of which he had already seen. So the members of the expedition, which included Rondon, Roosevelt, and his son, Kermit, foregathered on the boundary of Paraguay and Brazil and steamed for many days between the marshy banks of the Upper Paraguay river.

Soon the explorers left civilization behind them and sailed in a small launch along the River of Tapirs. Now they began to pass through woods of tall palms in whose fan-like branches were sometimes seen gorgeous flocks of rainbow-hued macaws. They also observed evil lance-headed snakes swimming in the river, and some of the lagoons were infested with giant cayman crocodiles or the bloodthirsty piranha fish. Although piranhas are only small fish, they are more ferocious than any shark, and once blood is spilled in the water they seem to be driven frantic, and in a short time will rend their victim to pieces. But the greatest trouble, both then and later on during the journey, was caused by the innumerable insect-pests which bit and stung everybody on all possible occasions.

In January, 1914, they turned westward away from the river on to the Paracis Plateau. One day they saw the local Indians play their strange game of football. This is played something like association football, the difference being that during the whole proceedings the natives use their heads instead of their feet to propel the ball. The rainy season had now set in, and all the outfit became either rusty or mouldy.

The unexplored Duvida, or River of Doubt, was reached towards the end of February. As the explorers embarked in their seven dug-out canoes they could not help wondering where the unknown stream would carry them. Was it merely a small head-stream of the Gy-Parana, or was it a great tributary of the Madeira? The rainy season was now at its height, and the swollen torrent was swift and brown. They took with them sixteen paddlers and provisions for fifty days. Progress was slow because at intervals Kermit Roosevelt would land with the sighting-rods so that Colonel Rondon might make charting-observations. Generally the forest was as silent as the grave. Sometimes they caught a glimpse of a cormorant or an ibis and more rarely saw traces of a jaguar. The air was scented with the exotic fragrance of forest-flowers. Camping was a difficult proposition, since it was usually necessary to hew and hack in the undergrowth before an open space could be cleared. Gradually the stream grew wider as small tributary-streams flowed in. On the fourth day the current began to quicken. Soon it was running like a mill-race, and they could hear the roar of rapids ahead. The canoes were hauled ashore, and Kermit went off to explore. He found to his amazement that the stream, which had been over a hundred yards wide, rapidly narrowed until it was barely two yards across. Through this deep, sheer-sided bottle-neck the waters boiled and rushed at a tremendous speed. A road had to be chopped through the forest, and the heavy dug-outs were man-hauled along rollers to a post below the rapids. So began the first of many arduous portages.

For the next twenty miles the widening river twisted and turned, and then once again rapids were encountered. Once more there were days of delay while the canoes were portaged. Although dripping with perspiration and stung by innumerable insects, the toilers paused to admire beautiful white and lilac orchids, or ant-thrushes and tanagers resplendent as a cluster of brilliant jewels. On March 10 a halt was made at the foot of the rapids; but then came more trouble, for two of the canoes broke their moorings and were smashed to pieces on the rocks. Although delays would imperil the food supply, there was no alternative but to build a new canoe. The woodsmen picked a great tree five feet in diameter and hollowed out the hard wood with axe and adze. Kermit and others went off on expeditions in search of game, but apart from a few monkeys they saw little. On the fourteenth the new canoe was launched, to the accompaniment of a torrential downpour. The course was still made dangerous by rapids, but they had to risk shooting many of these to avoid further delay.

On the following day Kermit's small canoe was caught in a whirlpool and carried over some dangerous rapids. The canoe filled and turned turtle. One of the two paddlers was pummelled to death on the boulders, but Kermit, breathless and half-drowned, managed to clutch an overhanging branch and, with the help of the second paddler, scrambled ashore.

Barely had the explorers recovered from this catastrophe when fresh danger threatened, for lurking Indians showed their hostility by shooting a dog. Shots were fired in the air, and apparently the Indians fled, for nothing more was heard of them. Soon afterwards more of the canoes were lost, and to save time a dozen of the *camaradas* volunteered to march along the bank until the danger-zone had been passed.

For many miles now the river had been running almost due north, and it was already evident that it was of considerable importance. At a confluence a tributary was called the Rio Kermit, and then Colonel Rondon insisted that the Duvida should be renamed the Rio Roosevelt. Two new canoes were built, and for some days better progress was made. By this time, however, fever had broken out, and the *camaradas* were beginning to show signs of fatigue. Then one day the explorers were cheered by the interesting discovery of some strange carvings on a bare mass of rock near some rapids. The carvings were carefully cut and consisted for the most part of multiple circles and inverted w's, and they probably represented the artistic efforts of a comparatively advanced Indian civilization.

Beyond this point the rapids seemed to get worse, and there were difficult portages in a rocky gorge. At one point the river rushed through a wild canyon between two previously unknown mountains. For some time the average rate of progress did not exceed two miles a day. The men were suffering badly from festering sores. Julio, one of the *camaradas*, had proved to be lazy, and he alone seemed to remain fat and healthy. Then it was discovered that he had been stealing food. This is the most heinous of all crimes on any exploratory expedition. One evening Paishon, a negro corporal, detected Julio stealing food and promptly struck him in the mouth. Julio's evil countenance blazed with malignant hatred. On the next day came swift tragedy. The envenomed Julio waited his opportunity, and when Paishon was returning along the trail to fetch a load of supplies, snatched up a rifle and shot his enemy dead. The cowardly assassin fled into the woods, but three days later appeared on the banks and offered to surrender. The explorers were placed in a dilemma, because it would be almost impossible to keep proper surveillance over an arrested prisoner. Eventually it was agreed that Julio should be captured, but when they went to seek him he had fled, preferring to take his chance among the hostile Indians and poisonous snakes.

Both Roosevelt and his son were now suffering from fever, and the leader of the expedition was laid up with an inflamed bruise. Fortunately the hunters now began to get fresh meat, and then they found traces of 'rubber men.'

34

They had travelled by this time over three hundred kilometres in forty-eight days over absolutely unknown ground. During the next few days they came across more pioneers, some of whom fled at their approach, since they believed that only Indians could come down the unknown upper reaches. Eventually the expedition came out on to the broad waters of the Madeira, and all told, they had added to the map a new river nearly nine hundred miles in length.

HAMILTON RICE IN SNAKE-INFESTED FORESTS

One of the most prominent of the modern explorers of the Amazon is Dr Hamilton Rice, of Harvard University. He has devoted most of his time to the north-west sector of the basin and particularly the Rio Negro and its mighty confluents. Much of this territory is very heavily forested, and the difficulties of exploration account for the fact that until recent years there were no reliable maps of the region.

In 1907 Hamilton Rice crossed the Andes from Bogota in an effort to trace the sources and course of the river Uaupes, which is one of the main tributaries of the Rio Negro. Paddling for four days down a stream called the Ariare, he passed numerous islands populated by giant alligators. One day a large macarel (a serpent of the rattlesnake family) cut across the bows of the boat in mid-stream. One of the paddlers struck the snake a heavy blow with a paddle. In a moment all was confusion. The furious snake leaped aboard the canoe, and there was a mad scramble for guns and cutlasses before a lucky blow killed the invader.

A few days later Rice and a companion disembarked, intending to procure monkeys for breakfast. They became separated, and both spent a miserable day floundering in a big swamp from which they could find no exit. To add to their difficulties, a violent storm arose, and then they had the bad luck to stumble upon a small herd of peccaries. The peccary is a kind of wild hog, and it is so courageous that even when badly wounded, it has been known to kill big hounds. Three of the charging peccaries were killed, and then, with ammunition and physical strength exhausted, the explorers took refuge on a providentially fallen tree-trunk.

35

Here they stayed until it was safe to seek a pathway back to camp.

Having crossed the head-waters of the Orinoco, at last they reached the mighty Rio Uaupes. This river runs for about four hundred miles before it flows into the Rio Negro at São Joaquin. At the point where they began the exploration, the Uaupes was twenty-five yards wide and varied in depth from a few inches to three fathoms. They found animal life very abundant. There were large jaguars, striped tiger-cats, peccaries, deer, monkeys, sloths, boas, and poisonous snakes. There were countless swarms of brilliantly plumaged birds, and the river teemed with lovely fish.

The voyage began in a large canoe with a crew of eight Indians. The stream was tortuous and less than two yards wide in places. Here and there the course was completely blocked by floating logs and *débris* which had to be cleared away with axes and cutlasses. Rapids, cataracts, and falls were frequent obstacles. Sometimes the river rushed through gorges with dizzy swiftness and was churned by the uneven, rocky bed into foaming whirlpools and maelstroms. The natives of the Uaupes proved to be extremely skilful at shooting rapids in their hollowed-out *ubas*. The little boys are brought up under a Spartan *régime* and are made to run the most dangerous cataracts in tiny *ubas*, so that long before they attain manhood they are already experts. They are capable of prolonged exertion on the smallest possible amounts of food, and they can swim like fishes.

Soon the explorers came to a region where the natives were hostile and reputed to be cannibals. Two years previously some Colombian *caucheros* (rubber-prospectors) had been transfixed with tapir lances by the inhabitants of a *maloca* some three miles inland. A number of *caucheros* had organized a punitive and peace-making expedition, and Rice found himself obliged to take part in their operations. Incidentally, he was able to learn a great deal about the natives inland.

The *caucheros* made it their practice to creep along the creeks noiselessly at night, and then at the first signs of dawning they would swoop down on the *maloca* with Winchesters and *machetes* ready for action. Parleys would follow, and compacts would be made by the interchange of gifts. The stealthy approach was essential, because if the Indians had any inkling of approaching strangers, they would abandon the *maloca* as it stood.

The Indians worship an evil spirit which lurks in jaguars, cataracts, thunderstorms, or pestilences. The gaudily painted *pagés*, or medicine-men, organize elaborate ceremonies intended to placate the Devil. The festivals are characterized by sottish indulgence in *mandioca* beer, incantations, curious dances, and weird music on a variety of instruments. The male dancers are adorned with pigments, circlets of feathers, and shell-garters. The medicine-men claim all sorts of miraculous powers and are greatly feared. When they wish to cure an Indian stricken with disease, they alternately blow and suck over the affected part of the patient's body and periodically go behind the *maloca* to spit out the evil spirit. Their fees are high, and often they are the wealthiest men in the community.

In the clearings round the *malocas* are cultivated plantain-groves, mandiocas, pineapples, grapes, and other fruits. Some of the *malocas* were a hundred and twenty feet in length and eighty feet wide, and they housed many families. Frequently they were defended by a kind of moat or fences made from tough palms. In the centre aisle of the hut are the big fires where *cassava* is baked. Here and there might be seen huge hollowed-out trunks which are used as casks in which to store their *mandioca* beer. Most *malocas* had a *trocana*—a hollowed-out log drum five feet high. The drum is slung in a cradle of rope from four posts and is played by means of sticks with rubber heads; the booming sound so produced can be heard for many miles.

Altogether Dr Rice spent nearly nine months making his investigations among the Indians, and he brought back with him a complete map of the Uaupes as far as its junction with the Rio Negro. Four years later he returned to the same region and explored the Inirida, one of the main tributaries of the Orinoco. Then he went across country to the Icana river, another great tributary of the Rio Negro. Since these rivers look so small on the map of South America, it may be just as well to point out that each of them is longer than any river in Great Britain.

The expedition started from a base at Calamar which had been used on the previous journey. A big raft was constructed to cross one of the myriads of head-waters in the neighbourhood. Unfortunately the raft capsized, and this resulted in a serious loss of food and supplies. When they reached the stream called the Macaya, some new canoes were built. Five Indians can build a canoe in five days. A big tree is felled near the river and then shaped and hollowed with axes; it is then filled with palm-leaves, overturned, and the leaves are lighted. When it has been sufficiently burned, the canoe is made water tight by a tar made of boiled palm-sap.

At first Rice tried to strike south towards a chain of mountains, but before going far the men became alarmed. Myriads of insects made life almost unbearable. Here and there the forest gave place to dense, tangled thickets on a surface of black boggy mud, which was specially trying for the carriers. When food ran short, a charge of dynamite was fired in a stream; but while the stunned fish were being collected, one of the men was badly wounded by a sting-ray. This untoward accident further upset the men. Fortunately they managed to catch some peccaries and tapirs, and this meat saved a critical situation so far as food-supplies went.

Most of the men, however, refused to go any farther into the unknown. Camp was made on a small island, and next morning there was open mutiny. Only two of the Indians would agree to continue, so the remainder were sent back to a *cache* on the Macaya river. Two days later Rice himself had to retreat. The advance-party lived on whatever they could get—small monkeys, palm-nuts, tortoises, and small birds. Thunderstorm followed thunderstorm. The hungry, emaciated men were drenched and chilled and began to look like grisly spectres.

In the end almost the whole of the equipment had to be abandoned so that they could reach the *cache* on the Macaya. Here they found the remnant of the mutineers, whose retreat had become a headlong flight. The man who had been

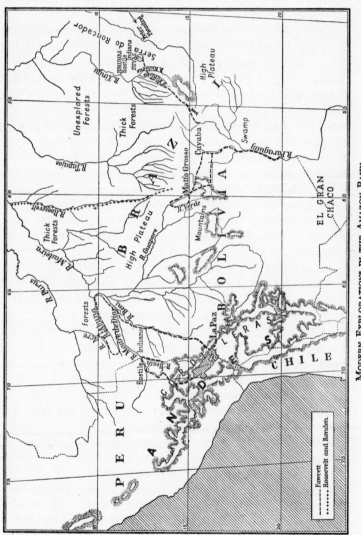

MODERN EXPLORATIONS IN THE AMAZON BASIN

wounded by the sting-ray was unable to keep pace with his demoralized comrades. For two days he crawled along, shadowed by a pair of pumas, and eventually reached the base-camp in a state of utter collapse.

Having reorganized the commissariat, the main journey—down the Inirida—was begun. Near the source, navigating the canoes was mainly a matter of chopping, pushing, and pulling. Tapirs were very numerous, and they were sufficiently curious to stand and stare at these rare intruders into their peaceful domain. Farther downstream, as soon as the camp-fire died down, jaguars began their nocturnal prowling and they had to be driven away like troublesome dogs when they approached too near to the mosquito-nets. Paddling downstream, the explorers frequently saw evidence of the wholesale destruction caused by sudden tempests. Great lanes had been blown down far into the forest.

When Indians were encountered, the Colombian crew became restless. Near the mouth of the Inirida, Rice turned aside into a small tributary and went southward towards the Amazon basin *via* the Icana river. At this point the Colombians returned home, and Rice had to await the arrival of Indian helpers. Eventually Rice and his assistant, Bauer, set off down the Icana accompanied by only two Indians. As often happened, the stream was choked with trees, and the whole countryside was flooded. Where the current could be traced, the canoes brushed against the banks, where spikes of bamboo or spiny bush-ropes tore clothing to shreds and dangerously threatened the eyes. During the heavy thunderstorms trees came crashing down into the water, and more than once narrowly missed the canoes. More often than not the men paddled among the trees, having lost the stream proper. At times the rain was so heavy that constant bailing was necessary.

When they reached a village of the Icana Indians they noticed that most of the men bore long scars. These were apparently caused by the severe whippings which are a feature of their festivals. The Icana Indians are also addicted to *caapi*, a potent liquor made from a forest vine, which seems to have effects similar to opium or hashish. The

Indians consented to assist the expedition, and went up-stream in their small canoes to collect the abandoned baggage. They were, however, very reluctant to leave their own hunting-grounds, and fresh helpers had to be engaged at nearly every village. Sometimes the porters deserted. Once, when Rice was camping on an island, his men deserted, and he had to wait until he could be rescued by friendly Indians.

Slowly the party made their way down the long tributary of a tributary of the Amazon. There were frequent rapids and scores of midstream islands to be avoided. On either side of the main current were innumerable lakes, lagoons, and ponds. At last, when they had been travelling for almost a year since crossing the Andes, they paddled out on to the broad bosom of the Rio Negro, and two hours later they were being regally entertained by a lordly Spanish planter of the old school. During the course of these two expeditions Dr Rice had examined the main waterways of a region larger than Great Britain.

During recent years Dr Rice has made a complete survey of the Rio Negro, and in 1924–1925 he made an important expedition down the Rio Branco. He has found aeroplanes very useful as an accessory for the land-parties.

CHAPTER II

THROUGH THE WASTES OF ASIA AND TIBET

A savage place! as holy and enchanted
As e'er beneath a waning moon was haunted
By woman wailing for her demon-lover!

COLERIDGE, *Kubla Khan*

THE ADVENTURES OF SVEN HEDIN

ALTHOUGH as early as the thirteenth century Messer Marco Polo had tramped the golden road to Kashgar and the stately pleasure-domes of Kubla Khan, few parts of the world were less known to Europeans than Central Asia when the twentieth century dawned. Tibet was still a closed land of mystery which had been glimpsed by few white men; over a hundred years had passed since an Englishman last gazed on the golden roofs of Lhasa's sacred shrines; the glacier-springs which feed the Indus and the Brahmaputra were veiled in misty legends; and there were towering ranges beyond the Himalayas as virgin as the mountains of the moon. What secrets of forgotten days lay buried in the deserts of Cathay? What mysteries of the high plateau inspired the zealous guard of the fanatical lamas? What unseen peaks on the roof of the world dwarfed Mount Everest? These and many other intriguing questions still remained unanswered in the year of Our Lord 1900.

It was Sven Hedin, the last great explorer of Tibet, who supplied many of the answers. He was born in Stockholm in 1865, and when still a young man he made many journeys into Central Asia. In particular he was interested in the great deserts to the north of Tibet. Beyond Yarkand, in the province of Sin-Kiang, stretches the Takla-Makan desert, which is almost equal in area to the whole of Great Britain. Farther east, in Inner Mongolia, lies the famed Gobi Desert, which sprawls for nearly a thousand miles to the north of the Great Wall of China. In the summer these deserts are

42

sun-scorched and parching, but in the winter they are bitterly cold, and the River Tarim, with its inland delta among the sand-dunes, is frozen solid. Here there are regions where even the hardy Kirghiz fear to go, and where the only animals are the rare wild camels.

In 1893 Hedin began a great journey which led him into the unknown across the mountainous sand-dunes of the

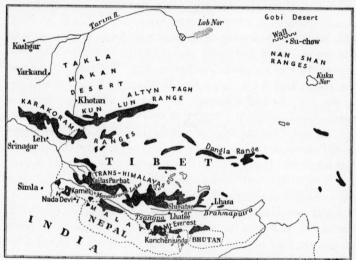

THE HEART OF ASIA, SHOWING THE REGIONS EXPLORED BY
HEDIN AND STEIN

Takla-Makan desert. Tragedy dogged the dusty footsteps of his tiny caravan. One by one the camels died. The weary men toiled up sand-dune after sand-dune until the water-supplies were exhausted. As a last resource the men drank the camel's rancid oil, and Hedin took some Chinese brandy which otherwise would have been used for a lamp-stove. This paralysed his muscles, and he dragged himself along far behind the caravan, ready to drop at any moment. In despair they slaughtered their last sheep, in order to drink its blood; but it was so thick and sickening that no one would taste it. Some of the men fell exhausted and could go no farther, but Hedin and his faithful servant, Kasim, crawled along with the waning strength of dying men. Kasim was

43

dreadfully giddy and confused. But at last their hopes grew lighter—they saw a dark line along the horizon. It was the wooded banks of a desert-stream, or *wadi*, the Khotan Daria. They walked into the leafy arbours, knowing that the river must be near at hand; but they were so exhausted with the heat of the day that they sank down under a leafy poplar.

That evening Hedin took a spade-handle as a staff and crossed the wood, creeping long distances on all fours. Kasim remained where he was, lying on his back, motionless, with his eyes wide open, and unable to speak. At last the wood ended abruptly, and a plain, lit up by the pale rays of the moon, spread out before him. This was the bed of the river; and it was dry! But Hedin determined not to die in the very bed of a stream, and he set off to search for a pool. All of a sudden a duck flew into the air, water splashed, and he stood on the edge of a little pool of fresh, clear water in the deepest part of the river-bed, where the stream had last lingered. Hedin drank freely, took some water to Kasim in his top-boots—the only available water-bottle—and soon afterwards they were both rescued by some passing shepherds.

Later on Hedin discovered two ancient cities buried in the sands, and then he went off to Tibet. In the early years of this century he was once more in the heart of the Takla-Makan. He had set out in the summer of the previous year on his fourth visit to Central Asia. At the outset he experienced some of the wild fluctuations of temperature which are characteristic of this wilderness. Where previously he had suffered agonies from parching thirst, he now had to contend with raging blizzards and Arctic frosts. Once his caravan was stricken by the *kara-buran*, the black desert-storm.

My tent-poles were snapped in two, and only the half-poles could now be used. With great difficulty my men had managed to pitch the tent in the shadow of a clay hillock. It was guyed with ropes and heavy boxes piled on its edges. The camels, freed of their loads, lay stretched out in the direction of the wind, their necks and heads flat on the ground. The men wrapped themselves up in their cloaks and huddled under their tent-cloth, which could not be pitched. The drift-sand beat against the tent-cloth, and the particles filtered through and covered everything within. The storm lasted all day, all night, and part of the next day, and when at last it had shot past, hurrying westward, and calm was again restored, we felt queerly dazed, as after a long illness.

Soon afterwards Hedin found yet another sand-buried city, but he pushed on, exploring the queer inland delta of the Tarim, and then returned to Tibet. Here he planned many salt lakes in a region where the wild black yak is lord of all he surveys, and where for two months they saw no signs of human beings. Even the camp-followers from Turkestan and Afghanistan found the rarefied atmosphere of these high plateaux too exhausting, and one of the hunters collapsed and died. Then they marched into the Gobi Desert, carrying enough ice in bags to last men and horses for ten days. When water ran short, and it seemed that the animals must be sacrified, they came across a cake of ice forty feet in diameter, and all was well for a time.

After some months of wandering the explorers returned to the strange desert-ruins which they had found on the previous journey. They made excavations in several houses, and there discovered some images of Buddha and many boards and papers inscribed with Chinese ideographs, or picture-writing. They found that the town had been called Loulan, and when the documents were interpreted they gave a clear picture of life about the period A.D. 270. Among the papers was a fragment of an historical work of the Han dynasty, and since this was made in the second century it is probably the oldest piece of paper manuscript still existing. Loulan had been a frontier-town on the great 'silk road' between China and the Roman Empire. References to large imports seem to prove that the town had a large population, and it was ascertained that it numbered among its important buildings a hospital, a post-office, a temple, and many warehouses. In this Pompeii of the desert the people had written of their simple joys and sorrows, of humble births and deaths, of menacing barbarians and military preparations. The discovery of old mollusc-shells near by showed that Loulan once stretched along the shores of a lake.

But it was in Tibet that Hedin made his most important explorations. This lofty plateau, which lies behind mighty

45

bulwarks of glaciated mountains and burning deserts, must always remain one of the most inaccessible of all the corners of the earth.

Sven Hedin next determined to attempt an entry into the forbidden city of Lhasa, and with that object in view he obtained an outfit of Mongol clothes and hired an errant lama as interpreter. So once again, with a large well-equipped caravan, he returned to high Tibet. Before long, however, the asses began to die off, the pasturage was coarse and scanty, and there were frequent storms of driving hail and snow. From time to time, as they plodded through the savage wilderness, the camp was invaded by bears or ravening wolves. Then came storm, wrack, and swamping deluge which churned the soil into a morass, engulfing the camels shoulder-deep.

In July, 1901, accompanied by the quaking lama guide and a Cossack, Hedin set off on his wild ride towards the forbidden city. There were many dangers to face; murderous robbers skulked in the rocky passes, and the Tibetan herders, lama-ridden and fanatically hostile to all strangers, were sure to be vigilant foes. In secret pockets beneath his crimson Mongolian cloak the explorer carried books, an aneroid, and a compass to plan the route. Round his neck he suspended a rosary of one hundred and eight beads and a copper case containing an image of Buddha.

On the second night they had their first adventure, when some lurking robbers stole two of the best horses. Thenceforth they found it necessary to keep guard during the nightwatches. The rain fell in torrents, and the little cavalcade almost came to disaster when crossing a ford over a swollen river. The horses were swirled away from the narrow passage, and they only reached the farther bank by plunging and swimming across the current. Eventually the party reached the main road to Lhasa, but by that time they were in a well-populated district, and one night they were surrounded by a force of quaint Tibetan warriors who informed them that the road to the south was blocked to all foreigners. Disguise and bluster were unavailing. Hedin had to agree to accompany an armed escort back to the Sachu-Tsangpo.

46

Hedin now returned to his caravan and tried to set off southward for India. Once again he found his way barred by a large force of Tibetan horsemen. Then the Governor of the province arrived with special orders from the Dalai-lama, saying, "It is quite beyond any need for Europeans to enter the Land of the Holy Books to look about them." As he had hoped, Hedin was forced to turn westward past lakes of fairy-like beauty where golden eagles soared among the cliffs. On several occasions he made use of a collapsible canvas boat, and he had many narrow escapes from drowning in the storms which swoop like sudden arrows from the mountains.

The escorted journey through the interior of Tibet lasted three months. Although food was plentiful, there was a shortage of fuel, and fires made of yaks' droppings were not very satisfactory or pleasant in regions where the temperature was Arctic in its severity. Several of the camels died, and all but one of the horses. Once the explorers had to wait for some days beside a lake until a sheet of ice sufficiently thick to bear the camels had formed. But as they journeyed through the rugged wastes many new areas were mapped, until in the end the frontier of Tibet was reached. Here they were met by a relief-expedition, and after a brief visit to India, Hedin returned home to Stockholm.

Three years elapsed, and then in the autumn of 1905 Hedin once again set forth—this time to explore the vast ranges of mountains which were suspected to exist north of the Tsangpo, or Upper Brahmaputra. Srinagar was the starting-point, and from there the caravan trekked to Leh and then over the snowy tops of the Karakoram range. At this point they turned aside into the forbidding region of desolate table-land. Many of the horses died from exhaustion or from the attacks of wolves, but the dauntless Swede plunged into a large triangular area where no European had ever yet entered. His objective was the large monastery of Tashi-lhumpo, on the Upper Brahmaputra—a shrine which ranks in importance next to Lhasa.

For months on end the wanderers met no human beings. The cold was so severe that horses and sheep were frozen to death, and the puppies had to be provided with felt sleeping-jackets. Once Hedin had a narrow escape from death when he was charged by an infuriated yak bull. Then at last they came across some nomads and were able to purchase some tame yaks. On they travelled through clouds of whirling dust, tormented by daily storms, and wrapped up like Arctic explorers. One night there were fifty degrees of frost.

Now they began to meet bands of pilgrims, and once again the caravan was stopped for interrogation by spies when on the very verge of the great unexplored area to the south. Here again Hedin was visited by the Governor of the province and ordered to turn back. Hedin replied:

"I started out on this journey with one hundred and thirty beasts of burden. I have eight horses and one mule left. How can you ask me to go back to that murderous Chang-Tang with such a caravan?"

"You may go wherever you wish, but not through my province," was the reply.

Eventually, however, for some reason best known to himself, the Governor changed his mind and opened the route to the 'Land of the Holy Books.'

Through labyrinths of winding valleys, with frozen water-courses and towering ranges as yet unmapped, the caravan wended southward, meeting on every pass cairns with clusters of votive streamers bearing the monotonous prayer, "*Om mani padme hum.*" (Oh, the jewel is in the lotus.) After crossing a pass 18,000 feet high, the travel-stained wanderers at last looked on the valley of the Upper Brahmaputra. Every step here, every slope climbed, meant a new addition to the knowledge of geography. Riding down from the steep slopes of the Trans-Himalaya, the caravan reached a wide valley which leads to Shigatse and the monastery of Tashi-lhumpo. Beyond, scintillating like a burnished blade, were the white snows of the Himalayas.

They passed through a land of many villages, of fertile barley-fields, and of fruitful gardens. For once in a while the camp-fires were fed with real wood. In order to minimize the risk of being turned back at the last moment, Hedin embarked on a rectangular boat make of yak-hides sewn together and fastened to a framework of light boughs. Floating along the rapid stream, they met many pilgrims sailing in similar craft to attend the New-year celebrations at Tashi-lhumpo. Here and there the black granite mountains sprawled down to the edge of the torrent. When Shigatse was reached, the Tashi-lama, who is second only to the Dalai-lama, sent a token of welcome—a long piece of light-blue gauze—and the white stranger was solemnly bidden to attend the festival.

On the appointed day Hedin walked through a maze of dark rooms and passages to a gallery from where he could witness the sacred ceremonial. White-robed lamas swung censers of gold, while others blew sonorous blasts on copper trumpets ten feet long. Then began a devil-dance. The holy lamas, who were arrayed in gold-embroidered, multi-coloured silk garments, and who enveloped their heads in masks of devils, dragons, or beasts, whirled and pirouetted in a frenzied ecstasy until the eyes of the beholder were bewildered.

On the next day the Tashi-lama summoned Hedin to an interview, and in the course of conversation he vouchsafed the information that he was the incarnation of the Dhyani Buddha, and that his successor would be chosen according to the same miraculous fashion by which a new Dalai-lama is elected. Rather surprisingly Hedin was given full permission to photograph and inspect any part of the strange temple-town. He saw a mighty kitchen where, in six enormous cauldrons, tea was brewed for 3800 monks. In another gloomy hall were the hundred and eight volumes of the Holy Scriptures. For forty-seven days Hedin freely explored the town, until urgent representations from Lhasa made it clear that he had overstayed his welcome; and so once again he had to set off on his travels.

Passing through wild and beautiful gorges, he visited several monasteries and crossed many crazy bridges whose rotting planks twisted across gaping chasms. At one monastery he saw a gigantic prayer-wheel which was kept ceaselessly turning by the zealous monks. At another he was shown a *dupkang*, or hermit-cave, at the foot of the moun-

D

tains. It had no windows, and the entrance had been walled up. Near the ground there was one small aperture through which food was pushed on a piece of board to a holy anchorite who had lived for forty years in permanent darkness. Elsewhere Hedin heard of another cave where a monk had spent no less than sixty-nine years. When the aged hermit realized that death was approaching he signalled that he would like to see the sun once again; but when he was released he was found to be stone-blind, and almost at once crumpled up and died. These hermits believe that as a reward for their voluntary imprisonment they will attain Nirvana, the Blessed Oblivion, immediately after death.

Toiling onward, Hedin once again crossed the Trans-Himalaya and then turned north-west. He tried to reach the holy lake of Dangrayum, but he was turned back by a horde of shrieking horsemen. Then he decided to be the first European to see the source of the Brahmaputra. He followed a river-valley towards the south-west, climbing ever higher into a world of gigantic snow-covered peaks and eventually saw the great blue-green glacier which suckles the infant Brahmaputra.

Thence he journeyed to the holy lake of Manasarovar. Hindus believe that bathing in the waters of this sacred lake ensures passage to the paradise of Brahma. The oval-shaped lake lies about 15,200 feet above sea-level. To the amazement of the Tibetans, who believed that the god of the lake would drag all defilers down to the depths, Hedin and a small party sailed across the lake and explored its shores. A gale arose; hail-stones as big as hazel nuts almost swamped their tiny cockle-shell, but finally the outraged lake-god withdrew his spuming water-devils, and they reached a monastery on the farther shore. The monks say that there is a sacred tree rooted in the golden sand at the bottom of the lake, and that the lake-god's castle is at its foot. Perhaps that is why there are no less than eight monasteries clustered round the shores.

Not far away there is a holy mountain called Kailas Parbat. Hedin decided to join the pilgrim-bands who come from far distant parts of Asia to complete the circuit of this peak. The way leads through a whole forest of votive cairns, and as the pilgrims struggle along they chant without ceasing, "*Om mani padme hum, Om mani padme hum.*" They believe that the paradise of Siva is perched on the white summit of this 'ice-jewel.'

Hedin rounded off this trip by seeking the source of the Indus, and in September, 1907, he reached a place where a spring gushes forth from a flat shelf at about 17,000 feet above sea level. Thus he was able to claim that he was the first white man to penetrate to the sources of two of the greatest rivers of Asia.

There still remained a huge area which had not been explored. Hedin gathered a fresh caravan, and in order to hoodwink the Tibetans, planned to take the main caravan-route towards the Karakoram pass, and, as he had done in the previous year, turn eastward into Tibet and reach the unknown area in disguise. This involved the dismissal of all his old servants, since they might be recognized. He knew that on this occasion—since it was December—he would be marching into annihilating winds and paralysing blizzards. The trail was strewn with the carcasses of dead caravan-horses. On Christmas Day they left the trade-route and turned eastward into the cold deserts.

Battered by constant storms, the expedition rarely advanced more than six miles a day. From time to time the onward march was delayed by deep snow-drifts or the death of a mule or a horse. It became necessary to jettison all but the essential packages. So they toiled on for sixty-four days before a small nomad camp was reached, and thereafter, in order to avoid arrest, Hedin adopted the disguise of a shepherd. Even now there were passes of over 18,000 feet to be traversed. One of his men, Abdul Kerim, pretended to be the leader of the caravan and told the suspicious nomads that he was a merchant seeking a new trade-route for wool. All Hedin's European clothes were burnt, and he dyed his face a deep brown. Sheep were purchased, serving both as food and pack-animals. Whenever the black tents of nomads were sighted, Hedin at once assumed his guise of shepherd and soon became an efficient drover. As they journeyed southward the risk of discovery increased, and to discourage inquisitive callers, Hedin purchased a fierce black watch-dog, called Takkar, which was tethered to a strong pole at the door of his tent.

By the end of April the party had climbed mountain-range after mountain-range, but at last the disguise was penetrated, and further progress was impeded by the arrival of a force sent by the Governor of the province. The explorers once again became captives of the Tibetans; but their captors proved to be lenient and provided new clothes and stores for the ragged vagabonds. Once again Hedin had to turn back, and he crossed the Trans-Himalaya for the seventh time by a pass over 19,000 feet high. Then he went off on a side-expedition, having arranged a rendezvous with Abdul Kerim. Before long, however, he was in sore straits, and he even tried to sell his Swedish gun in order to raise food-supplies. He was only saved from actual beggary by the belated arrival of Abdul Kerim, who had been first attacked by robbers and then forced by hostile chiefs to take a long roundabout route through rugged country.

Altogether Hedin had explored a region five hundred and seventy miles in length, which no European had visited before, and which on the latest English map was marked with nothing more than the word 'unexplored.' He now made his way to Lake Manasarovar again and then followed the Sutlej to the frontier of India. Here his party had to cross an immense river, which at this point is squeezed into a narrow channel between perpendicular rocks.

> Only a steel cable, as thick as my thumb, stretched across the abyss, which yawned about a hundred feet below. . . . Ngurup, our last guide, knew what to do. He wound a rope round the cable and hauled himself across.

A kind of wooden yoke was then improvised, and eventually the whole caravan swung across the gap. So in August, 1908, ended one of the most difficult journeys in the history of Tibetan exploration.

AUREL STEIN AND THE RUINS OF DESERT CATHAY

One of the most remarkable results of the journeys of Sven Hedin had been to reveal the existence of a number of ancient cities buried in the sands of Central Asia. These discoveries seemed to show evidence of climatic changes and therefore aroused the interest of archæologists, notably Ellsworth Huntington, whose theories about changes in climate due to sunspot-cycles have done much to throw light on the downfall of the Roman Empire and the history of the Tartars. It was, however, Aurel Stein who, in 1900, first revealed fully the great historical importance of the ancient culture in the oases of Chinese Turkestan. His excavations on the sites of Hedin's cities also showed the remarkable state of preservation in which age-old documents might survive under the sands in this extremely dry atmosphere.

In 1906 Stein began another journey, which extended these systematic explorations for almost a thousand miles to the east. Following the route of the famous Chinese pilgrim, Hsuan-Tsang, his expedition crossed the Pamirs to Sarikol, where he explored an old fort called the Tower of the Princess, about which the natives told a quaint story. They related that a certain Chinese Princess of the Han dynasty had been betrothed to a King of Persia. On the way to Persia she had reached Sarikol, beyond which point the roads were blocked by robbers. For safety she was placed by her escort on an isolated peak protected by precipitous cliffs. There the well-guarded Princess received visits from the sun-god. A son was miraculously born. Hence, when the route once more became open, the Sarikol tribes induced her to remain there and to rule over them. The chiefs of this mountain-region still claimed to be descended from that miraculous son. Stein was, however, driven to the prosaic conclusion that the fort was nothing more than an early Chinese frontier-post.

At Kashgar Stein gathered together a caravan which included a number of men who had worked with him on his previous expedition, and he also had the good fortune to engage a Chinese secretary, Chiang-ssu-yeh, who proved invaluable. Some months were spent in exploring the mountains to the south of the Takla-Makan desert. The dangers of travel in this region of great peaks may be illustrated by an account of the crossing of the Kash river. Just

where the river issues like a mill-race from a rock-cut channel
into a deep pool of whirling water the hillmen had constructed a crazy bridge which consisted of three roughly
hewn poplar-trunks jammed between the rock-faces. Only
one of the badly split trunks was broad enough to provide
a foothold, and it would have been quite impossible to transfer
heavy loads across. So a wire rope was slung across, anchored,
and then a raft of goat-skins was improvised to act as a ferry.
On the second journey the wire rope snapped, and only by
luck was the raft pulled ashore. Hours passed before this obstacle was overcome and the rope ferry satisfactorily refixed.

The party returned to Khotan and visited various
temple-ruins in the vicinity. At one oasis excavations
brought to light a number of paper manuscripts of Buddhist
Sanskrit texts. Other sites produced wooden documents of
split tamarisk and birch-bark sheets of Sanskrit of the
fourth century. Some of the tablets still retained intact their
original string fastenings and clay-seal impressions of Eros
and Hermes—tangible links with the art of Greece and
Rome. There were remains of chairs, weaving-tools, carved
cupboards, wood-carvings, and rags of silk, wool, cotton,
and carpets. The dozens of wood tablets which were dug
out revealed that the ruins belonged to a widely scattered
agricultural settlement which flourished in the third
century of the Christian era.

From this place the way led past many more ruins, and
then a hundred and six miles across the desert to Charchan,
along the route followed by Marco Polo. At Loulan, the
site discovered by Hedin, Stein made extensive discoveries.
Near Hedin's camping-ground there were ruins of timber and
plaster-built houses rising with their splintered and bleached
posts like the last remnants of wrecked boats. Before long
the excavators had turned up many records in wood and
paper. There were bales of yellow silk, bronze mirrors,
rings, bells, stone seals, and remains of ancient woven
fabrics. In the third century Loulan had evidently been a
walled station, and near by Stein found traces of an ancient
river-bed. Eventually four camel-loads of objects were
brought away.

In the early days of the new year Stein set off again to
the east. On the Miran site further fragments of ancient
records were found. One paper document was a private
letter to a high official recommending for his use a certain
medicine to be prepared of boiled sheep's dung mixed with
butter, barley-flour, and other savoury ingredients! At
Miran, too, there were ancient temples and remains of
colossal figures of seated Buddhas, seven feet across the
knees. From Miran the way led to Tun-Huang across the
Gobi Desert. Just before Tun-Huang was reached, Stein's
attention was attracted by a solid mass of brickwork about
twenty-three feet high. Was it an ancient watch-tower?
On the next day another tower was seen. Close by stretched
a line of reed-bundles which extended almost imperceptibly
for some miles to the east, gradually assuming the appearance of a wall. A little excavation soon proved that this
was the ancient *limes*, or frontier wall of China, and it
dated back to the Han dynasty. In places it was nine feet
thick, and it was somewhat similar in construction to the
famous Great Wall of China.

The most exciting of the discoveries made by Stein came
when he paid a visit to the valley in which are the 'Caves
of the Thousand Buddhas,' near Tun-Huang. In this sacred
valley, the cliffs are honey-combed with a multitude of
grottos arranged in irregular tiers. The caves were for the
most part untenanted except for images of the 'Enlightened
One.' There could be seen a myriad gorgeous frescoes and
square cellas covered with images and paintings. At Tun-
Huang Stein had heard rumours about a great hidden store
of ancient manuscripts which had recently been found in one
of the grottos. In May Stein paid a second visit to this
interesting sanctuary. He found that the shrines were in
the charge of a credulous Taoist priest. By a skilful use of
his knowledge of the Buddhist saints, Stein was eventually
able to persuade the priest to permit him to see the secret
hoard. Apparently one day a crack had appeared in the
wall of one of the grottos, and behind there was a small
room. To Stein's amazement, when he was allowed to peep
in, he saw a solid mass of manuscript bundles, rising to a

height of nearly ten feet. The Taoist priest permitted him to see a few specimens. Almost all were of great antiquity, and many were in the same condition as when they were deposited in their secret library. There were packets full of paintings on fine gauze-like silk, and temple-banners resplendent with painted Buddhas.

The priest was very chary about showing his sacred *chings*, or texts, for he feared the vengeance of fanatical pilgrims. Stein hinted that he would be prepared to make ample donations—for the holy purpose of restoring the shrines—if certain of the documents might be moved for 'closer examination.' Eventually a bargain was struck, and for four horse-shoes of silver Stein was permitted to remove twenty-nine large cases full of priceless manuscripts and art-treasures. One gigantic roll was over seventy feet long and a foot wide. The British Museum became the final depository for the numerous silk paintings and embroidered pictures which were thus acquired.

During the next few months Stein continued his work on the ancient wall and paid a fleeting visit to the caves in the 'Valley of a Myriad Buddhas.' Here he found that modern restorations had destroyed much of the archæological interest. Later he made important explorations in the Nan-Shan ranges and in the Kun Lun mountains, where he was severely frost-bitten, and he had to be carried back to India in a litter. When finally he reached London, he brought with him one of the most extraordinary collections of treasure-trove ever discovered, and enough to keep the scholars of Europe busy for many years.

RAWLING ON THE GREAT PLATEAU

Having obtained six months' leave of absence, Captain Rawling, accompanied by Lieutenant Hargreaves, set off from Kashmir on a journey into the regions of Tibet from which Deasy and Wellby had been turned back by armed Tibetans a few years before. The caravan was collected together at Leh, and all unwittingly they engaged as 'caravan-bashi' a scoundrel by the name of Abdul Khalik. Khalik was a cross-bred Pathan who could lie fluently in seven oriental languages. He proved to be a great nuisance, and more than once almost wrecked the expedition. The two white men were joined by Ram Singh, a native surveyor, and they set off across the high passes of the frontier with a motley collection of villainous-looking porters and miserable ponies which had been collected by Khalik. Khalik declared that he had bought the ponies a month before, and he presented a long bill for their feeding. Later on, however, it came out that he had only bought the ponies a few days before and had sold the grain to his brother.

On June 3, 1903, they left civilization behind, loaded up with heavy supplies for the porters and ponies. They had to cross several passes of over 18,000 feet, where the ponies floundered badly in the deep snow. When they looked back at the top of one ascent they could see a trail of blood left behind by the ponies, sheep, yaks, and men. They entered Tibet *via* the Changchenmo valley, down the centre of which rushes an icy torrent spanned here and there by snow-bridges. At one place the river ran close under a precipice, leaving a bare two-foot space between the rock and a perpendicular ice-wall. The way was so narrow that laden animals could not pass, and a piece of the cliff had to be knocked away. A little farther along they came to a herd of kiang or wild ass, and the camp-dog pluckily tackled a big grey wolf which was stalking the caravan-sheep. At the head of the valley they had yet another pass to cross, and here the cold was so intense that an ink-pot burst during the night, the spilled contents being frozen solid on the outside of the bottle before it had time to reach the floor.

Once in Tibet, they passed through desolate scenery across the huge Soomjeling plain, which lies at a height of 17,500 ft, and which is dotted with salt and fresh-water lakes. Soon they came to a large lake of about fifty square miles, from which the water escaped by an underground channel some miles away. At this point it was arranged that the caravan should split. Hargreaves was to remain by the lake to await some expected transport which had not yet arrived from the frontier. Rawling, Ram Singh, Khalik, and twenty-three ponies were to make a wide circuit of about fourteen days' duration, and then they were to meet at a place called by Deasy 'Antelope Plain.' This was the farthest point which had been reached previously.

Most of the country through which Rawling passed on his circuit was totally unknown. Turning to the south he soon came to a lake called Shemen Tso, which is about a hundred square miles in area. On the grassy slopes of the shore roamed herds of kiang and yaks. At their camping-place they found that the rich soil, in which the grass grew, was merely a deep covering over a mass of ice. In places the ice had melted and left small pools or dry hollows, which had been used as lairs by wolves waiting to pounce on antelopes. Snow fell at intervals, and during the night the ponies stampeded because of the presence of wolves, and they were only recovered after a day-long search.

On 'Kiang Plain' they met their first nomad. He was a short, stumpy man clad in filthy, blood-stained sheep-skins. His hair was matted with dirt and grease, and he carried a rusty old sword in his rope girdle. This unprepossessing old man turned out to be useful, however, since he was able to provide eight yaks for transport-services. So the march was continued. But now the going became very bad, and when they left the plain they soon found themselves in a narrow gorge filled with immense boulders.

Just when it seemed probable that they would have to turn back, one of the drivers saw the track of a wild yak high up the mountain-side. An hour's hard climbing brought them to a narrow ledge, which wandered into a maze of *nullahs* and precipitous cliffs. On one narrow ledge some of the ponies rolled over and plunged down the slope until their progress was arrested by a projecting rock some two hundred feet below. Here they lay kicking, but fortunately without any bones broken. It took nine hours to travel three miles, and then at last they found their way down on to a plain. Here there was an abundance of grass, and as so often happened in this district, there was an antelope waiting to be shot at the place where they decided to camp.

NOMAD FAMILY OF WESTERN TIBET

From Rawling's "The Great Plateau" (Arnold)

58

Then they entered into a rolling down-country where there were slow-moving streams but little vegetation. Once again they met nomads, who told them that there was a gold-field in the vicinity. Rawling inspected the nomad's tent, which consisted of thin rugs kept in position by sticks, string, and stones and was incredibly filthy. The nomads were living on the proceeds of their hunting, and the floor was strewn with large quantities of dried kiang-meat and the decomposing remnants of other animals.

It was now time to be making for Antelope Plain, where they hoped to meet Hargreaves. To the north of them the way appeared to be cut off by the high range known as the Deasy group, and before long they once again found themselves in a *cul-de-sac*, where a mighty glacier closed the end of the valley they were following. By this time the condition of the animals was causing some anxiety, since there was no grazing in this area, and they had used their last bag of chopped straw. Rawling and Ram Singh explored a ravine which looked hopeful, only to find that before them, barring the way to Antelope Plain, rolled a sea of unknown mountains. At length they had to climb a peak of 20,000 feet before they could find a pass which would take them to the plain. The caravan straggled into the pass through deep, soft snow, and at dusk they at last reached Antelope Plain.

Nothing could be seen of Hargreaves or his camp. Some hours later two men and a pony were spied slowly approaching. They proved to be two of Hargreaves' men. They bore a letter from Hargreaves in which it was stated that twenty of his ponies had died in a blizzard, no fresh stores had arrived, and some of the yak-drivers had thrown everything away and deserted. Sixty miles short of the agreed rendezvous the six remaining ponies had broken down, and so he had dispatched the two men ahead to find Rawling. Hargreaves was in no danger of starving, but he could come no farther without some means of transport.

Fortunately Ram Singh remembered that, when he had been exploring with Deasy in this region, a large store of supplies had been hidden beneath a cairn of stones. If this treasure could only be found, all would be well again, since the ponies would soon benefit from extra food. Two days' marching brought them to the spot, but by this time the supply of rations had given out. Moreover, to obtain fresh water they had to dig a deep hole in a dry ravine before they could find a trickle. Fortunately Rawling managed to bag two fine antelopes, so that the meat-question was solved for the time being. Early next morning Ram Singh located the *cache*, and the whole party set to work digging with sharp stones or with their bare hands. Soon they came upon a rotten tarpaulin, and below this they found many bags of Indian corn. The corn in the middle of the sacks was still in good condition, and soon they had garnered a fine harvest. A good feed revived the ponies, and some of them were sent off to rescue Hargreaves, who turned up two days later.

The whole party now returned to Antelope Plain, although Hargreaves was suffering from fever. Beyond them lay the unknown. Rawling climbed to the top of a ridge near the camp, and away to the north and east saw a vast plain where immense herds of antelopes were grazing on the fresh grass. Every moment fresh herds appeared from the east, until he estimated that he could see at least 20,000 of these graceful animals.

After all surplus baggage had been jettisoned, the explorers pushed eastward to a new lake about seventy square miles in area. This they called Lake Markham. Beyond this point there stretched a barren plain for about a hundred miles where there were no trees, and as far as the eye could see, not even a blade of grass. The expedition therefore turned to the south, hoping to meet Tibetans and grazing land. More often than not they had to dig a well to get even a meagre supply of water. Then they gradually marched into a land where animal life reappeared.

By the end of August they had covered seven hundred miles since leaving Leh, and the soles of their boots were worn to paper. Rawling and Ram Singh were able to obtain many fine views for mapping-purposes, and from one hilltop they had a clear view for fifty miles to the south. They could see five lakes, all of them so salt that even the surroundings were covered with a saline deposit. At last, however, they reached a fresh-water lake which they named the 'Drinking-water of the Giants.' This was the first sheet of fresh water they had seen for two months.

They now made for the lake called Aru Tso, and thence through the Aru mountains. There was an abundance of game, and once more they began to meet nomads. Once they met an old gold-digger who told them that the Dzongpon of Rudok had given orders that the expedition was to be turned back. He promised, however, to guide them for two days. At this juncture there was a minor outbreak of mutiny among the men. As usual, Khalik, the bully, was at the bottom of it. When the caravan-bashi was reprimanded for causing trouble among the drivers he threatened to desert. Since Khalik had been brought along for the express purpose of acting as interpreter should they meet any Tibetans, it was essential that his services, such as they were, should be retained. Hargreaves held up the departing Pathan, drew a line on the ground, and then stepped back ten paces. Khalik was given the choice of crossing the line and being shot or returning to his tent. For a moment Khalik hesitated; then he slunk away.

The next day the caravan crossed a low pass and unexpectedly found itself in a rolling, grassy valley, which was the main road to the forbidden city of Rudok. The whole country teemed with animal life, and the explorers pushed onward with great speed, hoping to reach the city before their presence was announced. Soon, however, they began to meet more nomads. One morning the shaky voice of one of the men gasped out the information that twenty armed Tibetans were approaching. Khalik was sent forward to parley, but all his vaunted blandishments were of no avail.

The villainous-looking soldiers came up. They were all armed with long matchlocks, long spears, and swords, and some also had bows and arrows. The explorers struck camp, loaded up the ponies, and went forward. The Tibetans apparently did not know what to do, but hung about in the rear. Gradually they were reinforced by small bodies of men, until a company of over fifty had congregated. Then, to add fuel to the fire, an irate old lama came bustling up, shouting out orders to stop. He urged the Tibetans to seize the explorers, and when they perceived that the white men did not intend to fire, they began to exchange blows with the caravan-drivers. Then, at the lama's command, the Tibetans suddenly dropped their weapons and made a mass attack. The caravan was submerged, and all the members of the expedition were firmly clasped about the arms and legs. Instead of struggling, the explorers now began to smile diplomatically on their captors, patting them on the backs and being soon on better terms. Rawling agreed to return as far as their last camp and there await the headman of the district.

Apparently the genial old nomad they had met a few days before had sent word of the approaching caravan. Now the way to Rudok was barred, and the expedition had to turn northward. The road led straight into the heart of the mountains, and the old lama persisted in accompanying the caravan to see that they did not diverge from the agreed path. Soon they were passing beside gaunt, crumbling pinnacles and barren ravines, where there was not a blade of grass or a drop of water to be seen. The ponies suffered severely, several of them dying.

The old lama now acted as guide and eventually led them to the banks of a large fresh-water lake, the Tai Tso. Here, for once in a while, the ponies had a good feed from the grass on the shores. Then followed another day of desert-crossing, until they came to a large river, which they followed until they were once again stopped by Tibetans. Once more Khalik nearly caused a disaster. He promptly quarrelled with the repulsive, swashbuckling leader of the band, and would have shot him had not Hargreaves intervened. Finally a truce was patched up, and the caravan was allowed to proceed, provided that it avoided the neighbouring village. They were now close to Rudok again, and soon officials arrived who had been ordered to provide transport and food to enable the expedition to return to Leh.

Accompanied by a small escort, they struck westward along a string of five lakes, a hundred and twenty miles in length, and then seven weary marches across the mountains brought them back to their starting-point. Altogether the expedition had resulted in the correct mapping of 35,000 square miles of hitherto unknown country. The troublesome Khalik met with his deserts when India was reached, for he was sent to jail because of his persistent frauds and ill-treatment of the natives.

THE GARTOK EXPEDITION

Owing to various breaches of the peace it became necessary in 1903 to dispatch a British Mission into Tibet. Eventually Colonel Younghusband marched his forces into Lhasa, and a treaty was signed between Great Britain and Tibet. One clause of the treaty agreed that a trade-mart should be set up at Gartok, the capital of western Tibet. No European had ever visited this place, and much of the route to it was through unexplored country. Thus it happened that four British officers—Rawling, Ryder, Bailey, and Wood—all of them famous explorers in Tibet, were appointed to survey a route to Gartok along the valley of the Brahmaputra, or Tsangpo.

A considerable caravan was organized, and thanks to the escort of an official from Lhasa, they met with no hostility, in spite of the recent fighting. At Dongtse they heard a story which reminded them that this courtesy was not of long standing. Twenty-five years before, an Indian explorer had been the honoured guest of the Abbot of Dongtse. For this indiscretion the old priest was taken to Lhasa, tried, and sentenced to death. Since the spilling of blood is forbidden, the venerable Abbot was sewn up in a leather bag and cast into the Tsangpo. Not satisfied with this punishment, the fanatical lamas proceeded to wipe out all his family, slaying some and selling others into slavery. There can be little wonder that so many Tibetan explorers have found the way bolted and barred before them by terror-stricken lamas.

At Shigatse the expedition was welcomed with the usual 'scarf greeting' and also a 'salaamy sheep.' The latter, although considered highly complimentary by the Tibetans, is a curious gift. A sheep, having been killed and cleaned, is

63

hung up to dry and to decompose. When the whole neighbourhood is redolent of decayed mutton, the flesh is considered fit for eating, and it is duly presented to the next
guest of honour. Needless to say, the British officers promptly
returned the 'salaamy sheep' to their host's servants, who
proceeded to feast upon it with evident relish.

Later, the members of the expedition were granted an
interview with the Tashi-lama. They were led through
broad passages, the walls and ceilings of which were covered
with beautiful paintings of gods, goddesses, and other
religious subjects. The Tashi-lama entertained them at the
inevitable tea-party, and he blessed the Buddhist servants
of the officers. They were also shown the golden tombs of the
previous Tashi-lamas. The gilded roofs rose high above the
surrounding white-washed houses. The sarcophagi were of
gold, beautifully ornamented with turquoises and other
precious stones. Curiously enough, among all this magnifi-
cence they noticed five coloured glass globes, obviously of
European origin, which had once been intended for a
Christmas-tree!

The fortress at Shigatse proved to be especially interesting. The fort stands some hundreds of feet above the town,
and it is supposed to garrison a thousand soldiers. But not
one warrior was to be seen; the *dzongpon*, or governor,
naïvely explained that they were all away on leave! They
also saw scores of dreary dungeons filled to overflowing with
decaying carcasses of sheep. These had been there for decades,
and had originally been intended as a store for the garrison
in time of war. The *dzongpon* did not consider it his duty to
remove the noisome supplies, and so there they stayed. In
this fort, too, they saw the remains of a noted robber who
had been sentenced to death. In order to avoid bloodshed,
the thief had been locked into a small room. A fire was
lighted underneath, and he had been roasted to death.

Slowly the expedition made its way along the unknown
banks of the Brahmaputra. Here and there they erected
their plane-tables and theodolites and made maps. They
passed many villages and scores of monasteries, each with
its crowd of red-robed lamas. Beyond Lhatse they entered

LHATSE FORT AND MONASTERY

From Rawling's "The Great Plateau" (Arnold)

western Tibet, and soon the character of the country began to change. There were fewer villages, and trees were scarce, although in places there was an abundance of game—gazelles, antelopes, kiangs, and the much-sought Tibetan ram (*ovis ammon*).

Ryder and Rawling crossed over to the south bank of the Tsangpo, and from the top of a hill they saw the towering pinnacle of Mount Everest fifty miles away to the south. From this vantage-point the giant peak appeared to dwarf all her satellites, and the northern face looked a sheer precipice.

The river now began to run through more open country, and since winter was approaching, great ice-floes came rushing down. Eventually the explorers came to a place where there was a leaking ferry-boat owned by some monks. To get the unwieldy contraption started the lamas had to wade waist-deep among the ice-floes, but at last the whole party reached the other side in safety, and soon afterwards they rejoined the main body of the expedition. They had been steadily rising since they left Shigatse and were now about 15,000 feet above sea-level, and the Brahmaputra was gradually dwindling in size. About here there were plenty of wolves, and whenever possible, the explorers shot them without mercy.

When they at last reached the holy lake of Manasarovar, the native porters collected some of the sacred water into small bottles so that they could carry back the precious fluid to their homes. For many days' marching Kailas Parbat, the sacred mountain, was in full view. This peak of 22,000 feet must be one of the most beautiful in the world. Rawling compares it with a vast cathedral the roof of which is regular in outline and covered with eternal snow. Below the roof are sheer precipitous walls of vivid pink, which form a lovely contrast to the purple-blue waters of the sacred lake beneath.

South of Gartok it became necessary to climb a high pass, where the yak-drivers suffered much discomfort from the cold during the night. Now they reached the Indus basin and had a clear view of the Gartok Plain, a desolate, flat, and barren region hemmed in by rocky ranges. They were told at the capital that in the height of the summer Gartok is the centre of a great fair which attracts merchants from all over central Asia. But at this time of the year there was not a shepherd or a flock visible, and many of the buildings were deserted.

When arrangements had been made for the trade-mart, the expedition turned into new country round the head-waters of the Sutlej. Here the country was divided up into strips by *nullahs* with precipitous sides. At a place called Tooling they came across a forgotten city on the top of a mountain. The town was reached by subterranean funnel-like passages, up which only one man could climb at a time. On the top they found ancient monasteries, temples, and palaces lying in silent ruin. The natives said that once Tooling was the capital of an independent kingdom of western Tibet.

From this point they made for the frontier of India. The track twisted along the beds of desolate *nullahs* or zigzagged down the face of cliffs to the bed of a ravine. The whole region was so gaunt and forbidding that it reminded the explorers of the infernal regions. When they finally reached the border they had to cross a high, snow-covered pass, and even then they were still two hundred miles from Simla. But soon they came to a fairly good road, and before long they were being welcomed at a Moravian Mission. In view of the many valuable maps which had been compiled, Ryder was awarded the Gold Medal of the Royal Geographical Society.

FREYA STARK IN THE WILDS OF PERSIA

Although the ancient Greeks knew a great deal about the geography of Persia, and although the modern petroleum-fields have brought the taint of commercialism to the land of the Shah, there are still regions in Luristan and other provinces of the country about which very little is known. The Lurs and the Kurds are a lawless, nomadic community. Thieving is the main national accomplishment, and the would-be explorer is in constant danger of attack by brigands.

The Government guards control some of the passes, but far more are in the power of local chiefs and robbers. Smugglers are as common as Jews in Whitechapel, and opium-smoking is a frequent vice.

One of the chief attractions of the unsurveyed parts of Persia is the ancient cemeteries. The Lurs are adepts at probing for the stone slabs which cover graves, and they are frequently rewarded for their sacrilege by the discovery of valuable antique bronzes. Miss Freya Stark, who is not only an accomplished student of languages, but is also interested in archæology and exploration, has been successful in penetrating the wilds of Persia on several occasions. Indeed, she has seen many places where white men have never been.

The way into Persia from the valleys of Mesopotamia is barred by a high mountain-range, the Pusht-I-Kuh. This is such a formidable barrier that beyond the range is a great expanse of hill-country which has never been surveyed. Here is the heart of Luristan, and here, according to some archæologists, the earliest Persian civilizations had their origin. Having failed to penetrate very far from the Persian side during her expedition of 1931, Freya Stark, in September, 1932, decided to make an attempt to reach Luristan across the Pusht-I-Kuh.

Just before she set off from Baghdad she met a young Lur who told a story about a treasure in a cave in the hills of Kebir Kuh. The Lur said that some years before, a tribesman had been caught by a storm on the slopes of the mountain and had taken refuge in a cavern, where he had found twenty cases of gold ornaments, daggers, coins, and idols. The tribesman had brought away all he could conceal under his cloak, and he had given some of the jewels to the Lur. Although Miss Stark's informant had a map of the way to the cave, he had never been there himself, because he was afraid that the Government would confiscate any treasure which was found. He now hoped that some European who understood the value of such antiquities and treasures would help him to get them out of Persia.

Such stories are common in all countries where archæologists have unearthed such treasures as the tomb of

Tutankhamen or Ur of the Chaldees. Freya Stark, however, was willing to take a chance—especially since there was some corroborative evidence for the yarn—and so she entered into the conspiracy. Unfortunately the young Lur had told his secret to a wicked ex-vizier who was planning to get the loot for himself. The consequence was that Miss Stark had to begin her journey without the Lur, whose passport was confiscated by a policeman under the thumb of the ex-vizier. The sketchy map, with pencilled ovals on it to mark the Lur's home and the cave, was handed into her keeping, and she set off.

Her guide was a dreamy quilt-maker who knew the country beyond the Pusht-I-Kuh, and who had by some secret intrigue managed to obtain a passport. Political differences had led to the placing of an embargo on trade across the frontier, so that smuggling had become the chief pastime of the hillmen. When the Persian border was reached, the guide led the way along a sunken river-bed among tamarisk trees which effectively hid them from the police-post on the ridge. Freya Stark's retainers were evidently of the opinion that she no more wanted to meet Government officials than they did.

Soon the caravan came to some typical Luristan huts made of a framework of poles, roofed with oak-branches, and with walls made of reeds woven into patterns with black wool. As they climbed into the hills two great peaks, each 9000 feet high, stood sentinel on either hand. It was a wild country, and the path led along corridors of rocks and through dry canyons. At last they reached the top of a pass and looked out over an unmapped country of parallel ranges, deep clefts, and dried-up rivers. The land was drought-stricken, and the ragged nomads were forced to eke out their scanty supplies of flour by eating soaked acorns.

Down in the Garua valley the travellers were welcomed at some mills in the midst of a tiny oasis. As they proceeded along the dry valley, the mass of the range called Kebir Kuh grew steeper, until the smooth slabs resembled a wall. At last they reached the home of the quilt-maker. Here

Freya Stark was told of two ruined cities near by called Larti and Hindimini.

Hoping to make important discoveries here, she turned aside from her 'Arabian Nights' venture, and made her way up the ravines to the old cities. A peasant, who said that he knew where the graves were, acted as guide. The walls of Larti were still plainly visible, and the lines of the streets were indicated by large boulders which marked the foundations of ancient buildings. A hurried examination was made of a few tombs, but with disappointing results, and no bronzes were found. Miss Stark had to be content with a skull which she carried away wrapped up in a Burberry. At Hindimini the story was the same. Beneath the precipitous walls of a ravine were foundation-stones, street-lines, and tombstones carved with a running Persian script.

On returning to the main valley the conspirators were considerably chagrined at the sudden appearance of three mounted policemen. Government-officials are never seen in these parts at ordinary times, but the news of a strange woman in Luristan had been carried to the Government-post at Husainabad, and the police had come to investigate. They were very surprised to find that Miss Stark had a pass-port, but insisted upon following her as a sort of escort, although they assured her that she was free to go wherever she wanted. In actual fact, however, the police intimidated the tribesmen, so that no horses were available for further travels into the unknown.

The search for the treasure-cave was now a matter for acute diplomacy. Having located the valley where the cave was supposed to be, Miss Stark announced her intention of spending a few hours looking for some ruins of which she had been told. At first the tribesmen and police tried to dissuade her, because this ravine, they said, was notorious for its brigands. At last her blandishments succeeded, and a start was made.

The problem now was how to escape the vigilance of her escort for a length of time sufficient to achieve her object. Fortunately the police exhausted themselves by chasing some fearsome-looking nomads, who were suspected of being brigands. When the party sat down to lunch, Freya Stark plied her escort with food, handed over a packet of cigarettes, and then, remarking that they must be tired, suggested that she should wander off by herself to look for ruins.

The wily stratagem succeeded. Once out of sight, the adventurous lady hurried along over the rocks towards the promised *wadi*. The ravine rapidly narrowed, and it was full of black rocks and clefts which suggested the entrances to caves. For almost two hours she scrambled about from rock to rock and then reluctantly had to give up the search because she knew that her escort would be looking for her. So the treasure, if it exists, is still carefully hidden in the cave. When she reached camp again, one of the tribesmen asked her if she had seen the cave during her walk in the ravine.

"What cave?" she asked.

"Far on the other side, a big cave near the river; it is a big cave, but with nothing inside it!"

The journey to Husainabad, the capital of Pusht-I-Kuh, was complicated by the fact that the lieutenant of the police-escort contracted fever, and his captive had perforce to administer pills of opium and quinine to keep him alive. So they rode into the town with the lieutenant lolling on the pack-saddle, and Freya Stark prancing on his Arab bay. In this outpost of civilization the explorer had to wait for four days until news came from Tehran that she was to be escorted to the border of Iraq by the shortest possible route. Visitors to Luristan are not officially welcome—probably the Government does not wish to have stories of the turbulent conditions there spread abroad.

Freya Stark also has many interesting journeys in northern Persia to her credit. In 1930–1931 she visited the famous 'Valleys of the Assassins' and 'Solomon's Throne.' These places are among the mighty Elburz Mountains, at the southern end of the Caspian Sea. The maps of this region are still very vague. The region, moreover, has long had a sinister reputation, chiefly because it was the home of the religious sect known as the *Hashishin*, or 'Assassins.'

The chroniclers of the Crusades first brought news of this strange sect to Europe. According to their accounts the leader, 'The Old Man of the Mountains,' had a secret garden where devotees were hypnotized by means of a drug (probably hashish, hence the name). The drug induced the sort of magnificent dreams which are described in Thomas de Quincey's *Confessions of an Opium-eater*, and the victims were told that this was a foretaste of the heavenly joys which awaited those who died in the service of the 'Old Man.' Some chroniclers said that the fanatics would hurl themselves from a high tower at the command of their chief. With such a band behind him, the 'Old Man of the Mountains' built up a strong political power based on blackmail and assassination. It was the biggest 'racket' in medieval history, and it struck terror through Islam and Christendom. The sect of the 'Assassins' still exists, although they are a peaceful people now, and the Aga Khan is now the official head of the sect.

Freya Stark's journey began at the town of Qazvin, and the trail led out of the plains until they reached the domains of the sturdy hill-tribes. Beyond the Chala pass (8000 feet) they came to a long ravine—the valley of Alamut. Away in the distance soared the magnificent peak known as 'Solomon's Throne.' Down in the 'Valley of the Assassins' were a number of villages grouped round small oases, and dominating the whole scene was the rock of Alamut, where stood the castle of the 'Old Man.' Since only two of the dozens of peaks were marked on the map, Freya Stark proceeded to collect the names of mountains from the hillmen and filled up the blanks in her maps as she went along.

A red-bearded old 'Assassin' took her up the steep rock to the ruined castle. Here wild tulips grew among the tumbled stones and mortar. It was possible to judge the extent of the enclosure from the patches of wall which hung precariously on the lip of the summit. There was little to show that this had once been the secret home of the dread chief of the *Hashishin*.

Freya Stark spent some days exploring the 'Valleys of the Assassins' and visited several of the oases. Farther down, the valley narrowed into a ravine with a rock wall on one side 3000 feet high. At the far end the exit was *via* a high pass. The 'Old Man' had chosen a lair with almost impregnable natural defences. From the pass the trail led through the forests of Mazanderan down to the Caspian Sea.

The Royal Geographical Society presented the Back Grant to Freya Stark in 1933 in recognition of her discoveries in Persia. She had travelled and made her maps in regions where even Persian officials fear to travel, and which for centuries have been notorious for lawlessness and brigandage.

In 1936 she made a two months' journey in the Hadramaut in search of Shabwa, the forbidden city, but was prevented by illness from reaching her objective. She again visited Southern Arabia in 1938 in the company of Gertrude Caton-Thompson and E. Gardner, and apart from exploring in a little-known area a great deal of information about ancient cities in that region was gathered.

IN SEARCH OF OPHIR

And Hiram sent in the navy his servants, shipmen that had knowledge of the sea, with the servants of Solomon. And they came to Ophir, and fetched from thence gold, four hundred and twenty talents, and brought it to King Solomon.

I KINGS ix

In modern times the seeker after treasure trove scours the tropic seas for the wealth of Captain Kidd or delves in the Wash for the jewels of King John. Sir Walter Raleigh and the swashbuckling privateers of Tudor times braved the unknown in search of El Dorado. But the most ancient of all the golden cities—the site of King Solomon's mines—remains a mystery. Moreover, modern research has been unable to identify with any certainty the fabled land of Punt, from where Queen Hatshepsut of Egypt procured her frankincense, aromatic woods, and 'green gold.' Many people believe that the key to these secrets is to be found in Arabia, the land which has sprawled on the fringes of the civilized world since the earliest days, but which still has its 'empty quarter,' about which very little is known.

At the beginning of the Twentieth-century that vast desert of South Arabia which is known as the Rub' al Khali had never been crossed by Europeans. This uninhabited wilderness stretches for about 900 miles east of the fertile oasis of Sulaiyil and is 450 miles from north to south—a total area as extensive as France and Spain put together. Over immense distances there are no wells, and what few Arabs do venture to cross have to exist almost exclusively on camel's milk. Apart from these obstacles two difficulties face the would-be explorer: the hostility of the Bedouin, who live on the fringes of the desert, and the problem of obtaining an escort willing to venture into this 'abode of death.'

Arabia is a land of perpetual vendetta. Every youth looks forward to the time when he can mount a swift camel and go off on a raiding-expedition which may bring him fame, camels, or ammunition. The tribes who live on the fringes of the steppe have an annual season for raiding. They travel light, without women, and swoop down on any caravan which is luckless enough to cross their path. Grazing-lands are so few and precious that they can only be kept by constant fighting. Then again, the typical desert Arab firmly believes in the existence of jinns and evil spirits who may play the most horrible tricks on those who venture far away from the beaten track. Little wonder that strange legends grew up about the unknown regions of the interior.

Then in 1930–1931 came the triumph of Bertram Thomas. Thirteen years of post-War service in Arabia had enabled him to acquire a peculiar knowledge of tribal dialects and Arab customs. He had been appointed Wazir to the Sultan of Oman and was known and respected throughout Southeast Arabia. In order to avoid official disapproval, he relates that his plans "had to be conceived in darkness, my journeys heralded only by my disappearances." During his holidays Thomas began to explore the fringes of the Rub' al Khali. In the winter of 1927 he made a 600-mile camel-journey through the southern border-lands, from the most easterly point of South Arabia to Dhufar. In 1929 he went 200 miles north of Dhufar to the very edge of the sands. To avoid religious and racial opposition he dressed as an Arab, spoke only the local dialect, and lived as one of the people, eschewing tobacco and alcohol to win a reputation for orthodoxy.

73

On October 5, 1930, Thomas left Muscat on an oil-tanker, and having transferred to an Arab dhow, was landed at Risut, in Dhufar. Here he heard bad news. There was war in the desert. The Rashidi and the Sa'ar, the implacable tribesmen of the hinterland, were busy at the ancient game of camel-raiding and stealthy slaughter. For some time it seemed that an expedition would be impossible, but eventually Thomas disclosed his plans to two Rashidis, who promised to try to raise enough men and camels for the adventure.

On December 6, at the eleventh hour, when Thomas was expecting at every moment the state-boat which was to carry him back to his duties at Muscat, two Bedouin came bustling through the crowded bazaar with the news that they were the advance-party of a band of forty ready and willing to help the Wazir. But when their leader, Shaikh Salih, arrived, he at once announced that it was quite impossible to cross the desert from sea to sea as Thomas has planned. At first he would agree to nothing more than to take Thomas to the grazing-grounds of his own tribe, the Rashidi. Eventually, however, the fine old campaigner agreed to go as far as the sands and then to ride on in search of a fresh escort. He warned the Wazir that for the first part of the journey a strong party of at least forty men would be needed to resist possible attacks by the raiding Sa'ar.

So the journey began. For many days the route lay through known country, where frankincense-trees flourished in desolate *wadi*-beds. Here, as from time immemorial, the natives still make their incisions after the manner of a rubber-collector and store the fragrant green, transparent oil which exudes.

From the beginning Thomas had to take great care not to arouse the superstitious hostility of his escort, and in order to take astronomical bearings (which they might associate with witchcraft), he had his own tent set up thirty yards away from the main camp. The Arabs, too, were persistently wrangling about the burdens which were placed on their beloved camels. Although the camel seems to be a singularly unfriendly beast, the Arabs so depend on them that they care for them as they would for their own children.

When the infrequent pastures were reached, the drivers would dismount and run hither and thither, garnering the most luscious shoots for their own particular animals. So the caravan straggled on from water-hole to water-hole, which were sometimes five or six days' march apart. The dividing-range was crossed, and the *wadi*-system of Mugshin reached.

Here is the true home of the South-Arabian Bedouin. To the north stretch the great sands, but here in the *wadi*-beds there are scanty pastures where camels could feed and where man could live chiefly on camel's milk. Arms and ammunition and camels are almost the only form of wealth, and raiding the age-old enemy is the only honourable profession. Their homes are caves or the shade of an acacia-tree, and their greatest terrors the jinn and the evil eye.

The next hundred miles lay along the southern edge of the sands, and were particularly dangerous because of the frequent murderous raids of the Sa'ar. Along the narrow track from one sandy water-hole to the next any approaching traveller must be assumed to be an enemy. Before camels were fed or a camp was pitched an Arab would climb the highest dune to spy out the land ahead. Once, after many days of parching heat, a thunderstorm was seen ahead. The caravan spread out in search of rain-pools.

> We soon breasted a rise in the plain to see our party beneath us upon a stony outcrop, with the camels' long necks stretched down and themselves frantically scooping handfuls of water into their water-skins. My thirst soon had me on my hands and knees beside them with my parched lips in the saucers of the rocky floor; and very sweet the collected raindrops tasted, after the water of our march, which had been sand-coloured or pestiferously green to begin with, and had acquired the taste of rank meat from its churning day after day in goat-skins 'cured' in crude Badawin fashion.[1]

For many marches which followed the only verdure was sparse willowy *abala* on the sides of the great red dunes. Thomas began to appreciate the advantages of the swathing Arab head-dress as a protection against the sun. One day, quite suddenly, the Arabs pointed to the ground. "Look,

[1] *Geographical Journal.*

75

Sahib," they cried, "there is the road to Ubar." They went on to relate the story of the great and fabled city of wicked King Ad which had been destroyed by heavenly fire, and which was doomed henceforth to be inhabited by jinns. It was a city rich in treasure, with date-gardens and a fort of red silver. Now, they said, it lies buried beneath the sands some few days' march to the north.

Thomas examined with interest the deep tracks in the arid earth. Was this the fabled road to Ubar? And was Ubar merely the Arab name for Ophir? Another Arab said that he had once been to the site of the old city, where he had picked up pottery and seen the drums of columns. It did seem possible that the tracks led southward to the ancient groves of frankincense; surely there was something to be said for the exciting theory? But no time must be lost; the caravan had to pass on. So the 'Ubar' of Thomas still remains unexplored. But as we shall see, there was a sequel to this incident.

Soon afterwards, when the column was floundering through steep dunes, the silence was broken by a loud droning on a musical note. The Arabs said this was the "bellowing of the sands," and they pointed to a sand-cliff a hundred feet or so high. The loud booming continued for about two minutes and then suddenly ceased. Thomas came to the conclusion that this strange phenomenon was due to the cooling of the sands in the evening. This causes a landslide, or rather a trickle, and so the musical note is produced.

At a grazing-ground called Dhahiya the weary wanderers met Shaikh Salih, who had ridden on and managed to collect a fresh relay of Bedouins. Above all, he had persuaded a Murra tribesman to be their *rabia* and guide. The Murra tribes inhabit the northern fringe of Rub' al Khali, and if Thomas wished to travel in their country he must have a hostage, or *rabia*, to guarantee his friendliness. The fresh relay took Thomas to the last of the wells at Shanna, where new camels were provided for the final dash across the interior sands. From Shanna the objective was to be Doha, on the Persian Gulf, 330 miles distant as the crow flies, across the barren ocean of Rub' al Khali.

The dash northward with a fresh party began on January 10, 1931. Now they had to endure many hardships. There was water at two fathoms, but it was so brackish and so beery in colour that Thomas relied almost entirely on camel's milk. The Murra proved to be a perfect guide and led them to a *hadh*-belt, where there was grazing for the camels on the small sage-coloured bush. Hereabouts the water was so brackish that it was undrinkable either by man or beast, and hence was termed *khiran*. In spite of the inhospitable terrain, animal life still persisted in these stricken wastes. They saw a sand-coloured fox, scarcely bigger than a cat, traces of sand-rats and wolves, and even a solitary eagle's nest. It was the fast of Ramadhan, and the Arabs faithfully observed the law that they should not partake of food until the sun went down.

Towards the end of January the caravan was stricken by a series of sandstorms, and men and camels had to huddle together for warmth. Eventually, however, the rolling red sand-hills began to be dotted with patches of vivid green, and so they came to the water-hole of Banaiyan. Here there was a real well, stone lined and with sweet water. The worst of the Rub' al Khali had been passed, and the sea was but eighty miles to the northward. For the next few days the way lay through known country, where ribbons of steppe alternated with sand-hills and salt plains. On February 3 Thomas was amazed to discover a large lake some seven miles long and a mile and a half wide. Two days later they saw before them the towers of Doha silhouetted against the waters of the Persian gulf.

PHILBY IN ARABIA

It seems strange that the Rub' al Khali, which had for so long defied the efforts of explorers to penetrate its mysteries, should be twice crossed in a twelvemonth. Indeed, but for a trivial incident, which delayed H. St John Philby at Riyadh, the Arab capital, the actual crossing might have developed into a race. As it was, the honour fell to Bertram Thomas, but Philby's expedition was none the less a remarkable achievement.

Like his predecessor, Philby knew Arabia well, and he was lucky anough to travel under the patronage of the King of Hejaz. Philby had long desired to cross the great desert, and also, if possible, to solve the great secret of the Arabian Ophir. His party consisted in all of nineteen persons, under the leadership of one Zayid, and a choice collection of thirty-two camels. Fifteen of these wonderful sand-bred beasts managed to cover a total of 1800 miles in ninety days—a remarkable record, when it is remembered that they had to be driven mercilessly and were at one time ten days without water.

Philby started from the northern edge of the desert, and the departure was somewhat depressing, for the Arabs were convinced that this journey into the 'abode of death' was little short of sheer madness. Their friends, who saw them off, wept bitter tears, as if convinced that they would never meet again. Moreover, it was bitterly cold, and every morning the frozen water-skins had to be thawed before breakfast. The fast of Ramadhan began on the third day out, and since all the travellers (including Philby) were Mohammedans, they were condemned to a day-long fast for the next month. Philby managed to avoid a really terrible thirst by taking a small pot of tea and a bowl of camel's milk before the dawn and another pot of tea after sunset.

As they journeyed southward to the last oasis, at Jabrin, the Arabs were full of tales of ancient kingdoms, and legendary cities, especially of 'Ubar,' or as they called it, 'Wabar.' After leaving the oasis, Philby did pick up a bronze arrowhead and saw traces of ancient trade-routes, which led him to hope that perhaps after all there was something in the story.

So they entered the great sands of the Rub' al Khali and plunged into a world of shimmering sand-dunes and undulating sand-ridges. For some days they followed the line of wells which skirts the north-west section of the 'empty quarter' and, on the way in the midst of a wide gravel plain, suddenly found a number of fresh-water shells and, what was even more intriguing, a fine collection of ancient flint implements. In times long past there had evidently been a river running through the desert at this point, and Philby was hopeful that he might find the ruins of 'Wabar' somewhere in the vicinity.

Two days' march across an ocean of sand-waves did indeed bring them to 'Wabar,' and a strange place it proved to be. Philby had brought with him two guides, both of whom claimed that they could lead him to the mysterious city. One spoke of ruins he had seen, and the other of a great piece of iron, as big as a camel, which was to be found there. In order to encourage the search Philby announced his intention of paying thirty dollars for the lump of iron and five dollars for every building found. Thus it was that on the very day when the caravan was due to arrive at the ruins, one of the guides went off on a private expedition of his own in the hope of getting the whole of the reward. Some hours later he reappeared with the news that he had found the place and produced from under his cloak a specimen from the ruins—a large vitrified brick pitted with numerous air-bubbles. These were evident proofs, thought Philby, of the story that the city had been destroyed by fire.

And we marched on till the ruins came into sight, a long black wall, as it seemed, riding on the sands. We drew nearer and halted at a suitable camping-spot, while I immediately hastened to the top of a low sand-hill near by to get a good first view of the site before dark. The great moment had at last arrived, the moment I had longed for for fourteen years, and I found myself looking down on the ruins of what appeared to be a volcano! So that was Wabar, the city of a wicked king destroyed by fire from heaven and thenceforward inhabited only by semi-human, monomembrous monsters. A volcano in the midst of Rub' al Khali! And below me, as I stood on that hilltop transfixed, lay the twin craters, whose black walls stood up gauntly above the encroaching sand like the battlements and bastions of some great castle.[1]

There were altogether five craters, which varied in diameter from fifty to a hundred yards. Most of them were filled with sand, but they were marked by fringes of black-ened slag. The Arabs were jubilant, and they were soon

[1] *Geographical Journal.*

busy digging in the 'ruins' for buried treasure, in spite of
Philby's persuasions. They filled their saddle-bags with
little jet-black shiny pellets which strewed the place, and
which, according to the Arabs, were the black pearls worn
by the ladies about the Court of King Ad. However, apart
from a few flint weapons, there were no signs of human
handiwork, and Philby set about seeking the reported mass
of iron 'as big as a camel.' Eventually a small piece of iron,
about the size of a rabbit, was found.

When the black pearls and the lump of iron were examined by experts it was definitely shown that the craters
were due to a gigantic meteorite. The pearls were fused
silica-glass, and could have been formed only by a very high
temperature, such as would be created when a large meteorite struck the earth. Meteorite craters of this sort are rare;
there is one in Arizona and another in Central Australia,
and in both these places silica-glass and meteoric iron has
been found in association with craters. So at last the secret
of 'Wabar' was out: it was not a city, but the site of a natural
catastrophe!

This anti-climax tended to dispirit the whole company,
but there still remained the conquest of the 'empty quarter,'
and that was the next objective. They marched south over
a bare plain, leaving Mr Thomas's route far to the east.
Strangely enough, soon afterwards Philby heard the
"booming sands" which had aroused the interest of Thomas.
He found that he could produce the desired effect by sitting
on a sand-hill and setting large quantities of sand in motion.

At the well of Ziqirt the scouts returned with the
information that the rumour of their coming had cleared the
desert to the south. They were to be left to fend for themselves. Philby's Arabs now began to get nervous. One
afternoon the look-out reported three men on camels
approaching in the distance. Immediately the alarm was
sounded. The camels were driven in from the pastures, and
the whole party manned the surrounding heights. Although
Philby guessed that this was an elaborate 'false alarm,' he
had to make a choice of either going to Dhufar along the
route followed by Thomas, or else striking across to Sulaiyil

from where they were. Since the latter course would mean
the crossing of the Rub' al Khali from east to west for the
first time, Philby agreed to take that course.

The Arabs evidently preferred to face the unknown
terrors of the waterless desert rather than the known terrors
of the hostile tribes to the south. Water-skins were re-

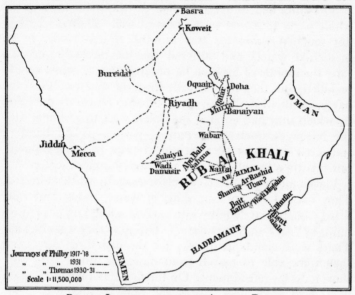

RECENT JOURNEYS ACROSS THE ARABIAN DESERTS

greased and patched, and the baggage was rearranged.
The distance to be traversed was about 350 miles in a straight
line, and Philby hoped to reach the western edge of the sands
in fifteen days. They set off on February 22. They crossed
many patches of gypsum, and in one stretch found immense
deposits of fresh-water shells—clear evidence that the
desert-area was not always so forbidding. Occasionally they
saw recent traces of onyx in this region, but as they advanced,
the vast wilderness became more and more barren and
desolate. For twenty years, said the Arabs, no rain had
fallen in this tract. The withered shrubs had thrust their
blackened roots along the burning surface of the sand as
if in a last desperate attempt to reach one drop of heavenly

F

dew. When they did see a living bush, it caused quite a sensation. The camels crawled along, thirsty and hungry, and before long the Arabs began to mumble threats of mutiny. They had grown tired of the perpetual diet of dates and began to demand food and water. Some of the baggage-camels collapsed, and finally the men refused to go farther.

So Philby had to accept defeat for the moment, and the whole party retreated to the nearest well. Philby, who had not touched water for two months, drank deeply of its medicinal waters and suffered the inevitable 'cure.' To raise the morale of his men he ordered that a camel should be killed, and they lived royally for a day or two. Then the party was divided. Those who wished to return by the route by which they had entered the desert were to go home with the baggage-camels; and Philby, with a picked band of stalwarts, was to make a second attempt to reach Sulaiyil, but this time travelling light and carrying more water.

Eleven men with fifteen camels once again struck westward. They carried twenty-four skins of water, dates, and raw, dried camel-meat. Philby also carried a large tin of peppermints to "suck on thirsty days." This time they were luckier. There were clouds in the sky for the first three days, and they were able to march from dawn to sunset with only short halts for refreshment. On the fifth day they were again in a dead wilderness, where the only pasture was a few moribund herbs. They crossed the vast gravel plain called Sahma, which is the very heart of Rub' al Khali, and now it mattered nothing which way they went for fresh water. The camels began to show signs of distress and had to be given 'refreshers' poured down the nostrils with a kettle.

Then they came to another vast expanse of gravel where there was neither a blade of dried grass nor a stick to make a fire. Philby resisted the temptation to drink water for a time (he had relied on coffee before) but now, since there was no chance of a fire, he finally succumbed and sipped the salty water as if it were the sweetest nectar. So they marched on, driving the thirsty camels without mercy for almost twenty-four hours. This decisive forced march broke the back of the Rub' al Khali. Next day they could see ahead the dark lines of the western mountains. Animal life began to reappear in the form of birds, lizards, and jerboas —and all over the vast plain they could see streaks of vegetation. By the evening they reached a large and luxuriant coppice and were close to Sulaiyil—the first outpost of civilization.

At the last moment it seemed that even yet they might be cheated of their victory. Early the next morning they perceived seven figures approaching stealthily from the bushes ahead, and seeming to be about to cut them off. In an instant rifles were unslung, and everything was made ready for an attack. But next moment some one laughed. The 'raiders' were a party of women, and soon they were exchanging greetings. For fifty-three days Philby and his men had spoken to no other human beings! The 'empty quarter' had been conquered again, but this journey had shown how utterly desolate and uninhabitable is that great and arid wilderness.

CHAPTER III

THE CONQUEST OF THE NORTH POLE

And now there came both mist and snow,
And it grew wondrous cold:
And ice, mast-high, came floating by,
As green as emerald.

C<small>OLERIDGE</small>, *The Rime of the Ancient Mariner*

PEARY'S JOURNEY TO THE POLE

O<small>F</small> all the fields of exploration none has produced more stories of heroism and endurance, of breathless escapes and heart-breaking tragedies, than that of the Arctic regions. Even the early Tudor mariners had cheerfully steered for the frozen north in the search for a route to Cathay, and old Robert Thorne had conclusively proved to his own satisfaction that it would be possible to sail over the very Pole itself. In 1588 John Davis, in many ways the most remarkable of the Elizabethan seamen, had reached 'Sanderson his Hope' at a point only 1128 miles from the Pole. An almost endless succession of discoverers followed along the same route, but all in the end had to admit failure, and many never returned.

During the nineteenth century a number of remarkable attempts was made to reach the North Pole. Parry, in 1827, from his base in Spitsbergen, had reached a point 435 miles from the objective. There followed in rapid succession the expeditions of Ross, Austin, Franklin, McClure, Greely, Nares, Markham, Nansen, and the Duke of the Abruzzi. Commander Robert Peary, of the United States Navy, had spent the best part of his life in Arctic exploration. He had crossed Greenland and explored much of Grant Land. In 1901 he reached a point 343 miles from the Pole. A Peary Arctic Club was founded, and sufficient funds raised to equip a strong ship, the *Roosevelt*, which was specially designed to resist ice-pressure. In 1906 Peary reached the farthest north, but it was not until 1909 that he finally succeeded in reaching the Pole.

By this time his twenty-three years of experience had made him familiar with every cape and creek of North Greenland, and he could claim to know every man, woman, and child of the Eskimo tribes who inhabit those regions. For eighteen years he had been training them how to modify their own wonderful ice-technique so that they would be useful assistants. Thus, on the journey up the Greenland coast from Cape York to Etah he was able to pick up a large number of Eskimos who were ready to follow him to the ends of the earth. Peary could speak their language, he knew their customs, and he respected them, even in the awkward moments when the superstitious natives disturbed his sleep by firing rifles to drive the devil *Tornarsuk* away. Another factor, which certainly helped Peary to succeed where others had failed, was that he thoroughly understood those wonderful animals, the Eskimo dogs.

During the summer the coast of North Greenland is not the abode of ice and snow which it is commonly supposed to be. The ice alongshore breaks up into floes, and the Eskimo travels about in his *kayak*, or hunting-canoe, from one floe to another, spearing the seals and walrus which lie basking in the sun. The frozen surface of the ground melts, and the soil becomes wet and swampy. Many brightly-coloured flowers appear, and along the shore are many kinds of grasses, ferns, and mosses for the herds of musk-oxen. The seal is, of course, the mainstay of life. Sealskin is made into clothing, into tents, and into coverings for the canoes. Seal-meat is the chief food, and the blubber is used for the lamp which warms their winter igloos and cooks their food. During the long winter the Eskimo has to sit patiently by a breathing-hole in the ice until a seal appears; sometimes the dogs will scratch away the snow above a seal-hole. Sometimes the Eskimo adds fish to his larder, his fish-hooks being made of bone or of ivory from walrus-tusks. The polar bear is the most highly prized catch, because it provides not only a large quantity of fresh meat but also a warm rug.

Although during the summer the Eskimos construct small houses of turf and stones, in the winter they are obliged to build igloos of snow-blocks. Peary became an adept at this work, and so saved himself a great deal of trouble in taking tents. The igloo is hemispherical, the blocks of snow being cut into shape by a special knife made of bone. The entrance is usually along a tunnel which also acts as a shelter for the dogs at night-time. The blubber-lamps make the interior of the igloo so warm that, more often than not, the inmates discard all clothing.

Having stayed for some time among his Eskimo friends at Etah, Peary set off for the north of Grant Land in August, 1908. He had planned to find a winter harbour for the *Roosevelt* at Cape Sheridan, on the north coast of Grant Land, while a base was set up at Cape Columbia, about seventy miles to the west. The voyage through the narrow straits which separate Grant Land from Greenland was hazardous in the extreme. There was a strong tidal current, which created a moving pack of chaotic ice-floes and icebergs in midstream. Then for days at a time the whole channel was frozen solid, and the *Roosevelt* had to seek a sheltered cove or hide behind a stranded floe until the opportunity to continue came. Even then gigantic floes, about an acre in extent, surged towards the ship, and it seemed likely at any moment that the expedition would have to take to the small boats or make for land. Once a charging iceberg smashed the bulwarks, and on another occasion dynamite had to be used to prevent that deadly 'pincers' effect of approaching floes which has proved the end of many a good Arctic ship.

Cape Sheridan was reached at last, on September 5, and in order to make it possible to moor the ship as near to the ice-foot as possible, the greater part of the cargo was unshipped. The boxes were piled in such a way that they made a series of huts which, when given a roof of sails and snow, were moderately comfortable. The Eskimos had brought their wives with them, and during the winter they made batches of Eskimo garments of sealskins and furs for the members of the expedition. During what remained of the autumn a base was arranged at Cape Columbia for the supplies to be taken next year on the dash to the Pole. The white men, too, had to gain experience in driving dog-teams.

Moreover, it was possible to arrange several hunting-trips, which provided the party with a plentiful supply of fresh meat during the winter. The 'bag' included a number of Arctic deer, several musk-oxen, and an occasional polar bear. The Eskimo dogs are extremely useful for this work. When they are on the trail of polar bears or musk-oxen they are indefatigable, and they are adepts at rounding up a herd of musk-oxen so that their prey can be picked off at leisure. When a herd is rounded up the oxen stand in a circle with their heads towards the enemy. Then the bull-leader will take his place outside the circle and charge the dogs. If this champion is shot, another beast will advance to the attack, and so the process continues until none are left.

Towards the end of the autumn the new members of the party—Borup, Macmillan, and Doctor Goodsell—were instructed in the art of building snow-igloos by Marvin, the chief assistant, Henson (Peary's negro servant), and the Eskimos. When trained in the art, four men can build one of these snow-houses in an hour by means of the strong snow-sawing knives which are utilized. When the igloo has been shaped into the form of a bee-hive, the builders crawl through a small hole at the bottom, fill up the hole with a block of snow, light the cookers, and in a short time the house is comparatively warm. The great advantages of the igloo over the tent, as used by Captain Scott and others, are that once made, the igloo will stand for some considerable time; that the igloo does not have to be packed up and taken away like a tent; and, above all, that on the return journey the weary explorer can be fairly sure that the end of his march will bring him to the igloos which were built on the outward journey.

The long winter night was spent in a number of useful tasks intended to increase the efficiency of the expedition. Some specially long sledges were constructed such as might be used in the difficult task of crossing the dreaded 'leads,' or lanes of water, which are to be met on the journey northward across the Arctic Ocean. A system of supporting parties was worked out, and it was arranged that one division, under

Captain Bartlett, was to act as pioneers and pick out a trail for the heavier sledges to follow. The fittest men and the best dogs were to be carefully reserved for the final marches.

The polar journey began on February 22. The air was filled with light snow, and the temperature was thirty-one degrees below zero. Altogether the party included twenty-four men, nineteen sledges and one hundred and thirty-three dogs. For the first few miles the journey was no pleasure trip, for the ice offshore was so uneven and full of pressure-ridges that pick-axes had to be used in many places to cut a road for the sledges. On the first day two sledges were smashed. Bartlett had gone ahead as arranged, and so when the day's march was finished, Peary and his section had a number of igloos ready waiting for them.

The first serious obstacle of the sledge-journey came on the second day out from land. During the course of the march Peary could see ahead the dark cloud which always means open water, since there is always a patch of fog in the neighbourhood of the leads. Marvin and Macmillan had been forced to halt, and it was not until the next morning that the raftering ice had closed sufficiently to allow a passage. On the other side of the lead, Bartlett's trail had disappeared, owing to the lateral movement of the floes, and some hours passed before the trail was found again, about a mile and a half to the west. All this time they had been travelling in the Arctic twilight, but now they saw at midday the flaming blade of yellow light which betokened the approaching sunrise.

Soon they came to a more serious obstacle—the expected 'Big Lead,' which apparently marks the end of the Continental Shelf, and which on a previous occasion almost caused the death of Peary and all his men. Captain Bartlett, too, had been held up by a lane of water about a quarter of a mile in width, which stretched east and west as far as the eye could see. There was no alternative but to wait until the floes drifted together again or until the water was frozen thickly enough to permit a crossing. So the days passed by, with the explorers in sickening inactivity. For ten days Peary had to arrange enough occupations and games to

88

prevent his Eskimos from getting fits of panic; and all the time the supplies were vanishing.

Finally it became possible to cross, and during the next few days good progress was made. Even in this region, however, there were many small leads. Borup almost lost his sledge when crossing a crack between two pieces of floating ice. On March 19, Borup, with three Eskimos, set off on the return-journey. A week later the party led by Marvin returned, but by this time the record established by the Duke of the Abruzzi had been passed.

There now remained Captain Bartlett, Master of the *Roosevelt*, Commander Peary, Henson, and six Eskimos, with the pick of the dogs and sledges, and everybody in the best of condition. There seemed every chance that Bartlett would realize his ambition and reach the farthest north yet attained before he had to return. Then an exciting episode almost caused disaster. The whole expedition had built their igloos on the edge of a wide lead, and Peary was just dropping off to sleep on his bed of deerskins when he heard some one yelling with excitement. Looking through a peep-hole, he was amazed to see a broad lead of black water between the igloos of his own party and those of Bartlett. These were slowly moving eastward on the ice-raft, which had broken off, and beyond, as far as they could see through the belching fog, there was nothing but black water. The dog-teams were rapidly hitched up, and as soon as Bartlett's floe had come close enough to permit him to escape across the lead, the whole party moved for safety on to a larger floe.

Fortunately the temperature dropped again, and it was soon possible to make further progress across the newly formed ice. This was some six or seven miles wide, and it was so thin that it buckled as they sped on at full speed for the other side. All the time there was a dreadful fear that the return-journey might not be so fortunate; that some impassable lead would be encountered; or that a storm would arise and set the whole world of floes adrift. During the next few days, however, they made rapid progress again, and when the time came for Bartlett to return, he had reached a point nearer to the Pole than any other man had ever been.

The final party consisted of Peary, Henson, the four Eskimos, Eginwah, Seegloo, Ootah, and Ooqueah, with five sledges and forty dogs. All were in excellent condition, and they had reasonable hopes that another eight marches would bring them to their goal. No sooner had they set off than Peary plunged off a pressure-ridge into the water under the surface-snow. This was no new experience, and since his clothes were water-tight, he merely had to scrape off the rapidly forming ice. There were still plenty of cracks in the ice where the sledges had to charge across from cake to cake, as if they were jumping across a series of swaying stepping-stones. Nevertheless, the picked party which remained were able to travel very fast, and for the next five marches an average of about twenty-six miles per day was maintained.

The Pole was reached on the morning of April 7, 1909. In order to make quite sure that the spot was the Pole, several different observations of the sun were made, and counter-marches were made ten miles in every direction so that an allowance might be made for any slight error in computation. Then, with due ceremony, flags were hoisted on a heap of snow, and a record was left with details of the expedition's progress. Altogether Peary spent thirty hours near the Pole, and he took a number of photographs of the desolate snow-swept scene in all directions. Then, after a short sleep in an igloo, the return-journey was commenced.

In order to avoid the danger of the spring tides, which would inevitably cause a number of leads, Peary decided that they must hurry the return, and he planned double-marches for the entire return-trip. Good conditions made it possible to follow this schedule, and for days on end they covered five northward marches in three return-marches. The trail was easy to follow, and the igloos were still there. As it had been impossible to obtain a sounding at the Pole itself, they had to wait until they reached a place where the ice was thin enough to allow them to drop a weighted line. Five miles from the Pole a sounding gave 1500 fathoms of water and no bottom. It seems likely, therefore, that the depths in the Arctic Ocean are comparable with those in the other oceans.

Since there were plenty of food-supplies remaining, it was possible to give the dogs double rations, and so for the first hundred miles the return journey was a glorious sprint. Very near to the eighty-seventh parallel traces of an Arctic fox were seen—these were the most northerly animal-tracks ever recorded. The weather remained good, and although they had to use ice-cakes as ferries in one or two places, the going was good also. Moreover, since the sledges were now much lighter, it was possible to rush places where the ice was thin.

A series of rapid double-marches brought the party within sight of the mountains of Grant Land. So far, says Peary, "it had seemed as if the guardian genius of the polar waste, having at last been vanquished by man, had accepted defeat and withdrawn from the contest." Even the region of the Big Lead provided few serious obstacles, and when at last they reached the glacial fringe of Grant Land, the Eskimos yelled and danced until they fell from utter exhaustion. As Ootah sank down on his sledge he muttered in Eskimo, "the Devil is asleep or having trouble with his wife, or we should never have come back so easily."

A few days later Peary reached the *Roosevelt* once more. The joy of the triumphant return was rapidly changed to grief, however, when Bartlett met them with the news that Marvin had been drowned at the Big Lead when returning to Cape Columbia. Apparently Marvin had hurried on ahead of his Eskimos and had not noticed the gradual thinning of the ice as he reached the centre of the recently frozen lead. The superstitious natives had found the hole in the ice, and realizing that their leader was drowned, they threw from the sledge all his personal belongings so that his spirit, if it came back that way, might find these things and not pursue them. Thus it was a sad ship which pulled slowly out of the melting ice off Cape Sheridan and began her uneventful journey homeward with the startling news that at long last the North Pole had been conquered.

THE AMUNDSEN-ELLSWORTH EXPEDITION

Although Amundsen had accumulated a fortune out of shipping during the early years of the War, by 1924 his expensive explorations had so reduced his capital that it seemed likely that only a long period of writing and lecturing could save him from bankruptcy. Then one day, when he was sitting dejectedly in his hotel in New York, the telephone-bell rang.

"I am," said a voice at the telephone, "an amateur interested in exploration, and I might be able to supply some money for another expedition."

So Amundsen met Lincoln Ellsworth, a wealthy American, who was himself to become a prominent explorer. Ellsworth was particularly interested in flying, and he offered to buy an Italian airship for a trip to the North Pole. Alternatively he offered to assist Amundsen with his proposed flight from Spitsbergen to the Pole with two Dornier flying-boats. So it was finally arranged that Ellsworth should be in charge of the N-24, while Amundsen should navigate the N-25 from a base in King's Bay, Spitsbergen.

It was the middle of May when the heavily loaded aeroplanes took off, and for two hours they flew over a thick blanket of fog. Soon they were flying fast over the great sheets of polar ice and making good progress. Early on the morning of May 22, however, when about half the petrol had been used, they came to a clear stretch of water and prepared to land. Suddenly the engine of the N-25 began to misfire, and instead of choosing the most convenient landing-place, Amundsen had to make a forced landing. The 'plane came down almost in a 'pancake,' and ploughed along through slush and small ice. This slowed down its speed but made it difficult to manœuvre. The aeroplane skidded and zig-zagged, missed one iceberg by inches, and finally stopped with her nose close up to another iceberg. A few more feet, and the 'plane would have been wrecked.

The situation was full of difficulties. The 'plane lay in a little pool surrounded by icebergs, and at any moment it seemed probable that the ice would begin to close in and crush the machine. For hours the crew of three tugged frantically to move the 'plane away from the iceberg, but all their efforts were unavailing. The companion machine, the N-24, was out of sight. As a precautionary measure Amundsen ordered that all the provisions and equipment should be transferred to solid ice. Then he made arrangements to use the 'plane as an improvised hut. The main cabin was used as a dining-room, a Primus stove was set up, and a meal was prepared.

Once again they tried to turn the machine, and once again failed. Then they decided to try to haul the machine on to a large floe which lay alongside. This scheme involved chipping away a level platform in the solid ice, and the only tools available were three knives, an axe, and an ice-anchor, which could serve as a pick. A sledge was prepared, and rations were reduced because it was clear that they would be some days before they could move. On the next day Amundsen climbed on to the top of the 'plane, and to his great delight he sighted the companion Dornier on the ice to the south-west. Communication by means of morse code was established with Ellsworth, who reported that his machine had begun to leak soon after they had started. Actually Ellsworth's aeroplane was damaged beyond all repair, so that the hopes of the whole expedition now rested on the dangerously situated N-25. When within ninety miles of the Pole, the Ellsworth machine had come down in a small lagoon, and it was now anchored to a large floe. Water was already above the bottom of the petrol-tanks, one propeller was broken, and only one engine would work. Moreover, the ten miles or so which separated the two contingents were a maze of ice-floes and young ice, which would obviously be very dangerous to cross.

By the twenty-fifth, however, the ice had drifted so much that the two camps were only half a mile apart, although it was still a very treacherous half-mile. Ellsworth and his two companions decided to take the risk, and they set off with heavy loads of provisions.

The crew of the N-25 were still working hard at the task of levelling the iceberg when they caught sight of their companions struggling through the floes only two hundred yards away. Since the last stretch was across open water, Amundsen got out a canvas boat and went to meet them. Then, as he passed behind an iceberg, he heard a succession of shrieks. He could not see what was happening on the other side of the berg, but he felt quite sure that there had been a tragedy. Actually what had happened was that Dietrichson, the pilot, had fallen through the ice and had yelled out. Then Omdal, the mechanic, had also gone in. Ellsworth quickly jumped off the sagging ice and lay down on a ledge of old firm ice near at hand, and from there he managed to save Dietrichson by fishing him out on the end of a ski. Omdal by this time was half drowned, but Ellsworth clutched his pack and held him up until Dietrichson had recovered sufficiently from his shock to render assistance. Jointly they succeeded in rescuing their companion, so that when Amundsen finally drew clear of the obstructing iceberg, he saw with great relief that all the men were safe.

So the whole of the members of the expedition crowded into the 'plane-hut. Now that six men were available, it was possible to make more ambitious plans for getting the remaining machine into the air. After a few hours' hard labour they managed to manoeuvre the N-25 on to a hard old floe, which meant that they were one step nearer safety. On the next day a quantity of petrol was rescued from the derelict N-24, and preparations began for the return flight.

By June 1 tons of ice and snow had been shifted, and a suitable run-way had been prepared; but when they tried to fly on the following afternoon, not only did the 'plane keep breaking through the ice, but a dense fog came down and made all further efforts impossible. The aeroplane was anchored in an open lead, and one mechanic was appointed watchman.

Scarcely had the weary explorers gone to sleep when they were awakened by the cry that the ice was closing in. When Amundsen arrived on the scene he found the open lead was now covered with ice, and all around were the menacing growls of pressure-ice. A catastrophe again seemed unavoidable. All the provisions were unloaded and placed on solid ice, and then began the task of moving the 'plane into a safer position. Rations were cut down to half a pound a day for each man, since now it seemed likely that they would have to make the long walk to Greenland over the ice.

During the next few days the process of hacking and levelling ice went on, but once again the N-25 refused to take off and kept breaking through the ice. Then they found an open lead about a quarter of a mile long, and they proposed to start from this lead, hoping that the speed attained would carry them on to the ice and so give them a chance of a run-way long enough to get the 'plane into the air. By the evening of June 4 the new track had been finished; then the fog came down again to prevent them from starting. During the night the pressure-ice once again ruined the carefully prepared run-way.

By this time they were almost despairing. Then they came across a large floe which was about a quarter of a mile square and about half a mile away. They thought that if they could get the 'plane on to this floe they would have a real chance.

So once again, day in, day out, they prepared a track from the lead to the 'life-saving' ice-floe. So intent were they on the work that they did not notice that the pack-ice was slowly approaching the aeroplane. Dietrichson, who had been left behind because he was suffering from snow-blindness, reported the danger, and all hands had to work hard to rescue the 'plane from an enormous, advancing ice-wall. A quarter of an hour after moving the 'plane, the spot where she had been anchored was smothered beneath the ice-pack.

Day followed day with little intermission in the labours of the stranded explorers. Finally the machine was hauled on to the great floe, and the men began the task of making a track from which they could fly. They well knew that this would be the final effort, for if they failed this time, then they would have to march across the floes to Greenland—a journey of such nightmare-perils that perhaps none would survive.

The snow was three feet thick and this had to be moved

before the 'plane could run along. At first they began the back-aching task of shovelling away the snow along a track a quarter of a mile long. But the continuous toil and the short rations had so sapped their strength that it soon became clear that they had attempted the impossible. Then Omdal proposed that they should try stamping on the snow along the track and then wait for it to freeze solid. This idea was adopted, and for the next four days they tramped backward and forward, making a firm run-way. Even so, large obstructions had to be cleared, and Amundsen calculated that altogether they must have moved about five hundred tons of ice and snow. Then the frost was not severe enough to make the trodden snow solid, and twice the 'plane refused to budge.

All spare equipment was thrown away, and on the fifteenth, when a sharp frost had hardened the track, they made the final—and this time successful—effort. The 'plane gathered speed and was soon travelling at top speed. It was now or never. She charged across a wide crack in the floe; then the scraping noise stopped, and only the humming of the engine could be heard. At last, after more than three weeks on the ice, they were in the air again. A flight of eight and a half hours brought them in sight of Spitsbergen, and they came down on the sea close to a ship which towed them to King's Bay.

THE ADVENTURES OF NOBILE AND AMUNDSEN

The lucky escape from the N-25 expedition did not diminish Amundsen's interest in aviation as a means of reaching the Pole, and three weeks after he had returned to Oslo a telegram was sent to Colonel Nobile, of the Italian Air Service, to make inquiries about an airship which was for sale. The negotiations which followed were somewhat complicated by the fact that Nobile wished that the proposed flight across the Pole from Spitsbergen to Alaska should be under the Italian flag. Eventually, however, Amundsen and Ellsworth went to Rome, and three days later the Norwegian flag was hoisted on the airship, which was christened the *Norge*.

THE CONQUEST OF THE NORTH POLE

On May 7, 1926, the *Norge* reached Spitsbergen, and the explorers found that Commander Byrd's Fokker had also arrived. There was little question of rivalry between the two expeditions, since Byrd's sole object was a flight to the Pole, whereas Amundsen and Nobile wanted to fly across the Arctic Ocean, and the Pole was only to be 'an interesting incident.' When Byrd's machine safely returned to Spitsbergen after her famous flight, Amundsen was sincerely pleased at his success, especially since it now meant that he could go ahead with his own plans instead of possibly having to undertake a search for Byrd.

The *Norge* took the air for her great flight on the morning of May 11, and she was favoured by good weather for some time. Soon after 1 A.M. on the next morning they passed over the Pole, and the flags of Norway, the United States, and Italy were dropped to honour the occasion. Some hours later they ran into thick fog, and until six in the evening they could see very little. The fog also caused trouble by freezing on to the exposed metal parts of the airship. When this ice broke away, it was thrown by the force from the propellers against the envelope, which was in consequence damaged considerably.

At six o'clock on the next morning land was sighted. Very soon they were passing over Wainwright, Alaska. By this time the crew were terribly tired, and since petrol was running out, a landing had to be made near a small village called Teller. In seventy-two hours the *Norge* had covered 3391 miles across Arctic wastes. No new land had been seen, but the possibility of islands north of Canada could not be dismissed, since for long hours visibility had been reduced to zero.

Many public celebrations followed when Amundsen returned to Norway. Nobile, who had quarrelled with Amundsen, proposed to repeat the polar flight, and he set off in May, 1928, in the airship *Italia*. Then came the dramatic news that the *Italia* had come down on the ice when returning from the Pole. Immediately all past grievances were forgotten. Amundsen procured a seaplane, and in company with Dietrichson, he set off from Tromsö to the

G

rescue. Wireless-messages came through for some hours, and then followed a great silence. The conqueror of the Arctic had answered the "one clear call," and he had died as he always said he hoped to die—a martyr in the cause of humanity and exploration.

BYRD'S FLIGHT TO THE POLE

One day in April, 1926, the good ship *Chantier* steamed out of New York Harbour with a strange crew and on an even stranger mission. There were, it is true, eight real sailors on board, but the remainder of the crew of fifty were volunteers from many walks of life. Some of them had never even handled an oar, and when the boatswain instructed one of the hands to "get the fire-hose started" (to carry out the routine-washing of the anchor-chain as they set off) the amateur, thinking that the ship must be on fire, seized a patent fire-extinguisher and dashed to the forecastle. There were also one or two stowaways, bitten with the lure of adventure, and willing to be useful, even if it only meant washing dishes. On the deck was a mingled assortment of flying-gear, and stowed away in the hold was a large 'plane, the *Josephine Ford*. This was a Fokker three-engined monoplane in which the leader, Commander Richard Evelyn Byrd, hoped to fly to the North Pole.

In the previous year Byrd had gained valuable experience of flying under Arctic conditions in a series of flights across Ellesmere Land and above the Greenland ice-cap. But Greenland had proved to be unsatisfactory as an air-base, and so now Byrd was sailing to King's Bay, Spitsbergen, where there is a landing-ground only 750 miles away from the Pole.

On arriving at King's Bay they found that preparations were already under way there to receive the Italian airship, the *Norge*, for the Amundsen-Nobile expedition. They found that the little harbour was choked with ice, and there were no facilities for landing the heavy 'plane. Moreover, the only available landing-stage was occupied by a Norwegian gunboat, which had just narrowly escaped disaster in the drifting ice. Byrd was therefore obliged to anchor as close as possible to the shore and send the aeroplane through the drift-ice on a raft improvised out of the ship's life-boats. After a struggle the 'plane was lowered on to the raft, but

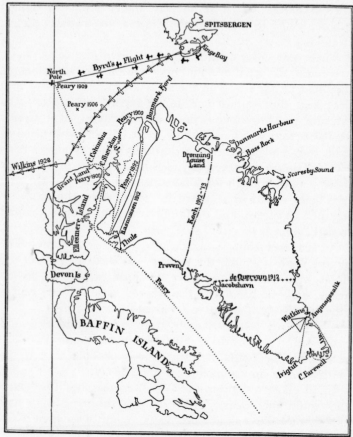

THE CONQUEST OF THE NORTH POLE AND RECENT JOURNEYS IN GREENLAND

just as they were about to hoist the wings out and bolt them on to the fuselage, the wind rose and almost wrecked the whole mission. Since they had only one aeroplane, an accident would have meant complete and final failure. Then the ice started moving, and a great iceberg came charging in with the tide. Owing to the drifting snow the berg was not visible until it was near enough to threaten not only the raft but the ship as well. As quickly as possible they dynamited the monster, and then went on battling their way to shore. When at last the 'plane had been hauled ashore, it had to be pulled about a mile up a snowy incline to the top of the landing-field.

There was still a considerable number of difficulties to be overcome. Before they could pour the oil into the machine they had to dig a hole in the snow and warm the tins in a fire; and the engines had to be heated by means of a pressure gasoline-stove. Since there was no level stretch available that was long enough for a take-off with a heavy load, they had to arrange a downhill run-way across deep snow. The men worked eighteen hours a day to make the snow smooth enough for a take-off, and even then the first trial flight ended in a snowdrift. Three times the skis were smashed to pieces, and eventually the ship's carpenter had to make a fresh set out of some oars.

At last everything was ready for the great flight. The motors were warmed, the fuel-oil was heated, and all the stores were put aboard. But the load proved to be too heavy, and the friction of the skis too great. They went a little too far and taxied off the end of the run-way at a terrific speed, jolted roughly over snow-hummocks, and ended up in a snowdrift. Fortunately the 'plane stood up to the terrible pounding, and it was possible to taxi the *Josephine Ford* up the incline for another try.

In an effort to lighten the load Byrd searched the 'plane and found that nearly every man in the expedition had hidden some souvenir aboard. Even so, one of the men managed to have his ukulele carried to the Pole and back!

Just after midnight a second attempt was made, and at last the heavy 'plane took the air and was off on her great adventure.

In case they should be forced down on the ice, they took with them a short-wave wireless-set, a hand-made sledge, and enough food for ten weeks. They had a rubber boat for crossing open leads, rifles and ammunition, and plenty of seal and polar-bear clothes. Byrd and his companion, Floyd

Bennett, aviation-pilot, shared the task of steering and navigating.

The *Josephine Ford* climbed to a height of 2000 feet, and they got a good view of the coast and the magnificent snow-covered mountains in the interior of Spitsbergen. Within an hour they were over the polar ice-pack, and for fifty miles ahead they could see the sea-ice gleaming in the rays of the midnight sun. Soon they were far out of sight of land, and it was now vitally important that they should reach the Pole, or at least a place where they knew where they were; there was always a chance that on the return-journey they might miss Spitsbergen altogether. They could not navigate by means of the magnetic compass, because apart from the fact that the compass-needle points to the magnetic pole, which is on Boothia peninsula, a thousand miles away from the Pole, they had no means of knowing what the local deviation was. So they had to depend on a sun-compass, which is something like a reversed sun-dial. Another navigational difficulty was due to the fact that when sights were taken from the trap-doors, or figures were written on the chart with bare hands, the observer's fingers and face were frozen.

Looking down at the ice-sheet, they saw that it was criss-crossed with pressure-ridges, and near the open leads they estimated that the ice was forty feet thick. Flying-conditions were good because, owing to the flatness of the ice and the steady temperature, there were no bumps in the air. Every now and again the observer would relieve the pilot, and empty oil-cans would be thrown overboard to get rid of any superfluous weight.

Suddenly, when, according to their calculations, they were about an hour's flying away from the Pole, Byrd noticed through the cabin-window a bad leak in the oil-tank of the starboard engine. Bennett was pessimistic. "That motor will stop," he wrote. Then he suggested that they should attempt landing in order to mend the leak, but Byrd decided to trust to luck and keep straight on for the Pole. The remaining two engines would, in any event, keep them afloat for some time. Just after 9 A.M. on May 9, 1926, they reached the Pole. They took some photographs and some moving-pictures, although the scene below was a desolate expanse of blinding whiteness. In order to make quite sure that they had reached their destination they made careful observations and then circled round the place which they estimated to be the actual Pole.

Fifteen minutes later they were headed back for Spitsbergen. To their astonishment the leaky engine continued running. Actually they found later that the leak had been caused by a rivet jarring out of its socket, and when the oil got down to the level of the hole, it stopped leaking. The chief danger now was that they would fall asleep, for they frequently dozed at the wheel, and the constant lulling roar of the motors had a narcotic effect. Soon they were going at a hundred miles an hour. Speechless and deaf from the motors, they felt strangely lost in the centre of those 10,000 square miles of visible snowfields.

Fifteen hours after leaving their base they came back to King's Bay, flying at about 4000 feet. Soon they were in the midst of a yelling, cheering crowd of shipmates, and a few minutes later the news was being flashed to all the corners of the earth that for the first time an aeroplane had flown over the North Pole.

THE PAPANIN EXPEDITION

From May 1937 to February 1938 a gallant band of Russian scientists made their home on an ice-floe which drifted steadily from the North Pole southward along the east cost of Greenland. The leader, Papanin, had already had much experience in polar regions, and his three companions were interested respectively in marine biology, physical geography, and radio-telegraphy. The party was landed near the Pole by aeroplane from Franz Josef Land. Altogether four 'planes reached the Pole, bringing provisions and scientific gear. During the long drift southward wireless communication was maintained; for several months weather reports were issued from near the North Pole. Soundings of the ocean depths were also made. In the end the explorers were rescued by Soviet ice-breakers.

CHAPTER IV

AMONG THE HEAD-HUNTERS OF NEW GUINEA

My travels' history:
Wherein of antres vast and deserts idle,
Rough quarries, rocks and hills whose heads touch heaven,
It was my hint to speak. . . . And of the Cannibals that each
    other eat.

SHAKESPEARE, *Othello*

THE ADVENTURES OF STANIFORTH SMITH

NEW GUINEA has for long defied the efforts of explorers to learn the secrets of its forested and mountainous interior. There are many difficulties to be overcome. New Guinea is one of the largest islands in the world and is nearly 1500 miles long and over 400 miles wide. On either side of the great backbone of snow-capped mountain-ranges are dense jungles, where progress for a hundred yards through undergrowth like barbed-wire entanglements may mean a whole day's hard hacking. Here only scanty patches of the sky may be glimpsed. The soil is so fertile that not one foot remains untenanted. There are giant trees whose topmost boughs are fully a hundred and fifty feet above the ground, and a lower stratum of bushes and shrubs which attain a height of forty feet. Creepers and lianas twine snake-like round every stem, as if intending to strangle the life out of their hosts. Their tentacles twist out from branch to branch, forming a dense, matted super-structure which prevents even the stricken giants from falling to the ground. There are deadly swamps, roaring mountain-torrents, poisonous snakes, deep rocky chasms, and hostile head-hunting natives.

The natives of New Guinea are some of the most primitive in the world. Very often they go naked except for a grass kilt. They wear the black plumes of the cassowary or the feathers of a cockatoo for head-dresses and plaster their hair into fantastic rolls with bees-wax and honey. They are very superstitious and carefully destroy all their remnants of cooked food lest an enemy should seize them and work a spell on those who had partaken. Tribal warfare is endemic, and explorers frequently meet bands of natives in full war-regalia, carrying arrows and gruesome battle-clubs. On such occasions their very appearance is enough to alarm the traveller, for it is their habit to paint themselves with yellow or red clay, stick pencils of bone or cane through their noses, and hang skulls or human jaw-bones round their necks.

Much of the work of exploration has been done in the ordinary course of business by Government-officials. In 1910 Staniforth Smith, the Administrator of Papua (*i.e.*, the British portion of New Guinea), set out across the centre of the unexplored area of his province to find the sources of the rivers emptying into the Papuan Gulf. He started with four other white men, twenty-five native police, and fifty native carriers from the head of navigation on the Kikor, or Aird, River. His first objective was Mount Murray (7000 ft.), and when this had been climbed he sent back most of his party. Then he turned westward into the unknown, accompanied by Mr Bell and Mr Pratt (two officials), eleven police, and seventeen carriers. The way led along a high limestone plateau. They soon came to a fertile valley in which there were a number of native villages. Fortunately the natives were friendly, and they even gave the explorers some sweet potatoes. They were evidently a very primitive tribe, and many of them had never seen a white man before.

The expedition now turned along a tributary of the Kikor, and the men were soon in difficulties. The limestone had been cut up into a series of precipitous ridges and deep gorges, and they were constantly scrambling up or down mountain-sides clothed with thick jungle. For days on end they could see no more than a few yards ahead, and they had to hack their way through, like moles burrowing underground. The compass was their only guide, and on an average they advanced about three miles each day.

One day they had a great surprise, for the tributary suddenly disappeared into a huge cave and flowed on under the limestone mountains. The rock hereabouts was so porous that the rain-water sank immediately into the ground, and sometimes they had to travel for twenty-four hours without a drink. The rivers, too, they discovered were always disappearing underground and then reappearing farther on. At one place they had the good luck to come across some sago-trees, and so were able to add to their food-supplies. They cut down the trees in the approved fashion, split them open, and extracted the edible floury pith.

Before long the tributary which they had been following turned sharply to the south, but Staniforth Smith pushed on westward until he was forced by the mountains to follow a more southerly route. He came to a large river called the Mobi, where there were native canoes and other evidences of inhabitants. They found that the savages in this region inhabited long thatched houses not unlike the *malocas* of the Amazonian Indians. Some of the houses were perched on steep rocky ridges and raised on wooden piles some ten or twelve feet above the ground. The whole of the tribe, sometimes seventy or more, lived in the one building. Sometimes the native villages were further protected by rickety wooden drawbridges which spanned deep ravines, and which could be quickly removed in times of danger.

At one of these villages the explorers had a very narrow escape. The natives were evidently hostile and they had never seen white men before. When they saw Smith approaching, they mustered their forces, armed themselves with bows and arrows, and began to shout their blood-curdling war-cries. Staniforth Smith ordered his party to sit down on the ground before the huts, and instead of preparing for a fight, they held up pieces of red cloth. The savages did not quite know what to make of their strange visitors, and eventually they all disappeared, leaving the hut empty. Knowing the danger of offending the native ideas of *taboo*, Staniforth Smith did nothing to interfere with the house except to leave presents, and the next morning the expedition continued its journey. The Administrator's diplomacy had a good result, for on the next afternoon they were overtaken by the natives, who were now very friendly and made presents of food to the party. Moreover, in that mysterious fashion which has often puzzled westerners, the news of the peaceful intentions of the expedition were spread abroad, and on several future occasions the natives came to the rescue when food-supplies were at a low ebb.

Then followed many days of arduous travel along first one river and then another, until the explorers reached the crest of a range of mountains, and away in the distance they could see a large river, which according to their calculations, should have been the Strickland, a tributary of the great Fly river. Staniforth Smith thought that once this river was reached their troubles would be over, for it would be possible to build rafts and float down the river to the coast. Unfortunately they found that the mountain-side was so precipitous that they were unable to reach their immediate goal and had to turn again in to the forest. That night they camped on the banks of a creek in which they could see some shiny black rocks, which they found to be coal. All the next day they followed this stream, which they realized must be a tributary of the broad river they had seen from the mountain-top. Then they came to a mighty waterfall down the side of a gorge 300 feet high, and further progress in that direction was effectually barred. They pitched camp on a mountain-ridge and had to go waterless, though they could hear the tumbling roar of the stream far below.

As they travelled on, the gorge seemed to get deeper, and since they had to have water, they decided to risk a descent down the precipitous cliff-face to the torrent. The descent was extremely difficult, but thanks to the assistance of some ropes manufactured out of strong creepers, they managed to reach the bottom safely. But there they found that they had jumped out of the frying-pan into the fire! At the foot of the cliff there was a small piece of flat ground bounded by the roaring rapids of the torrent; behind was the precipice, up which it was next to impossible to carry the provisions. On either hand the river churned furiously through gorges, which were so narrow that there was no possibility of walking along the banks of the stream. Staniforth Smith decided that the only thing to do was to build rafts from the trees growing on the little plain and then trust to luck that they could shoot the rapids.

Smith embarked on the first raft with three police and two carriers. For two hundred yards they pitched and tossed along the boiling waters, and then they came to a sudden sharp bend. The raft turned turtle, and the passengers were all thrown into the swirling torrent. By good luck they managed to cling to the upturned raft, and so they dashed along, swept by great waves and dazed in rapid whirlpools. Suddenly the river divided into two branches. The raft went careering along down one of the channels, and then to their horror they saw a huge timber-barrage which stretched across the stream. The raft charged the obstruction like a mad buffalo and was dashed to pieces. The battered crew managed to scramble ashore, but they were in a desperate plight. One of the carriers was so badly injured that he died the next morning. They had lost all their food, clothing, and baggage and had nothing left but three rifles, a revolver, some ammunition, and their sheath-knives.

The survivors started to cut a track back along the river in an attempt to join their comrades, but they soon found that they were on an island between the two channels. With sinking hearts they improvised a camp for the night.

The next day they found a place where it was possible to ford the river, although the current was so strong that they could hardly keep their feet. Continuing to slash his way along, Staniforth Smith eventually met two of the native police from the other party, who informed him that Mr Bell and Mr Pratt were on the other bank of the river. It was quite impossible to cross at this point, and Staniforth Smith had to turn back downstream, hoping against hope that they could find a native village, for they had already been two days without food. But no natives were to be found. For five days they hacked and hewed their way along, slowly starving in the midst of tangled vegetation. At night the white man had no covering from the torrential rain other than a rough shelter of boughs put up by the police.

On the fifth day they suddenly saw a sight which gladdened their hearts. It was a group of natives on the opposite bank holding up baked sago. Faint with starvation, the men hastily built a crude raft, and they reached the other side of the river in the last stages of exhaustion. While they were eating the food given to them by the natives they had another surprise, for they heard a sudden hail, and looking up, saw Bell and Pratt and some of the police and carriers emerging from the jungle. They had also had their adventures. Pratt had narrowly escaped drowning when sucked under in a whirlpool, and seven of their carriers had lost their lives.

It was now clear that the river along which they were travelling could not be the Strickland, for it was running to the east, so that they were travelling in the direction from which they had begun their journey. Smith decided to travel downstream in search of a native village. They had no means of making fire and no food other than that which they could beg from the few natives they met. For the next hundred miles they passed rapid after rapid, and for twenty-nine days they had to exist on a few handfuls of soup-powder and a few tins of cocoa saved from the capsized rafts. They slept in caves and under palm-leaves, and since they had no matches they had to keep a fire burning day and night. After a long tramp under such conditions they came to another native house, where they were well treated and fed.

Now the river became smooth enough to allow them to embark in two frail dug-out canoes. On the first day they covered fifty miles. On the next day, however, they came to more rapids, and once again the canoes were upset. Clinging like limpets to the upturned boats, they were swept along for ten miles before they were able to land. They spent that night in the pouring rain, without food of any sort. Starting again at daybreak, they passed successfully over several rapids, and about nine o'clock in the morning they saw some tents on the river-bank. The camp belonged to a relief-expedition, and Staniforth Smith found that they had encamped at the precise spot from which he had begun his overland journey from the Kikor. In fifteen weeks he had covered the round trip of 500 miles through the heart of unknown country. Few explorers have earned more thoroughly the gold medal which is awarded every year by the Royal Geographical Society.

CAPTAIN RAWLING DISCOVERS THE PIGMIES

Dutch New Guinea is sharply divided into southern and northern districts by a mighty backbone of snowy ranges, which culminate in the peak known as Carstensz Top, 16,000 feet high. Although this range approaches to within thirty or forty miles of the southern coast, for many decades the forested coastal plain provided such a pestiferous, malaria-ridden obstacle that no white man succeeded in reaching the snows visible from the coastline.

In 1910 a British expedition, which had the assistance of the Dutch Government, undertook to explore a huge area of the coastal plain between the Mimika and Utakwa rivers —a total of 3000 square miles of unknown land. Captain Rawling, who was in charge of the surveying, was accompanied by a number of naturalists, who hoped to learn more about the wonderful variety of gorgeously plumed birds which are the gems of the New-Guinea jungle. Rawling's main object was to reach the snowfields of the dividing range and, if possible, to climb Carstensz Top. The Mimika river-mouth had been visited previously, and he hoped that if he followed this river it would lead him across the plain to the mountains.

The Dutch Government provided forty Javanese soldiers and sixty convicts as an escort. Many of the latter were convicted murderers, and some were even brought to the ship in chains. The shackles were struck off as soon as they boarded, for it is well known that there could be no chance of escape from New Guinea. The Dutch also promised to provide coolies, but when they arrived Rawling gasped in astonishment. Most of them were sixteen-year-old Javanese who wore the pseudo-civilized dress of black frock-coats, bowler-hats, and brilliantly coloured *sarongs*. Those who were actually halt or maimed were promptly shipped back to Amboina.

As the expedition-ship, the *Nias*, approached the coast, a thin column of smoke was seen rising from the nearest promontory. This alarm-signal was repeated with astonishing rapidity every few miles along the coast, and at the same time swarms of canoes shot out from the inlets and were paddled along behind the steamer. Finally a launch was lowered, and one of the natives guided them to the mouth of the Mimika.

The launch crossed the bar and was soon passing between slimy banks covered with mangrove-trees. Alligators basked on the shores of the dank and gloomy creeks, and sometimes a flashing ripple indicated the startled flight of a water-snake. Overhead white cockatoos screamed with fear, and the cry was taken up by flocks of parrots, lories, egrets, and pigeons.

Soon they reached a place where the river divided, and close by they saw the rickety huts of a native village. There was a wild yell from the banks, and as if by magic a dozen well-filled canoes appeared. Then Wakatimi gave itself over to transports of welcome. The men, already anticipating a plenteous supply of trade-goods, turned somersaults into the water, while the women, not to be outdone, threw themselves into the mud, rolling over and over until they were plastered from head to foot. Yet as soon as the white men landed, the women scuttled to their rudely constructed communal houses, and scores of frizzly heads peeped out from the dozen doorways.

Eventually a large base-camp was set up on the opposite bank of the river, and in the following months a wide area of forest was cleared and gardens were laid out. Then began the tedious process of transporting food-supplies and tents upstream in dug-out canoes. The natives were willing to assist and would work for days on end in return for a steel axe-head. But the Mimika proved to be useless as a line of approach to the high mountains. Continuous soaking rain and fever caused terrible sufferings among the coolies. Soon it was decided to cut across country to the Kaparé river. From this point they had a grand view of the mountains, but at this moment the dozen Papuans who were accompanying Rawling took it into their heads to desert. This was by no means an unusual occurrence. Once out of their own hunting-grounds the natives were nervous, and there was always a chance that they would turn on the explorers with their terrible jagged stone clubs. This time, however, the savages thought better of their desertion, and Rawling returned to the base-camp safely.

But fifteen miles away he had seen a saddle-backed mountain about 7500 feet high and, far up the valley, an immense precipice running east and west—a sheer wall of rock, bare of vegetation, and over a mile high. So, a few days later, Rawling returned up the Kaparé river and reached a point a little higher up than on the previous occasion. The Papuans then refused to go farther. They seemed to be afraid of what lay beyond. To shame them into activity Rawling shouldered a load and plodded on up the river-bed. There was a sudden guttural cry, and the sulky savages, galvanized into life, dashed on over the stones into the jungle. Rawling, thinking that they were hunting a wild pig, dumped his load and pounded along after them. Then, to his amazement, he saw that the footprints along the trail were not those of a pig but were human. Before many minutes had passed a confused mass of yelling savages emerged out of the forest. In the midst of the crowd were two very small naked men who were struggling frantically to escape from their burly captors.

When they had been hauled before him Rawling ordered that their bows and arrows, grass helmets, and string hold-alls should be returned to them. Then, as a further friendly gesture, he gave them some brightly coloured beads. They proved to be members of a mountain-tribe called Tapiro, and when measured, they were found to be four feet seven inches in height. They were, however, in no sense deformed; indeed they were quite strong and wiry. One of the pigmies consented to stay with the expedition for a couple of days, and that evening he proudly displayed his prowess in making fire by rubbing two sticks together. A day or two later two more pigmies—even smaller than the first two—were captured. These also were released, because

Rawling wished to make friends with this hitherto unknown people and if possible to visit their homes.

That evening Rawling spied through his glasses the edge of a forest-clearing high up the mountain-side. Since this had the appearance of being cultivated, he guessed that it must be near the home of the pigmies. During the next few days attempts were made to reach this place through a trackless labyrinth of deep ravines, and at last a way was found to the clearing. There was a shrill yodelling, and soon eight little men appeared with their bows and arrows ready for instant use. One of them was one of the former captives, and with his help a certain amount of bartering was carried on. Rawling discovered that the clearing had been made partly by burning down the mighty tree-trunks and partly with the help of a tiny axe made out of a piece of old hoop-iron. There were no signs of huts, and Rawling could not persuade the pigmies to take him to their homes.

Since the labyrinth of ravines, from which issued the Kaparé, were obviously no use as a means of approach to the mountains, Rawling had to retire, to seek a route more to the east, and for some time he saw nothing more of the pigmies. Later in the year, however, he paid a return visit. This time a well-defined trail was discovered along the crest of a spur, and soon they reached the pigmy-village. The women promptly fled high up into the mountains, and during the whole course of the expedition no pigmy women were ever seen. At first the little men were very hostile, and as the explorers ran up they were fitting arrows to their bows. But when beads, knives, and cloth were displayed, they became more friendly and allowed Rawling to examine their huts.

The men were all about four feet six in height, and their only dress was a bright yellow gourd. Over the shoulder they carried large net bags of coarse string in which they treasured all their portable wealth—fishing-lines, fire-sticks, boar's tusks, plumes from birds of paradise, and other odds and ends. Some wore earrings of banana-seeds and necklaces of wallaby-bones or red seeds. Their huts were erected on piles and roofed with palm-leaves. To reach the hut a ladder had to be climbed.

TAPIRO PIGMIES

From Rawling's "Land of New Guinea Pigmies" (Seeley Service)   112

The task of finding a practicable route to the mountains seemed to be insuperable. Tracks were hacked for weeks on end across the head-waters of the numerous streams which run down from the dividing range to the coast. Always it was the same story. A river would be followed, but soon impassable spurs or gorges were reached which held up further progress. Most of the difficulties arose from the unsuitability of the coolies. Many of them died from fever or beri-beri. Others were incapable of struggling through the dripping forests for more than one march. The natives were only reliable until they had obtained a steel axe-head or some other tool which aroused their cupidity.

The Papuans could never understand why they were always rewarded at the base-camp when they took along the slips of paper which served as pay-checks. On one amusing occasion, when the men were being paid according to what was written on their chits, four or five loafers joined in the line and calmly proffered labels and pieces of wrapping off beef-extract tins. They were highly indignant when these 'bank-notes' were not honoured.

The difficulty of transporting supplies from the base to the advanced camps was never satisfactorily overcome. It took six days to paddle a canoe to the head of navigation on the Mimika river, and by that time a large proportion of the cargoes had been eaten. Motor-launches were tried, but they collided with sunken logs and were put out of action.

Eventually, after weeks of hacking a trail through the jungle, a path was made to yet another river, the Iwaka. Directly to the east was a ring of mountains, and if this could be reached, a good deal of planning could be done. Down in the jungle, where the visibility rarely exceeded a few yards, it had been almost hopeless trying to find a route to the interior. Unfortunately the Iwaka was a wide, raging torrent, and unless some means of crossing it could be found, the expedition would have to retreat without any chance of success.

At first the explorers tried to bridge the stream by chopping down trees, but these either broke in two as they fell across the chasm or were swept away by the torrent. The two Gurkhas, who had been the most valuable of the servants brought by the Britishers, volunteered to find a way. One of them swam across with a line of rattan fastened round his waist; on the other side he felled a tree with such precision that it spanned the river. That night, however, an immense flood swept the bridge out of existence, and only the single rope remained as a connecting-link with the farther bank. Moreover, the torrent was now so swollen that any attempt at swimming across would have been fatal.

One of the Gurkhas quietly fixed a girdle of rattan round his waist, lowered himself into the river, and, hand over hand, started on his perilous journey, clinging to the rope. The line was weak and flimsy, but there was a hope that if he were torn from his hold he might be saved by the line round his waist. The force of the current was so strong that his body was level with the surface, but on he went until he was three-quarters of the way across. Then the rope round his waist caught in the water, and the extra weight stopped his progress completely. It would have been useless to pull the line tight, and it seemed that at any moment his arms would be torn away, and then his life would depend on the waist-line. Then the waist-line suddenly snapped. This made the situation critical, but now that he was relieved of the weight the Gurkha was able to continue. The line held, and soon he lay gasping on the farther bank.

Now it was possible to stretch more ropes across, and soon a serviceable rope-bridge had been built. Good progress was made for the next few miles, and then came the old story of ravines and forested spurs making long detours necessary. At last it was decided to cut a way through the jungle up the hills in an attempt to reach a spot where it would be possible to construct a map. Four cutters went ahead, slashing at the tangled undergrowth, and for the last thousand feet of the ascent they had to walk on a thick layer of live or dead timber which covered the soil. At last the summit of the spur, over 5000 feet high, was reached. Here there was a bare patch, and they knew that if only the mist would clear from this vantage-point they could examine the country spread out around them.

114

The next morning at daybreak they were on the peak, and soon the longed-for vista unfurled. Not a moment was lost. Steadily the detail of the map was filled in, the courses of the rivers were plotted, and the mountains were sketched in. At their feet stretched the interminable jungle where for months they had struggled against appalling difficulties. But to the north, Mount Godman stood clearly out, and beyond that, the great precipice stretching for eighty miles—black, forbidding, and with an unclimbable scarp nearly two miles deep. The planning of this gigantic cleft was one of the outstanding accomplishments of the expedition.

Now the work was virtually done. A small expedition went down the coast and plotted another river, and then after fifteen months the explorers left New Guinea. For one reason or another the loss of life had been terrible. Out of a total of four hundred coolies, convicts, and other servants who had been taken to the island only eleven remained. All the rest had died either from beri-beri, fever, or exhaustion, or had been so affected that they had to be invalided out of the country. But a huge area had now been planned, and it was now only a question of time before Mount Carstensz and the interior would be reached.

THE CANNIBALS OF THE CENTRAL HIGHLANDS

The discovery of gold in many parts of New Guinea has, in recent years, led to the opening up of large areas in the interior. Since Australia was given a mandate in the island there has also been a good deal of activity by the Government in exploring the central highlands. One of the most intrepid of the present generation of New-Guinea explorers is Michael Leahy. During the period 1930–1934 he made ten journeys into the unknown plateaux and ranges and made many important discoveries. Although aeroplanes are to-day used for reconnaissance-surveys, many of the difficulties faced by the pioneers still have to be overcome if a more detailed survey is required. Moreover, the natives of the interior are numerous and frequently hostile. Leahy has had more than one narrow escape from death.

Leahy has made a special study of the Purari river and its confluents. The river rises in a high plateau which is difficult of access and where the natives have rarely seen white men. They are mostly bow-and-arrow fighters, using oblong-shaped wooden shields to protect themselves. All of the people on the Purari plateau are cannibals. Although a father will reverently bury his son's intestines, he does not hold any malice against his fellow-villagers for eating the flesh of his offspring. Most of the villages are surrounded by a barricade of timber twelve feet high and protected with outworks. Fighting between the villages is so common that a man will never stir without his bow and arrow.

Leahy reached the plateau from Salamaua, on the coast, and soon found himself among natives who would not exchange a pig for a tomahawk because they did not know how to use any weapon not made of stone. On the whole the natives were friendly, but they persisted in following the expedition in hundreds. The country was mainly limestone, and it was greatly cut up by streams and gorges. On one timbered range 7000 feet high, Leahy camped at the edge of a gorge where the river ran about 3000 feet below! After a few days in such country food-supplies began to run out, and the explorers had to seek a native village. They now decided to follow a large stream called the Tua river, which turned out to be one of the main confluents of the Purari river. Progress was difficult, because at every few miles a side-tributary had to be crossed, and as yet it was not practicable to raft down the main stream. Once, when they went down to inspect the river, which was flowing like a mill-race, they saw the bloated corpse of a Kanaka float past. "Possibly the victim of some argument here about," was Leahy's laconic comment. A little later they saw their first sago-tree, and thus knew that food-supplies would be safe for a time.

Gradually the river increased in size, and Leahy began to look forward to the time when it would be possible to build a raft, because there were millions of leeches eating the men and the dogs. But the track steadily got worse, and at last Leahy reached a side-tributary so wide that it was impossible to cross immediately. A makeshift punt was constructed out of sticks and a fly-sheet, but when the boys tried to swim across with a line made of lawyer-cane ropes, the current proved to be too strong. The presence of rapids just below made it dangerous to risk a crossing without a tow-rope. By this time the food was about all gone, and they were living on a little sago. Eventually, however, the boys cut out a big canoe, and with some difficulty the whole party crossed over.

Now the explorers were able to continue following the Tua river, and they soon came to Kanaka houses. One day they found the bottom of a glass bottle and knew that at last they were approaching civilization. The river was now over a hundred yards wide, and Leahy had almost decided to take a raft when he heard a rumble from down the river; he decided to go and investigate. He found that a little farther down the river ran through a deep limestone gorge and over a series of rapids which would have smashed up any raft. The cliffs on either side of the gorge were 1000 feet high, and a path had to be made to get over them. Some natives volunteered to show the way. They led the explorers back along the trail and then to the top of the range. Below the gorge, the river was found to be 300 yards wide, and the mountains were giving way to low hills and heavily timbered level stretches. The men still continued to cut a track along the river-bank through the bush, because they were not yet quite sure that it would be safe to trust to a raft or canoe. Eventually four canoes were obtained from the natives. At first these natives were frightened of the white men and thought that they would tie their hands (presumably as a preliminary to a cannibal feast).

Drifting along at ten miles an hour, the expedition now made rapid progress towards the coast. Sago-swamps began to appear, and this meant the onslaught of millions of mosquitoes. Then they began to meet natives who spoke the dialect of Papua, and who told them that there was a magistrate five days away. So at length they reached Port Moresby, having crossed New Guinea and definitely discovered where the Purari rises.

The expeditions of 1931 and 1932 were undertaken on behalf of the New Guinea Goldfields Company, who maintain aerodromes on the known goldfields. The region which Leahy proposed to examine is inhabited by the fierce Kukukukas. This tribe in recent years have killed several prospectors entering the Mount-Hagen district, on the border between Papua and the New-Guinea mandated territory. In 1933, for example, Patrol-officer McCarthy, looking for natives concerned in the murder of two prospectors, was attacked from an ambush. McCarthy and six of the native policemen were wounded by arrows, but they rallied and managed to drive off their assailants. This party was finally rescued by aeroplane. The dangers of travel among the central highlands are increased by the fact that certain valleys are thickly populated, and round Mount Hagen explorers are frequently surrounded by crowds numbering as many as a thousand. In April, 1931, Michael Leahy and his brother and fourteen native carriers left the Upper Watut aerodrome for the troublesome area. They cut their way across heavily timbered ranges until they reached the thickly inhabited grass-country. At the first Kukukuka village they reached, the inhabitants were very hostile and opened fire with bows and arrows. Leahy's men were forced to fire in return, but after one of the assailants had been killed the Kukukukas became friendly and brought along plenty of native food.

Following the top of the Papuan water-shed, they were again surrounded and attacked by Kukukukas just before daylight. There was a fierce battle. Six of the cannibals were killed, but Pat Leahy got an arrow through his left arm and another one in his right lung. Michael himself was knocked out by a blow on the head with a pineapple-club, and his cheekbone was grazed with an arrow. Two of the carriers were also wounded, but in the end the Kukukukas were driven off. In view of the various injuries, it was decided to return to the coast for a doctor as soon as possible. Leahy soon began to feel better and was able to walk to a place where rafts could be built; then the whole party sailed down the Markham river to Lae, on the coast.

Six months later the indefatigable Leahy Brothers were once again back in the Mount-Hagen district. This time they took with them a geologist, who joined the party by aeroplane on the Ramu river. In a creek they found traces of gold, but a few days later they were once again troubled by the natives. A local native snatched an axe from one of Leahy's carriers. Leahy was loath to use force to recover the axe, and so moved his camp to the top of a near-by grassy ridge. Here they felt safe from a surprise attack, since all the approaches were across open land. However, thinking that the camp was being moved because the white men were afraid, and being under the impression that the explorers were merely armed with sticks, the natives began an attack on the outskirts of the village. A well-directed volley stampeded them, and four of them were killed.

A few days later a native asked that he might be allowed to accompany the explorers to the coast so that he might see the wonders of the white man. Leahy agreed, but he had much trouble to preserve the native from the vigorous assistance of his friends, who were quite convinced that the white men were taking him away to eat him! When Leahy reached the temporary aerodrome on the Ramu river, this native was sent on a trip by 'plane to the coast. He came back the next day with two bottles of salt water, a collection of ironware, and a handful of hairs out of a horse's tail— this last item to prove to his friends that the white man "has big pigs on which to ride"!

The aeroplanes sent out by the gold-mining company were very useful. A system of signals was arranged so that the ground-party could communicate with the airmen and arrange for landing-grounds where the terrain was suitable. For example, the landing-ground at Ramu was cleared of all obstructions and served as a base from which journeys were made in all directions. In February, 1933, near the Kubor mountain (14,000 feet) Leahy made the important discovery of the huge Wahgi valley. The new valley was sighted from a cleared look-out on a timbered range, and it was so long that it melted away into the smoke-haze in the distance. The discovery of this valley, which is about a hundred miles long, meant that a route across to the Sepik river, in northern New Guinea, could be found. While he was in this district Leahy saw a typical native raid. The villagers were clustered round his roped-off camp, when enemy natives crept into the village, shot an arrow through

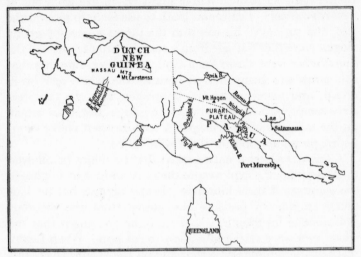

THE MODERN MAP OF NEW GUINEA

an old man, who was too feeble to go sightseeing with the rest, and then set fire to a house before dashing away.

The discovery of the new route was such an important event that arrangements were made to charter a Junker 'plane and set up aerodromes on the flat, grassy areas; then by a system of smoke-fires, they would be able to signify whether it was safe to land or otherwise.

Then Leahy started up the valley. There were big areas of planted *casuarinas*, and there was evidently a large population. Most of the natives seemed to be friendly; more often than not, a crowd of hundreds followed the explorers as they made their way along the northern bank of the river. In places they were held up by terrible swamps, where the dogs had to be assisted by tying bundles of reeds under their bellies to keep them afloat. Later native tracks were found high up above the stream, and also gold was

AMONG THE HEAD-HUNTERS OF NEW GUINEA

located in a creek. The return-journey to the air-base was made without incident.

In the spring of 1934 Leahy went exploring to the west of Mount Hagen and was ambushed on two occasions by hostile natives. He found that the natives in this district lived in long houses over a hundred yards long. Here and there he saw small cages with the skulls of deceased natives inside. He also saw one native wearing a spoon as a neck-ornament! At one village about two thousand natives collected round the roped-off camping-area. One pugnacious savage ran into his house and armed himself with two spears and began to urge his friends to attack. Finally he threw a spear at one of Leahy's boys, and then a general assault with stone axes began. The savages, apparently thinking that rifles were meaningless pieces of wood, hoped to garner a rich loot of the shells which Leahy carried for bartering. Fifteen natives were killed before the battle ended, inevitably in favour of the riflemen. Twice more Leahy was attacked by native bands before he reached his base again. Ultimately, however, Leahy was able to prove that the great new river ran into the Purari. As a recognition of his important discoveries he was awarded the Murchison Grant of the Royal Geographical Society in 1936.

Other expeditions undertaken recently include the famous journey of Karius and Champion from one side of New Guinea to the other. After undergoing great privations on the limestone barrier they found their way to the headwaters of the Sepik and explored a vast area of unknown country.

Equally remarkable is the work of J. G. Hides. Hides, an officer in the Papuan Police, made several important journeys during his patrol duties. On his most notable expedition he discovered a large, thickly populated area to the north of the great limestone barrier, and despite several attacks by natives brought his party safely back to the coast.

Other expeditions, some using aeroplanes, have explored other parts of the interior during the course of journeys in search of new goldfields.

CHAPTER V

ACROSS THE HEART OF AUSTRALIA

Away, away, from men and towns—
To the silent wilderness,
Where the soul need not repress
Its music.

SHELLEY, *The Invitation*

THE RECENT EXPLORATIONS OF MICHAEL TERRY

ALTHOUGH the greater part of settled Australia has been systematically explored, there still remain large areas in the deserts of the interior which are 'blank spaces' on the map. For many years after the first crossing of the deserts by Burke and Wills, in 1860, Central Australia was condemned as a 'no man's land.' Then hardy prospectors began to search far and wide for a new Kalgoorlie, and they located numerous 'soaks' and 'rock-holes' where water-supplies could be replenished. Along some routes wells have been sunk, and ranchers are already making tentative efforts to open up the country beyond Alice Springs.

But there are still huge areas where there are no known wells or 'soaks,' and where the explorer must carry all his water-supplies on drays, motor-trucks, or the patient Afghan camels. Mackay, one of the most famous modern explorers of the interior of Australia, has also used aeroplanes for his important explorations, but although the aeroplane is useful as a means of getting a rough idea of the general physical features, it can give no information as to the mineral or commercial possibilities of the land surveyed. The motor-truck has many advantages. In many regions the country is moderately flat, and speeds in excess of twenty miles an hour are possible. Large quantities of water and petrol have to be carried, of course, and everything depends on the engines. If they break down, then the explorer may be faced with a march of hundreds of miles, or he may even die of thirst. In those regions where there are steep hills or

122

sand-dunes the camel-train is still the best means of transport.

Unlike the sand-seas of the Sahara or the Rub' al Khali, the deserts of the interior of Australia are not entirely devoid of vegetation. In 1908, S. Weston explored much unknown country among the mountains of Central Australia, and he reported that although there was a complete absence of surface-water, the country was covered with trees and scrub which would provide good feeding for camels. The wiry spinifex grass seems to grow almost everywhere in scattered circular clumps. There are also various species of *mulga* scrub and occasionally thickets of larger trees. The battering and scratching, which travel through such country involves, means the packing of camel-loads in strong cases, and the all-important water-supplies have to be stored in sheet-metal canteens.

Although Weston reported the complete absence of surface-water, it is a significant fact that the native blacks are able to exist almost everywhere. They must have water, and it is certain that there are many 'soaks' and little oases which are unknown to white men. Even in districts where white explorers have been forced to rely on carried water for weeks, the bush-blacks still manage to exist. Sometimes they root up yams, which retain moisture even during drought, but more often they repair to a private little cavity in the rocks where there is a spring or where rain-water collects. Some of these are so artfully hidden that white men have stood within a few feet of a 'soak' and yet been unaware of its presence until it was revealed by a 'Jacky.'

Probably the most distinguished of modern explorers of the interior of Australia is Michael Terry. During thirteen years (1923–1936) he led more than a dozen expeditions—principally in search of mineral deposits, but incidentally making accurate maps. On his first expedition he crossed, with one companion, from Winton, in Queensland, to Broome, in Western Australia. Funds were low, and the only means of transport they could afford was an old Ford car. The journey involved the crossing of eight hundred miles of roadless and largely unsurveyed country. They set off with insufficient

123

petrol-supplies to complete the journey, but contrived to pick up further supplies *en route* from scattered stations or from the north coast. In places they had a very rough ride indeed. In the unmapped Muranji country the tyres were wrenched right off the wheels on two occasions, and sometimes the bush and scrub were so thick that it took an hour to travel a hundred yards. The most thrilling moment came when they encountered a roaring bush-fire. The scrub was ablaze for miles across the line of their advance and roaring like an express train. A retreat would have meant losing many valuable miles already gained, and, in the event of a hold-up they might find themselves completely trapped. So they decided to run the gauntlet. They tied wet rags over their faces and then charged with all the speed that the old Ford could muster. It was quite impossible to see the ground for smoke, and they had to risk striking a pot-hole or a tough ant-hill. When they reached the line of blazing scrub, the flames actually licked their faces, but the old car won through and brought them to safety beyond.

Soon after they had crossed the boundary of Western Australia their petrol-supply ran out. They were still some miles away from a station to which they had been directed, and they set off on foot with enough supplies for one day. They boiled out a gallon petrol-can to use as a water-cask, but unfortunately the boiling was not effective, and their precious drinking-supply was contaminated. By midday they had hoped to reach the station, or ranch, but instead they found themselves in thick scrub-country. All that day they stumbled on. They could not drink the contaminated water, and their throats were parched and burning. When night fell they tried to sleep, but since they had brought no camping-equipment with them, they were chilled to the bone by the cold night air. The following night found them still wandering in the trackless bush.

On the next afternoon, when they were almost at the end of their endurance, they found a small spring. This brought some relief, but they were still lost, and they had no clear idea in which way to turn in order to reach the homestead.

After another day's struggling, Terry decided to remain at the spring and send his companion on with all the remaining food-supply in one last effort to find assistance. Fortunately this last effort proved successful, although the weary wanderer was so exhausted that he collapsed as he reached the fence surrounding the station. Here he was found by blacks, and a little later Terry was rescued. Beyond this point the expedition was more or less straightforward, and when at last they reached Broome they were able to claim that they had made the first crossing of northern Australia by car.

During his subsequent expeditions Terry has received considerable assistance from an Adelaide syndicate who are interested in opening up the undeveloped interior. He has used motor-transport of various kinds, combinations of trucks and camel-parties, and, for exploration in sand-dune country, camel-strings alone. As a result a reconnaissance survey of a huge area bounded by the deserted gold-field of Tanami on the north, by Alice Springs on the east, and by Lake Amadeus on the south, has been accomplished.

The difficulties which have to be overcome are not confined to poisonous snakes, lack of water-supplies, and thick, tyre-splitting scrub. Many of the blacks in the interior are definitely hostile to white settlement. During his 1928 expedition, for example, when Terry pioneered a route from Tanami to Alice Springs on six-wheeler Morris cars, he found that the 'Wallmullas' were on the warpath. Some of the half-dozen or so settlers north-west of Alice Springs were attacked, and some were killed.

When the Morris cars went 'off the map' at Tanami there was ample evidence of nomadic 'Jackies.' Every day smoke-signals and hunting-fires were visible. Even in regions where there were apparently no water-supplies of any sort, thin columns of smoke would rise up and be repeated at intervals of about a mile. Clumps of spinifex grass are very inflammable—one touch with a torch, and the whole plant blazes fiercely. At rare intervals they came across the tracks of prospectors looking for 'Wyckham's claim.' A prospector of that name had turned up in 1925 with a sugar-bag full of rich gold specimens which he said he had found in a valley between two sandhills. He had never been able to locate his claim again.

Mirages of various kinds were common. Sometimes hills well below the horizon would be thrown up, especially just after dawn. Terry calls it 'seeing round the corner.' At a place which they named 'Ivy Leases' the prospectors with the expedition found traces of gold and went back to Tanami to register their claims. Meanwhile an advance-party went forward for fifty miles across scrub-country to lay a depôt of petrol- and water-supplies on the way to Lander Creek. The actual journey across the unexplored area was accomplished without any great difficulties, in spite of the fact that dense mulga scrub made navigation complicated. At last they reached Lander Creek, and found there a mass of trees and grass four hundred yards wide. Along this creek are a few scattered stations—tentacles of civilization thrown out from Alice Springs. The first farm they reached was called Wyckham's Camp.

Wyckham's nearest neighbour, called Morton, was forty miles away, and three days earlier he had been attacked by blacks. Morton had been preparing a camp near a large water-hole on the Lander when he saw some blacks behaving suspiciously. He therefore moved his camp a mile away into the scrub. At breakfast-time next morning two 'bucks' came up and asked for food and tobacco. As he was handing them the food, Morton's arms were pinioned. A group of blacks immediately rushed to the attack from the cover of some trees. Morton fought desperately to reach his saddle, where his revolver was. Fortunately his assailants were so numerous that they hindered one another and did not strike a vital blow. At last, half-blinded by head-wounds, Morton reached his revolver, and the blacks immediately fled for cover.

Terry followed the course of Lander Creek towards Coniston and Alice Springs. Soon he met another settler, who told him that Brooks, his neighbour, had just been killed by blacks. Tilmouth, the settler, had himself recently had a very narrow escape. Near his bough-shed (a sort of temporary shelter from the heat) some blacks had started to beat a piccaninny, hoping to lure the settler into an ambush. A loyal boy warned Tilmouth of the danger, and he did not go out. A little later another 'buck' came up and said:

"This one black-feller country; nothing want 'em white man, white feller shift, can't sit down longa black feller "

Tilmouth, however, with the doggedness characteristic of the frontiersman, had no intention of shifting.

A few days later Terry reached Alice Springs. The main pioneering-trip as far as the Lander had been accomplished in three days, during which they had crossed a hundred and fifty miles of new spinifex plain.

CHAPTER VI

THE HOME OF THE BLIZZARD

What miracle of weird transforming
Is this wild work of frost and light,
This glimpse of glory infinite!

WHITTIER, *The Pageant*

SCOTT'S FIRST EXPEDITION

CENTURIES ago, every one believed that there must be a huge continent in the southern hemisphere which would balance the land-masses of the northern hemisphere. They called this land 'Terra Australis,' and on some maps of the sixteenth century it is shown to extend from Cape Horn to Java. The explorations of Captain Cook showed that if such a land did exist, it was entirely within the Antarctic circle —a land of ice and snow useless to man. Thus it was not until the twentieth century, when most of the valuable land of the world had been explored, that expeditions were organized to penetrate to the southernmost limits of the globe. Antarctica is a vast continent, although not so huge as was once imagined. Not allowing for the major indentations, such as the Ross and Weddell seas, it has a coastline of about 12,000 miles, of which even the latest maps only show about one half with any accuracy. Although the heart of the continent has been reached on three occasions, there are probably several ranges of mountains awaiting discovery, and it was not until 1935 that it was at all certain whether Antarctica was one land-mass or two separated by a wide strait. Apart from penguins, seals, and gulls round the coast, this huge area, as large as Australia, is a white, empty, uninhabited waste, the very approach to which involves weeks of battering through ice-floes and icebergs so large that they have been mistaken for ice-covered islands.

The exploration of the continent has provided many tales of brave adventure and a roll of heroes—Scott, Shackleton, Amundsen, Byrd, Mawson, and Oates, to name only a few

—whose names are immortal. In the first year of the present century Commander R. F. Scott sailed in the *Discovery* to Cape Adare, on the Ross Sea. He discovered land on the other side of the Ross Sea to which he gave the name of King Edward VII Land, showed that Mount Erebus was an active volcano on an island, made a journey inland for two hundred miles, and then struck westward on to the high inland plateau. One of his companions on the sledge-trip across the Great Barrier, which chokes the Ross Sea, was Ernest Shackleton. After travelling for two months, they had not reached the end of the Barrier, and they had to return because all their dogs were dead and all the men were suffering from scurvy.

THE DISCOVERY OF THE MAGNETIC POLE

In 1907 Shackleton published his intentions of following the barrier to its limit to reach the South Pole, and also to solve the important question of the exact position of the South Magnetic Pole. Early in 1908 the *Nimrod* reached the Ross Sea, and a hut was erected for the winter. Then a party of climbers succeeded in reaching the crater of Mount Erebus. Depôts were laid along the great ice-barrier in preparation for the polar trip.

On October 29, 1908, Shackleton, Adams, Marshall, and Wild set off with four sledges drawn by four Manchurian ponies. They were thrilled with the idea that in the south of the Great Barrier they would make astounding discoveries, and they hoped to look on land never before seen by human beings. It was like setting off from the east coast of England across a frozen North Sea, and they had not the faintest idea what the southern shores were like, or even if there was a southern shore. So they plodded onward, ever to the south, across crevasses, through snowdrifts, and over sastrugi, or ice-waves, caused by the frequent hurricanes. Sometimes they suffered from snow-blindness; this affliction begins by making the eyes run, causing double vision, and ends with temporary blindness. The tears rolled down the men's cheeks into their beards, and, freezing there, created a muffler of hoar-frost. When stricken by a howling blizzard, they rolled themselves in their sleeping-bags and read the few books they had brought with them. The ponies made good progress for over a hundred miles, and then, as they grew lame from stumbling in crevasses or from sheer exhaustion, they were shot and eaten. Here and there depôts were laid for the return-journey, and some of the horse-meat was stored. Actually, on the return journey, they were so short of food that once they were glad to eat the frozen blood which had fallen on the place where one of the ponies had been shot.

November 22 was a memorable day, for soon after they had deposited some of the pony-meat, they caught sight of new land to the south. They could see, rising high above the level barrier, great snow-clad mountains towering to a height of 10,000 feet. For the next few days there was always some new discovery to be made. Range after range, peak after peak opened up before them, with mighty glaciers sweeping down to the ice-covered sea. On November 26 they passed the previous 'farthest south,' and soon they were passing beneath enormous granite cliffs. They pushed on along the barrier until December 4, when they made for the base of one of the mountains, hoping that from the summit they would see an opening to the south. With great difficulty they scrambled up the rocky face, and when they reached the top of a ridge, they could see an open road to the south. Before them stretched a mighty glacier running almost due south between two mountain ranges.

So they turned on to the 'Gateway to the South' and began toiling up the glacier. Soon they found that the way was much broken by crevasses. The ice was so slippery that they often fell and were bruised. 'Socks,' the only remaining pony, often sank to his belly in the drifts, and just after lunch on December 7 they heard a cry for help from Wild. The pony-sledge was half down a crevasse, with Wild hanging on desperately. Poor Socks had plunged to his death thousands of feet below. The pony's weight had snapped the sledge-bearers, and this alone had enabled Wild to save their valuable stores.

Henceforth the men had to pull the sledges. They were

on short rations, for the hard work on the slopes of the glacier had caused so much delay that the chances of reaching the Pole were rapidly vanishing.

Day after day they trudged along, until they realized that they were climbing what must be the greatest glacier in the world. Often they journeyed no more than three miles a day. Always they hoped that the next day would bring them to the top, but always the glacier rose ahead, until at last they had reached an elevation of about 11,000 feet. On Christmas Day they were still climbing, but on January 1 they passed all records for polar journeys and at last had reached the great plateau on which stands the Pole. Gradually the mountains disappeared, and they tramped over an immense level expanse of ice and snow.

By this time, however, their food-supplies were very low, so they decided to dump everything possible and make a dash for the Pole. Their sledge was broken, and often they sank in the snow to their ankles. The altitude also gave them splitting headaches, and the slow rate of progress told of waning strength. For days on end they were confined to their flimsy tent by shrieking blizzards, with the temperature ranging from 60 to 70 degrees of frost. On January 9 they reached their 'farthest south,' in the latitude of 88° 23' south. If their food-supplies had allowed them to continue for a few more days, they would undoubtedly have reached the Pole.

The return journey was one long struggle against hunger. Fortunately the weather was good, and a following breeze enabled them to put up a sail which helped the sledge along. To add to their troubles, however, they all began to suffer from dysentery—probably as a result of eating infected horse-meat. Frequently they ran completely out of food before they could stumble to the next depôt. A few crumbs of biscuit were treasured more than anything. Worn out with their exertions and ill with dysentery, they at last reached the big Bluff Depôt, where at last they were able to eat their fill. By this time Marshall was suffering from paralysis of the stomach and could go no farther. A tent was set up, and then Shackleton and Wild set off on a race to reach the ship. They reached the hut without any food or sleeping-bags, but on the following day the *Nimrod* was sighted. A rescue-party was quickly organized, and all safely reached the ship on March 4, after one of the most courageous of all Antarctic sledging-trips.

Meanwhile Professor David, Mawson, and Mackay had travelled northward along the shores of the Ross Sea in an effort to reach the South Magnetic Pole. Altogether they dragged their heavy sledge a distance of about 1260 miles and were absent for 122 days. For the first two hundred miles the way lay across the sea-ice round McMurdo Bay, and then along the western coast of the Ross Sea. Since they had to carry all equipment necessary for determining the situation of the Magnetic Pole, for long stages they had to go on short rations. To eke out their supplies they made a cooker out of an old tin which served as a blubber-lamp in which seal-meat could be cooked. They found that a diet of seal-blubber and blood was delicious when one got used to it.

After they had been travelling north for about two months, they came to a most formidable obstacle—the Drygalski glacier-tongue. This is a mighty cape about twenty miles wide, and jutting out into the sea for about forty miles. They had to find a way over this maze of seracs and crevasses in order to reach the place where they could turn inland towards the Magnetic Pole. Actually it took them a fortnight to get across, and of course their supplies were correspondingly reduced. They had one or two very narrow escapes from disaster on this glacier. Mawson, who seems to have fallen into more crevasses than any explorer on record, suddenly fell into a chasm, and found himself suspended by the harness from the sledge. Although he was in grave danger, he occupied his time, while the Alpine rope was being fetched and lowered, in throwing up some interesting ice-crystals from the sides of the crevasse. Professor David was no less courageous. A day or two earlier, when Mawson was snugly lying in his sleeping-bag, changing some plates in his camera, he heard Professor David politely asking for his assistance. Since the tone of voice did not sug-

gest any immediate need for help, Mawson continued his
work for a few moments, and then, when he heard a second
polite request, he scrambled out of the sleeping-bag and
peeped out of the tent. To his utter amazement he could
see nothing of David except his head and outstretched arms.
The Professor had only just stepped outside the tent when
he had suddenly fallen into a crevasse, and he was only
saved from a ghastly drop by flinging out his arms and
staying himself on the snow lid on either side. Even as it
was Mawson had some difficulty in rescuing him, but finally
he managed to extend the shaft of an ice-axe across the hole
so that the leader could grasp it and be hauled to safety.

On January 16 the explorers at last reached the Magnetic
Pole, and hoisting a flag, they claimed the land for the
King. Then they began a forced march back to the sea.
They had to average sixteen miles a day in order to pick up
the *Nimrod* at the meeting-place near the Drygalski glacier.
Bruised from falls, frost-bitten, half starved, they pushed
along as fast as the deep snow and ice-ridges would let them.
They were a day late when they reached the coast, and there
was no sign of the ship. They began to discuss the gloomy
prospect of wintering in that bleak place on a diet of seal-
blubber. Then, on the afternoon of February 3, they heard
a sudden report. "A gun from the ship!" yelled Mawson,
diving for the tent-door. David and Mackay quickly followed suit, and there they saw the welcome *Nimrod* in the
bay. Mawson ran ahead towards the ice-edge, and promptly
fell into a deep crevasse! So the first task which the sailors
had was to fetch out a strong plank and lower ropes so that
Mawson could be rescued again. With his usual fortitude
he was calmly awaiting rescue with his feet on a little ledge
just above the sea-water. That evening the three explorers
gorged themselves on all the dainty dishes they had dreamed
about for the last three months.

MAWSON IN THE ANTARCTIC

Dr Douglas Mawson had been a member of the expedition
which sailed southward from New Zealand under Sir Ernest
Shackleton in 1907, and he had taken part in the great

sledge-journey to the South Magnetic Pole. He was a lecturer at Adelaide University, and was anxious to learn more about Antarctic conditions in the segment south of Australia. The winds and currents from this region have an important effect on the climate of Australia. Therefore, when, in 1911, he announced his intention of organizing a new Antarctic expedition, his plans were given an enthusiastic welcome by the Governments of the Commonwealth and Great Britain.

Mawson set sail from Hobart, Tasmania, in December, 1911, on the *Aurora*, a converted whaling-ship. A halt was made at a rocky island called Macquarie Island, which is situated about half-way between Tasmania and the Antarctic circle. Here a wireless-station was established, to act as a relay-station for messages from the expedition. Thus was inaugurated the first attempt to use wireless telegraphy in Antarctic exploration.

From Macquarie Island the *Aurora* pushed southward, and eventually came to a bay called Commonwealth Bay, on an unexplored part of the coast of Antarctica. Here a base-camp was organized, and then the ship went westward through the ice-pack for about 1500 miles and landed a second contingent, which was to be known as the western party. The main expedition, under Mawson, erected a comfortable hut for the long winter. They soon found that the blizzards here were just as severe as they had been in the Ross Sea. Once, in a blizzard which reached a force of 100 miles an hour, the explorers heard a loud crash. Several sledges had been picked up bodily and flung with terrific force against the sides of the expedition-hut. All the sledges were rescued except one, which drifted away in the direction of Australia.

Mawson was anxious to send out sledging-parties to explore the unknown interior, but the blizzards were so persistent that they had to wait seven months before sledging was possible. Even then, after the first sledging-party had penetrated fifty miles to the south, their tents were torn to ribbons by a blizzard, and the whole party had to return, badly frost-bitten. To avoid a recurrence of this trouble it was decided to dig two ice-caves, one at a distance of six miles from the base, and the other at twelve miles. These caves were stocked with supplies and given the picturesque names of 'Aladdin's Cave' and 'Cathedral Grotto.'

On November 10 Dr Mawson and two companions, Mertz and Ninnis, set off to the south-east to explore the region which was to be called King George V Land. They took with them three sledges, which were hauled by dogs. At first progress was very rapid, and the explorers were often able to sit on the sledges and ride along. But before long the usual Antarctic difficulties—ice-ridges and crevasses—were encountered. Here and there they had to cross ice-covered hills 3000 feet high. The crevasses were specially dangerous, because many of them were completely snow-covered. One day, without warning, half of Mawson's dog-team suddenly plunged into the depths, and they were discovered swinging by their harness in a deep crevasse. Fortunately the sledge held fast, and Mawson found that he was standing on the middle of a snow-bridge across a crevasse twenty-five feet wide. Many anxious minutes passed before the dogs could be rescued and the dangerous bridge passed.

A day or two later, while Mertz was preparing lunch in the tent, Mawson and Ninnis went off to take some photographs. Suddenly Mawson heard a crash, and turning round, could see nothing of Ninnis but his head and arms. He had fallen into a crevasse fifteen feet wide. He was soon dragged to safety, but then it was discovered that the tent was hanging partly over the edge of the death-trap into which Ninnis had fallen. The explorers did not waste much time taking lunch on that day!

The crevasses were an endless source of trouble and accidents, and before long a fatal accident occurred. One of the sledges had been damaged, so the three explorers had packed all the stores on to two sledges. Mertz went ahead to pioneer a track, while Mawson and Ninnis followed with the dog-teams. Just when they were making good progress, Mawson happened to glance ahead, and he saw that Mertz had halted and was gazing anxiously to the rear. Mawson quickly looked behind. He could see his own sledge-tracks, but Ninnis and the other sledge were invisible!

Mawson hurried back along the trail and soon came to a black chasm about eleven feet wide. On the far side were tracks of Ninnis and his sledge, but the whole outfit had evidently fallen into the crevasse. Mawson leaned over and shouted into the gloomy depths. There came no reply save the moaning of a dog which he could just see caught on a ledge about 150 feet below. Close beside it were the remains of a tent and another dog. Quickly Alpine ropes were knotted together, but the total length was not sufficient to reach even the ledge where the dogs lay. For three hours the men shouted into the depths, and then reluctantly they had to agree that Ninnis must have been killed outright by the fall into the icy depths. Mawson read the burial service, and then, stricken with grief, they turned in the direction of the base-camp.

The loss of Ninnis's sledge was a serious blow. He had been in charge of all the best dogs, and on the sledge had been all the food for the dogs and the greater part of their own food. Fortunately Mawson's sledge had a spare tent-cover and enough food to last ten days. They were 316 miles from the base-camp, and the outward journey had taken a month. Now only six dogs were left, and they were in poor condition, so that often the men had to drag the sledges along. It was indeed a desperate situation.

One by one the dogs had to be killed, and the meat shared between the men and the remaining dogs. This diet appeared to have a bad effect on Mertz, and after a fortnight of hard pulling Mertz became so weak that he could not walk. Mawson tried to pull the sledge along with Mertz as passenger, but progress was very slow. Moreover, the sick man became so cold that they soon had to stop and pitch a tent. On the morning of January 7 Mertz could hardly move, and soon after midnight he died.

This second tragedy placed Mawson in a most perilous position. There were still a hundred miles of snow and crevasses to cross before he reached the base, and he would have to do all the work himself. With dogged pluck, which must be for ever admired, he set about the tremendous task of saving his own life. From a coat which Mertz had worn he contrived to make a kind of sail, which helped him along a little; but by this time his feet were so sore and painful that he could only make slow progress. Snow fell heavily, and it was difficult to keep to the correct course. A few days' hard pulling, however, brought him in sight of a glacier which had been named after Mertz, and he knew that just beyond lay the base-camp.

This gave Mawson fresh courage, and he pushed steadily along until he met with an alarming accident. When climbing up a steep slope, which was deeply covered with soft snow, he suddenly fell into a crevasse and found himself dangling from the end of the rope with which he had been hauling the sledge. Slowly, inch by inch, the sledge glided towards the lip of the chasm, and Mawson felt that this really was the end. But by a miracle the sledge stopped short of the edge and supported the dangling explorer. Slowly Mawson began to haul himself up. On the very edge, just when he was about to climb out, the snow gave way under him, and once more he fell back into the crevasse. By this time he was exhausted and rapidly freezing. He felt his strength fast ebbing, and then he made a final supreme effort. Inch by inch, with muscles aching, he scrambled to the surface. At last the safe ice was reached. For an hour he lay there, exhausted but reprieved for a further struggle with the elements.

For the next few miles a merciful wind helped the sledge along, but by the time he had come in sight of Commonwealth Bay, Mawson had only two pounds of food left. This was scarcely enough to see him through, but his anxiety was suddenly relieved by the discovery of a cairn on which was placed a bag of food. This had been left by a search-party which had reached this place only a few hours before. Revived by the fresh supplies, Mawson pushed on, and three days later he reached 'Aladdin's Cave.' Then came a blizzard which kept him confined to the cave for a week. Finally there was the last lap down to the hut, and soon he was welcomed by his comrades, who had given him up for dead.

The *Aurora* had already departed for home, and so the expedition had to spend another winter in the hut. As a result of the explorations which were carried out, over 800 miles of new coast-line were mapped, and Mawson was knighted in recognition of his services and intrepidity.

JEAN CHARCOT AND THE "POURQUOI PAS?"

On September 16, 1936, disaster overtook a very famous ship and resulted in the death of one of the most notable French explorers. The ship was the *Pourquoi Pas?* and her leader, Jean Charcot. Charcot was bringing home a party of French scientists who had made a trek across the Greenland ice-cap when the ship struck the rocks on the west coast of Iceland and sank. Jean Charcot was then sixty-nine years old, and this was his last polar voyage.

Originally trained as a doctor, Charcot led his first expedition in 1903, and a few years later had the 800-ton *Pourquoi Pas?* built specially for work among the ice. His most important expedition was that of 1909, which resulted in the discovery of Charcot Land. The ship sailed from Punta Arenas, in the Strait of Magellan, and was held up in the ice near Berthelot Island, to the west of Graham Land. Charcot and two of his men set off in a picket-boat one day to make a reconnaissance of the islands round the anchorage. They reached Berthelot Island safely, and from a high peak had a clear view on to the main continental mass. But when they tried to return to the ship, they found that the ice-pack had drifted, and it was now impossible to force their little boat back to the *Pourquoi Pas?* The party had brought only a light ration, but for the next few days it was quite impossible to make any headway, so that they had to make one biscuit serve as a meal for three. The motor-boat was badly damaged during the ineffectual attempts to reach the ship; and when at last they did find a clear lead, after three days without food, the engine broke down.

This was almost the last straw. Already weak and exhausted from hunger and exposure, they decided to

CHARCOT'S POLAR SHIP, THE "POURQUOI PAS?"
Photo the "Daily Mirror"

attempt a march across the ice to a point where it would be possible to signal to their comrades. Fortunately they were saved from this ordeal because the *Pourquoi Pas?*, smashing her way to the rescue through the ice, came into view, and soon the explorers were aboard again.

A few hours later the *Pourquoi Pas?* ran on to a rock, and all the lifeboats had to be launched. Fortunately when the ship was lightened she slid off the rock, and all was well again. In the vicinity of Charcot Land the sea was covered with great icebergs, and once a splitting iceberg touched the stern of the ship and smashed one of the lifeboats. Still the *Pourquoi Pas?* pushed southward, until she had passed all previous records for that region and had sighted a long stretch of new coast-line to which the name of the leader was given.

During the winter at Petermann Island a great deal of important astronomical and magnetic research was carried out, but a great deal of time had to be spent in repairing the defences of the little harbour, which was always being invaded by icebergs. Scurvy broke out, but a diet of fresh seal-meat did much to improve the health of the expedition. Charcot himself was so badly affected that he was unable to join the sledging-parties, which explored many miles of the new coast-line during the ensuing spring.

When the *Pourquoi Pas?* finally returned to Punta Arenas she had sailed farther south than any ship in the South-American sector of the Antarctic, and had been for eighteen months continually among the ice.

THE VOYAGE OF THE "ENDURANCE"

When Ernest Shackleton heard of the double conquest of the South Pole by Amundsen and Captain Scott, he began to plan to accomplish the last remaining Antarctic journey of major importance—the crossing of the continent from the Weddell Sea to the Ross Sea. This journey would be roughly 1,800 miles, and the first half, from the Weddell Sea to the Pole, would be over totally unknown land. In order to complete the march it would be essential to have depôts laid out from a base on McMurdo Sound, in the Ross Sea. Hence two ships had to be commissioned. The *Endurance*, with Shackleton in command, sailed into the Weddell Sea, while the *Aurora*, under Captain Mackintosh, went into the regions made familiar by the previous expeditions of Scott and Shackleton. Altogether it was a most ambitious programme, and although it ended in failure, the survivors came back with a saga of high adventure and grim endurance such as transcends any tale of fiction.

The expedition sailed from London on the eve of the outbreak of the Great War. When, on August 4, they learned that war had been declared, they promptly offered their services to the Government and suggested that they might be transferred to a destroyer. But so much money and time had been spent on acquiring equipment that Shackleton received explicit instructions from the Admiralty to proceed on his voyage. In the circumstances many of the men were disappointed, but all of them shared the common belief that the War would soon be over. As it happened, almost the whole personnel were able to take an active part in the campaigns of 1917, after spending two years in the Antarctic without hearing any news of the progress of the mightiest conflict in history.

The *Endurance* left the whaling-station in South Georgia on December 5, 1914. The good ship made steady progress to the south-east, but when two days out, it began to meet great tabular icebergs and soon ran into pack-ice. The pack was loose in the early stages and did not present any great difficulties. Towards the end of December the jig-saw puzzle of ice-floes became more confused and menacing, in spite of the fact that this was the height of the southern summer. On all sides loomed huge icebergs as big as the Rock of Gibraltar. One floe was estimated to cover about 150 square miles. Sometimes, when the way was barred by a floe of only moderate thickness, the *Endurance* would charge the obstruction repeatedly until a long, sinuous crack appeared and opened out into a passage.

The coast of Coats Land was sighted on January 10, 1915, and soon afterwards the *Endurance* was steaming along an open lead between the high barrier and the heavy pack-ice. On January 12 new land was sighted; it was named the Caird

Coast, in honour of one of the benefactors of the expedition. The ship pushed on southward towards Luitpold Land, passing high barrier-ice and immense glaciers. The explorers saw no bare land or rock.

A few miles before they reached the desired landing-place, the *Endurance* ran into very heavy pack-ice mixed with 'growlers.' The next night the ship was firmly beset, the ice being packed heavily all round as far as the eye could reach. A north-east gale had crowded the floes into the south of the Weddell Sea, and the *Endurance* began to drift with the imprisoning floes in a south-westerly direction. Now and again leads opened up for a few hours, and steam was raised in an attempt to force a way through. But all efforts were unavailing. After ten days of helpless drifting, the fires were put out. Land still showed to the east, tantalizingly near, yet absolutely unapproachable.

There were plenty of seals and penguins about, and the men soon gathered a good store of fresh meat for themselves and the dogs. Low temperatures during the first week of February further cemented the pack, and by this time the delay was becoming serious. At the end of this month the *Endurance* reached the most southerly point of her drift, and already it was practically certain that the expedition was doomed to a winter among the floes.

So the *Endurance* was converted into a winter station and began her long death-struggle with the pounding ice. The dogs were installed in kennels, or 'dogloos,' on the floe, and sledge-team practice was started. Now and again the men made trips to the big bergs seven or eight miles away. There was plenty of opportunity to observe the extra-ordinary effects of ice-pressure. The floes would groan and creak, buckle and crash, or be catapulted into the air when nipped suddenly between two moving, heavy masses. Sometimes football and other games were played on the ice. The greatest fun of all were the Antarctic 'Derbys'— races between the dog-teams.

The long winter night closed down, and it became dangerous to move far from the ship, except in the moon-light. There were many anxious days when areas of disturbance approached and threatened to overwhelm the ship or to pinch her in gigantic, icy nut-crackers. During May and June the *Endurance* continued her drift to the north-west. July was a bad month, and the party often heard the grinding and crashing of the floes as they rafted upward to a height of ten feet or more. During the next two months the ship received many severe nips, and the beams were buckled under the terrific stresses. The rudder was torn away, and the decks shuddered and arched. The ice all round was five feet thick, but the returning sun caused great leads to open up at times. On no occasion, however, did the *Endurance* have a chance to escape from her crushing prison.

On October 17 the pressure became so great that the iron plates on the engine-room floor buckled up and over-rode one another with deafening clangs. On the following day the ship heeled over until the boats almost rested on the floe. But this was not the end of the gallant ship; the floes opened again, and she righted herself. A week later the position became desperate. Thick floes and pressure-ridges attacked from three sides at once. The ship was twisted and bent like a bow by the enormous strain, and at once began to leak dangerously. Three days later came the final squeeze; millions of tons of ice pressed forward inexorably, and gaps four or five inches long were opened on the starboard side.

The boats, sledges, gear, and provisions, which had been made ready for this eventuality, were lowered and moved to flat ice a little distance away. They were now shipwrecked 180 miles away from the Barrier and 360 miles away from Paulet Island, the nearest point where they could find food and shelter. Slowly the gallant ship, which had put up such a magnificent fight against tremendous forces, began to sink. Great beams snapped with a noise like the firing of artillery, and water began to pour into the hold.

The floe, on which the expedition was now camped, began to crack and steadily grow smaller. Preparations for a march across the moving floes to Paulet Island were hurried along, and the three ship's boats were fitted on to big

THE " ENDURANCE " CRUSHED BY ICE
From Shackleton's "South" (Heinemann)

sledges. Shackleton and Wild, the second-in-command, pioneered a route for about a mile and a half, and the next day a start was made.

It was heavy work to men and dogs. Cracks opened up as they tugged along, and 'killer' whales pushed their evil heads through the holes. The sledges were cumbersome, and with fifteen men hauling the boats across rough ice, the total gain for the day was only one mile. And they were faced with at least 300 miles of this sort of travelling before they could reach open water! Was ever an expedition faced with such a superhuman task?

Three weeks later they were still only a few miles away from the battered hulk of the *Endurance*, and one morning Shackleton saw her stern rise high in the air; she gave one quick dive, and the grinding ice closed over her grave. By this time all effort to haul the boats along had been suspended. 'Ocean Camp' had been set up on a big flat floe about a mile square. This was to be their home for nearly two months.

Large quantities of supplies of all kinds had been rescued from the sinking ship. The ship's wheel-house was rigged up as a galley, and a large blubber-stove was constructed out of the ship's ash-shoot and some oil-drums. Over an observation-post made from deck-planks and the binnacle the King's flag still proudly floated. Regular observations were taken, and it was discovered that the strange craft was slowly, but surely, carrying them northward to the open sea.

There was no danger of starvation. All seals and penguins which appeared were promptly killed. 'Ocean Camp' even boasted a small library, in which the greatest treasure was a portion of the *Encyclopaedia Britannica*. As far as they could see they might have been on dry land, but the navigating officer was able to report an advance of as much as ten miles on some days. Blizzards—usually the curse of the Antarctic —were welcomed, because the howling winds increased the rate of drift. Now, however, it was the height of summer, and sometimes the temperatures rose above freezing point and melted the surface of the floe into a slushy morass.

On December 23 it was decided to strike camp and attempt a march westward to Paulet Island, which was now much nearer. Christmas Day found them relaying the loaded sledges and hauling the heavy boats. Progress was, however, painfully slow, and when they had advanced only a few miles in seven days, the task was abandoned as impracticable, and a new station, 'Patience Camp,' was established. For the next three and a half months the explorers had to rest content with this ice-floe as a home. Gradually they drifted away from Paulet Island, and now their hopes were centred on either Elephant Island or Clarence Island. These small, ice-capped islands are quite close together, and Clarence Island was sighted 60 miles away on April 7, 1916.

After drifting so long at the caprice of wind and current through a world of ice and snow, the glimpse of black lines of scree was a cheering sight. But they were not out of the ice yet by a long way. The floating home, with its crew of twenty-eight men, was slowly diminishing in size, and although the heavier pack and bergs had been left behind, it was still too dangerous to attempt to launch the boats. Gradually the pack began to open; and on Sunday, April 9, the floe suddenly split right across. The boats were launched, stores were thrown in, and the party moved out towards an open pool, in the middle of which floated a lonely berg. Then a tide-rip brought masses of ice charging into the pool, and they had to take shelter on an old flat floe, where they camped for the night. The new floe was no haven of rest, for in the middle of the night it split directly under one of the tents. Quickly the gap widened to about four feet. Shackleton, who was on watch, saw a sleeping-bag, with a man inside, floating in the water. He just had time to heave the man out when the ice-jaws snapped together again with tremendous force. There was no more sleep for anyone that night. Their floe was now only seventy yards long by thirty yards wide, and 'killer' whales were blowing in the surrounding lanes, as if in anticipation of an interesting change in diet in the near future.

The following night the boats were hauled up on a big floe-berg after they had made some progress. Slowly they drifted towards the open ocean; for three more days they rowed along and camped on ice-floes. Most of the men were now suffering severely from exhaustion, lack of food, and the combined attack of icy-spray and bitter winds.

On April 13 Shackleton decided to risk a run across to Elephant Island. About noon the explorers suddenly emerged from the loose pack into the open ocean. For once in a while they could now navigate the boats in the desired direction. They had escaped so suddenly from the encompassing ice that they had been unable to collect enough ice for drinking or cooking-purposes, and in the darkness of the following night they suffered from the additional torment of increasing thirst. They chewed pieces of raw seal-meat in order to slake their thirst with the blood, but the salty flesh only increased the agony.

Dawn came at last, tinting the peaks of Clarence and Elephant Islands with a rosy pink. All that day the men sailed and rowed through a clear sea; and on the next day, after a narrow escape from a gale which separated the boats, the whole party made a safe landing on a narrow beach beneath the towering cliffs and sheer glacier-faces of Elephant Island. Some of the men were so delighted at reaching solid earth again that they laughed uproariously, in spite of cracked and bleeding lips. Some picked up pebbles and let them trickle through their fingers, after the manner of a miser gloating over gold. The next day, however, they had to move to a safer camping-place on a little spit a few miles away. Here was a bleak, inhospitable acre of rock and shingle bounded on the landward side by a glacier. By this time most of the tents were useless, and an effort was made to dig an ice-cave in the ice-slope. When this failed, two of the boats were turned upside down and converted into a kind of 'Peggotty's Hut.' In these cramped quarters twenty-two men lived for four and a half months!

The long struggle with the ice and the unrelieved privation had left its mark on the men. One man was so badly frost-bitten that he could not walk out of the hut. Food-supplies were low. The rations, at a pinch, could be spread out over three months; and for the rest they must live on what seals, sea-elephants, limpets, and sea-weed they could find.

Shackleton immediately decided that a boat-journey would have to be made to fetch relief. It was most unlikely that any search-party would look for the survivors of the *Endurance* on an unexplored island some hundreds of miles away from the proposed base. The nearest inhabited place was South Georgia, 800 miles away. With luck a select party might make the voyage in under a month and bring back a whaler to relieve the castaways.

The perils of such a journey were obviously extreme. During May the ocean south of Cape Horn is notoriously the most tempestuous in the world. The only boat available was the *James Caird*, a twenty-foot whale-boat, and the largest salvaged from the *Endurance*. Already she had been seriously buffeted and holed during the weeks of struggling through the pack, but the carpenter thought he could make the boat sea-worthy. In the intervals between the blizzards the little boat was provided with a deck made out of sledge-runners, box-lids, and canvas. A month's supplies for six men were taken aboard, and a number of boulders selected to act as ballast.

The crew of the *James Caird* who made this remarkable boat-journey must be remembered with pride by every Britisher. They were Shackleton, Worsley, Crean, McNeish, McCarthy, and Vincent. The voyage started badly, for the boat almost capsized among the rocks, and one of the two water-casks was slightly stove in. This proved to be a serious misfortune, because sea-water got into the cask and made the water brackish. During the next sixteen days the battle amid the raging waters of the worst sea in the world went on without ceasing. It was almost impossible to get any sleep on the floor of the boat because of the multitude of cases, bags, and sharp ballast-boulders.

Continually drenched with spray, cramped by the narrow quarters and the necessity of crawling about on all fours under the improvised decking, and always in danger of frost-bite, they battled grimly along. The canvas decking leaked, and constant baling was needed. Their meals con-

sisted of Bovril, a piece of biscuit, and a pannikin of milk.
Then a south-westerly gale sprang up, bringing zero temperatures, and a heavy coating of ice formed over everything.
The *James Caird* began to wallow with the increased weight,
and a thousand times it seemed that one of the mountainous
waves would engulf her. On the eleventh day Shackleton
suddenly saw a gigantic wave surging along like a monstrous
bore through the breaking seas. The little whaler was picked
up bodily and thrown into a seething chaos of foaming
spume. Somehow she lived through the next few moments,
and then the gallant crew began baling with every available
receptacle. Fortune favoured the brave, and they survived
to struggle on.

By this time the men were reduced to the cask of brackish
water and were soon assailed by a dreadful thirst. The next
few days were agony. Then, on May 8, they saw some land-
birds sitting on a mass of kelp, and they realized that they
must be within fifteen miles of the coast. On the fourteenth
day South Georgia was sighted, and two days later, after a
severe buffeting in a storm, they found a way through the
fringing reefs into a little cove at the mouth of King Haakon
Bay on the western side of the island.

Even now their wanderings were not at an end. The
nearest whaling-stations were on the other side of the island
150 miles away by sea; and by land the alternative route led
across high mountains and ice-sheets which were reputed to
be impassable. But the first essential was to recover some of
the strength which had been lost on the boat-journey. Vincent
and McNeish could scarcely walk. So they found a small
cave about eight feet deep and strewed the rocky floor with
tussock grass to form a soft bed. Much to their delight they
came across some albatross fledgelings, and before long they
were feasting on the best meal they had had for months.

After five days in the cave the men were fit enough to
sail the *James Caird* for eight miles to the head of King
Haakon Bay. Here they found a colony of huge sea-
elephants—enough food and fuel to last for years. The
James Caird was turned over and converted into a temporary
hut to shelter the weaker members of the party, while

Shackleton, Worsley, and Crean prepared for the overland journey. They arranged to take with them three days' rations, because although Husvik, the nearest station was only seventeen miles away in a direct line, they correctly anticipated a good deal of trouble in crossing crevasses and high ranges in the totally unknown interior.

The overland party set off on May 19 at 2 A.M. on a moderately clear morning. Two hours' steady climbing up a glacier brought them to a point about 2500 feet above sea level. The surface was bad, and they often sank above the ankles in the soft patches. When they reached the top they had a wonderful vista of steep glaciers, seemingly impassable cliffs, and a maze of high peaks. Then a thick fog settled down, and for the next two hours they travelled 'blind' and roped together. Soon they found themselves walking down a glacier to the sea at the uninhabited Possession Bay. It was quite impossible to follow the coast-line, so they had to climb up again and strike to the south-east. Steadily they plodded on, thinking anxiously of their marooned comrades on Elephant Island.

The journey across South Georgia was in itself a remarkable piece of exploration. Time and again they had to change direction because of vertical cliffs, deep ice-precipices, and huge crevasses. They took brief rests, when they ate scanty meals, and then plunged on again, marching, stumbling, tired to death, and more than half-frozen, but with a grim determination to win through.

At 6.30 A.M. on the following day Shackleton suddenly heard a steam-whistle! That whistle put fresh life into the three adventurers; it seemed to promise that help and success were not far ahead. The final stretch led down a steep slope where they cut steps with the carpenter's adze, and by noon they had reached a flat plateau with only one more ridge to conquer before they reached Husvik. Even now, however, the battle was not ended. Shackleton sank up to his knees when they were crossing a newly frozen lake; and when they were actually in sight of the station they still had a steep precipice to climb down. The only way seemed to follow a stream. Half-way down they found that the stream ended in a waterfall, and since there were impassable cliffs on each side, they had to lower one another down with the Alpine rope through the actual water of the fall.

So it was that three soaking-wet vagabonds, with no other possessions than their tattered clothes, a carpenter's adze, a cooker, and a log-book, returned to civilization,

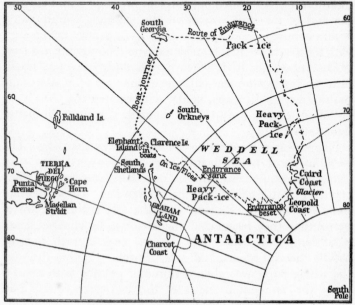

SHACKLETON'S EXPEDITION, 1914–1917

whence they had departed a year and a half before with a fine ship and a comprehensive equipment.

As quickly as possible Shackleton organized relief-expeditions—first for the three stranded men on King Haakon Bay, and then for the large party at Elephant Island. The main relief proved to be extraordinarily difficult owing to the fact that the ice-pack had closed round the island, and it was only after attempts from South Georgia and the Falklands had failed that Shackleton was successful, on a fourth relief-expedition, in a small tug-boat from Punta Arenas on the Straits of Magellan.

Wild, who had been left in charge of the twenty-two men

149

on the island, had contrived to keep everybody well and as happy as the circumstances permitted. The hut made out of the boats had been improved in various ingenious ways, and in spite of the fact that quarters were very cramped and filthily dirty with smoke from the stove, they had been well sheltered from the blizzards. For four and a half months they had waited patiently for the 'Boss'; and towards the end of the time, whenever the ice had cleared away, Wild encouraged the men to pack their scanty belongings, with the assurance that Shackleton would be coming any day.

On August 30, 1916, when they had only two day's seal-meat and penguin-meat left, one of the men on watch came panting across the snow, hoarse with excitement.

"Wild, there's a ship!" he shouted. "Hadn't we better light a flare?"

There was a frantic dive for the narrow doorway. The precious hoosh-pot with its limpet and sea-weed soup went flying, and as the crew tumbled out, there, sure enough, they could see a little ship flying the Chilian flag. No sooner had some one lighted a beacon with the sole remaining tin of petrol than they recognized Shackleton as he climbed down a ladder into a boat. Soon he was near enough to hear Wild's cheerful report, "All safe, all well." Within the hour the whole party was aboard ship and hearing with amazement the momentous news of the two years which had elapsed since August, 1914.

Meanwhile, the party in Ross Sea had also met with misadventure. The *Aurora* reached McMurdo Sound safely in January, 1915, and Mackintosh proceeded with the work of laying preliminary depôts. The dogs, which had become soft on board ship, were unfitted for the strenuous work of laying depôts, and most of them died. A shore-party had been landed, but before all the equipment had been put ashore, the *Aurora* was beset. The ship drifted with the ice and narrowly escaped the same fate as the *Endurance*. As it was, when the *Aurora* reached New Zealand in April, 1916, she was a battered, rudderless ship with only a few tons of coal left in the bunkers.

The shore-party fared badly. In spite of the difficulties

due to lack of proper equipment and dogs, the depôts were laid out as far as the Beardmore glacier, so that the Shackleton party on their way down from the South Pole should not be disappointed. The work was only completed at a tremendous cost. Scurvy broke out, and the advance-party narrowly escaped the same fate as Captain Scott. First Spencer-Smith, and then Mackintosh, collapsed and had to be hauled on the sledge by the remaining four men, Joyce, Wild, Richards, and Hayward.

Progress was so slow that supplies ran out, and Wild had to be left behind with the invalids while the others raced to Bluff Depôt and back for food. For several days blizzards kept them helpless in their tents. Then Hayward began to develop scurvy and had to hang on to the sledge to get along. When they were still four days' march away from Hut Point, Spencer-Smith died, and once again Mackintosh had to be left behind in a tent while the remainder made a dash for help. Luckily there were no more casualties on this journey, but the explorers were disappointed to find that the *Aurora* had not returned. They lived the primitive life at Hut Point for the rest of the summer, because the sea-ice had gone out, and it was impossible to reach the base on McMurdo Sound.

During the following winter Mackintosh and Hayward, who had recovered from the scurvy, made an ill-advised attempt to reach the base across the young ice and were drowned. Joyce, with the remainder, reached the base in safety later on, and eventually the survivors of the party were rescued by Shackleton in January, 1917.

CHAPTER VII

THE ROOF OF THE WORLD

The rocky summits, split and rent,
Formed turret, dome or battlement,
Or seemed fantastically set
With cupola or minaret.

SCOTT

THE CONQUEST OF MOUNT KAMET

THERE are over seventy peaks of over 25,000 feet in the Himalayas, and until 1931 not one of these had been conquered. It is true that greater heights than this had been reached on Mount Everest, and that airmen had risen to far greater elevations with the help of electrically heated clothing and other scientific equipment. But the actual attainment of a Himalayan peak means something more than a mere physical triumph over appalling obstacles of rock-precipices and glacier-slopes. The mountain-people say that on the topmost peaks live the Gods of Ice and Snow, and it requires a good deal of patience to persuade them to carry loads beyond a certain point. An example of this was provided when Kamet was conquered. Lewa, a magnificent Sherpa porter, actually reached the summit, but he was so severely frost-bitten that he lost his toes, and the porters all believed that he had been burned by the divinities of the eternal snows.

Mount Kamet (25,447 feet) lies near the sources of the Ganges, not far from the mighty Nanda Devi. Various attempts had been made since 1855 to reach its summit, but although a great deal was learned about the glaciers and cols which surround it, nobody succeeded until Smythe's expedition of 1931. The climbing party which assembled at Ranikhet in May of that year included some famous mountaineers—Smythe, Shipton, Birnie, Greene, and Holdsworth. They brought with them eight Darjeeling porters and picked up two Gurkha N.C.O.'s on the march.

Following the Dhaoli river from Niti, they reached a

glacier called Raikana which flows down from the vicinity of Kamet. Here, on a terminal moraine which looked like a gigantic slag-heap, they made a level platform and pitched their base-camp. A few miles up the Raikana glacier they had to branch off on to a tributary glacier called the East Kamet glacier. This they hoped would lead them to an ice-covered col, which would give access to the slopes of the mountain.

The East Kamet glacier is a very different proposition from the well-known Rongbuk glaciers on Everest. The East Kamet gradually narrows until it runs through a gorge half a mile wide. On the south side is a mountain-wall 6000 feet high crowned with fantastic, towering ice-walls, hundreds of feet thick. A passage on this side of the glacier would mean an imminent peril from avalanches of cataclysmic proportions. Smythe called it a "bowling-ground for the gods." The explorers followed a moraine on the safer side of the glacier and established Camp 2 near a boulder the size of a house and conveniently near water. As they proceeded, they heard a sullen thunder, like a warning shot, and some hundreds of tons of ice-blocks toppled over the edge of the precipice and swept down to the glacier. A day or two later Smythe saw another ice-avalanche. An enormous square piece of ice the size of a cathedral slowly tore away from a hanging glacier and then, toppling like a felled factory-chimney, it crashed in a cloud of ice-shrapnel on the glacier below.

The route to Camp 3 led up a wide snow-gulley to a little glacier plateau. The gulley forms a natural route for avalanches after a heavy fall of snow, and as the climbers ascended they often heard the vicious 'ping' of falling stones. On the plateau they were exposed to the biting rapier-thrusts of the winds, and at this height (20,600 feet) they were beginning to feel the effects of the lack of oxygen, which is found on all Himalayan peaks. But they had not yet reached the crux of the climb. Camp 4 had to be established on a bulge of ice which crowned a 1000-foot precipice of rock and ice, and a good deal of risky prospecting had to be done before this point was reached.

At first the explorers thought that they could surmount the precipice by ascending a couloir; but they were alarmed at the outset by a large boulder which fell from the cliffs and then rolled down the couloir with a terrific velocity before plunging into soft snow. A little higher up they found that the snow in the couloir lay unsteadily over a sheet of black ice, hundreds of feet in extent. So the couloir proved a fiasco, and they had to make a direct assault on the precipice. Snow had to be cleared away from every hold, and soon they reached a rock wall twenty feet high, which took them half an hour to surmount. Eventually, after much heaving and struggling, Smythe plunged his ice-axe into the firm snow on the ice-bulge and pulled himself to the top. From this vantage-point he was able to find a better route along a shelf beneath the precipice and down a little couloir. When ropes had been stretched along the shelf and a staircase cut in the upper ice-slopes, it was possible for the laden porters to ascend. Cutting steps in the leathery ice at 22,000 feet was a weary job, but at last a safe route was discovered round a patch of green-black ice, and the party eventually stood panting for breath on the little plateau which formed the summit of the bulge.

Above Camp 4 there were further ice-slopes to be surmounted, and at one place was a vertical ice-wall fifty feet high. Here the men had to cut steps, and having reached the top they were endangered by huge crevasses. The snow became softer and softer and collected in clumsy balls round their boots. Their progress was like that of a weary marathon-runner who suddenly finds himself in the midst of a soggy ploughed field. Slowly they toiled on; first one took the lead, and then another, and sometimes they leaned on their ice-axes, gasping for breath. One of the porters collapsed, but the magnificent Lewa actually took up the discarded load and ploughed on with a double cargo. The slope eased off, and at last, on a horizontal shelf, Camp 5 was pitched. Above them rose the final slopes of the mountain, and they knew that one more great effort would lead to victory.

The final assault came on the morning of June 21. As

ON THE SUMMIT OF MOUNT KAMET

Reproduced by courtesy of F. S. Smythe, Esq., from "Kamet Conquered" (Gollancz)

the slope gradually grew steeper, the climbers took it in turns to lead, and in the first hour they had climbed 500 feet. A short rest, and then on they plodded through crusted snow which broke beneath their weight. Here and there they had to cross crevasses, which were snow-bridged, but which on the upper side necessitated step-cutting. Eventually, they reached a very steep slope 400 feet high immediately beneath the summit-ridge. At one point they could see a large boulder of reddish granite which projected from the ice, and slowly they hacked steps in the ice towards this possible resting-place. The work was terribly exhausting. Heart and lungs strove desperately for oxygen, and after every few steps a rest had to be taken. Then they had to use the ice-axe again; after an hour's work of this they had climbed 100 feet. Then, when they reached the boulder, they found it smooth and sloping with no place for a rest. Above, however, the snow was deep, and they all sank down gratefully. After a few minutes they went on again, the slope steepening until it was practically a wall. They had to use the ice-axes once again, and Smythe drove in his axe and hauled himself up, to find himself sprawling across the summit-ridge. Soon the four climbers were gathered on the sloping roof-top, and then they began toiling along towards an eminence which appeared to be the summit. They came to a shallow gap, and there, a few yards away, was a small cone of snow—the summit at last!

With numbed hands Smythe set up his ciné-camera and took a number of 'shots,' while Holdsworth smoked half a pipe of tobacco to celebrate the victory. The view was one of the most remarkable in the world: thousands of feet below were the moraine-girded glaciers; on three sides rolled a vista of purple-shadowed clouds riven by snowy island-peaks, like so many rocks of glaring salt protruding above a sea of misty billows; on the extreme horizon the explorers could glimpse the Karakorams—280 miles distant; and only in the north was there any relief from this over-powering maze of pinnacles—for there, beyond barren, snow-streaked hills, gleamed the golden plains of Tibet.

But there was not much time to admire the view; in less

than three hours it would be dark. So one by one they climbed down the ice-wall again and set off for Camp 5. Lewa was very exhausted and suffering from severe frost-bite. On they stumbled along the track, and as the sun sank, they saw Birnie advancing to meet them with hot drinks. Kamet had been conquered; and the conquerors had safely returned. On the next day the second party, consisting of Birnie, Greene, and Kesar Singh, also reached the summit, though they, too, had a difficult struggle to climb the ice-walls. Then the whole party set off on the downward trail which led to the base-camp and comparative luxury.

THE STORY OF NANDA DEVI

What boy has not dreamed that some day he might find a secret valley walled round by a mountain bulwark where, amid verdant pastures and flower-bedecked meads, he might rule a kingdom all his own? The inaccessible valley has, too, been a long-loved theme with imaginative novelists. It is given to few to find such places, however, but that they do exist is revealed by the following story.

Nanda Devi (25,660 feet) is the highest mountain entirely within the British Empire. It lies in the heart of the Garhwal Himalaya, not far from the pilgrim-haunted sources of the Ganges. Yet until 1934, though several expeditions had tried to reach its mighty twin peaks, nobody had penetrated even as far as the glaciers which sweep down from its feet. This was due not merely to the fact that the usual difficulties of Himalayan travel had to be overcome—landslides, raging torrents, mountain-sickness, and insect-pests—but because the peaks are surrounded by a unique system of natural defences infinitely more formidable than those of the most impregnable medieval castle. Even when the outer bastions of forested foothills and icy passes have been stormed, there still remains what is probably the most gigantic natural rampart in the world. This seventy-mile encircling barrier is nowhere lower than 17,000 feet, and at intervals stand craggy turrets, at least twelve of which soar to over 21,000 feet. For those who seek an alternative to storming these icy curtain-walls there is a way through the 'moat.' But

like everything else about this Gargantuan fortress the
'moat' is built on heroic lines. Raging down from the ramparts at one point is a glacier-torrent, the Rishi Ganga.
This, according to the local tribes, is the abode of demons,
who guard the entrance to the secret shrine of the Blessed
Goddess, Nanda Devi. This gorge, or 'moat,' as we have

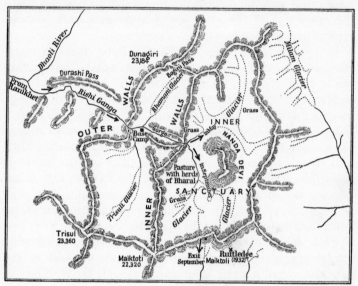

THE APPROACHES TO NANDA DEVI

called it, might seem to be the natural means of approaching
the central keep.

In 1883 W. W. Graham, accompanied by two famous
Swiss guides, tried to reach Nanda Devi by this route. They
made their way laboriously along the sides of the steep
cliffs on the northern side of the Rishi Ganga, clambering
over wild rocks and broken gullies, with the river churning
along some 7000 feet beneath their feet. A day's hard
climbing took them three miles, and when they pitched their
tents they had to sleep on a rock sloping so steeply that they
built a wall of stones to prevent them from rolling over the
precipice! The next day brought them to a most magnificent
gorge with sheer sides falling thousands of feet. Then their

coolies deserted, and since it seemed impossible to go farther, Graham had to retreat.

In 1905 Dr Longstaff tried to reach the Nanda Devi basin by climbing the eastern ramparts, and eventually, after three days' climbing up the glaciers, he reached a ridge whence for the first time men looked down into the secret basin. But they found it quite impossible to descend on to the other side of the ridge and had to turn back without setting foot in Nanda Devi.

In 1932 Mr Ruttledge, of Everest fame, tried to reach the basin by climbing the southern ramparts, but having made good progress up the glaciers, he was brought to a sudden stop by a vertical wall of six thousand feet of rock and ice. Near the top of the wall, for about a mile and a half, was an overhanging terrace of ice from which masses were constantly breaking to sweep down the polished cliffs and thunder into the valley below. For all the world it seemed as if the guardian spirits of the fortress were bombarding the invaders, just as in ancient times the defenders of a castle were wont to hurl down rocks and molten metal from their man-made machicolations.

Early in 1934 Eric Shipton, who had had considerable experience of mountaineering both in Africa and in the Himalaya, had a letter from an old friend, H. W. Tilman. Tilman announced that, having successfully ridden across Africa on a bicycle, he was ready and willing to accompany Shipton in an attempt to reach Nanda Devi. The party which forgathered at Calcutta in April, 1934, was a very small one. There were the two white men and three Sherpas, Angtharkay (who had been as far as Camp 6 on Mount Everest), Kusang, and Passang, from the wilds of Nepal. This expedition was indeed in marked contrast to the elaborately organized armies which have attacked Mount Everest, and the total cost amounted to only £287.

Eventually, after nine days' wandering through the lovely foothills beyond Ranikhet, in Almore Province, the explorers hired twelve Dotial porters and began the assault of the Rishi Ganga. Steady plodding through rhododendron woods and over snowy passes brought them to the junction of the Dhaoli and the Rishi Ganga; from there they reached the little vale of Durashi *via* a track running along the face of a steep precipice. For about half a mile there was a narrow ledge, just wide enough for shepherds to drive their sheep along, winding round the sides of cliffs, which fell in a breath-taking plunge for 8000 feet. In places the way was covered with ice, and at any moment it seemed probable that the carriers might stumble with their heavy loads into the chasm.

In the evening the explorers wandered down to the end of the Durashi vale and looked down a 5000-foot precipice into the Rishi Ganga gorge. Dimly down in the depths they could just see the torrent, the 'Demon's Lair,' where no man had ever been. On the farther side of the river rose tier after tier of steep slabs and slippery rocks which towered upward to a crenelation of sharp, menacing peaks some 10,000 feet high. On the next day they came to a beautiful little alp bordered by tall, stately pines, where there was soft grass and a carpet of wild flowers.

Two days later they reached the Rishi Nala and began to work their way along a line 2000 feet above the river-bed. Not only was the side of the gorge steep, but it was cut by innumerable gullies and bare cliffs, which forced the party to turn back again and again to seek an alternative route. Eventually they decided to descend to the river-bed, and for this purpose they sought out a deep-cut gulley, down which it was possible to climb. Here and there the loads had to be lowered by ropes, and once Shipton was struck on the head by a rock dislodged by one of the porters above him. At last, after scrambling through a tangle of brambles, they reached a place where a number of large boulders enabled them to cross over the stream to the northern bank.

Next morning the men pushed along through tangles of thorn-scrub for a few hundred yards, where they came to a big scar in the hillside, beyond which it was impossible to travel at that level. Having climbed up to 1000 feet they followed a terrace which took them for a further half a mile; but then Tilman reported that, farther on, that ledge became so narrow and so sloping that there were not even any hand-holds. So once again they had to descend to the river, where they cut down trees to make a bridge. At this point of the southern shore there was a strip of pine-forest, and after another hour they reached the junction of the Rhamani river, where they had arranged to place the base-camp.

Snow fell heavily, and Tilman's tent collapsed under the weight, so that he took refuge with Shipton and Passang under the cover of a small, overhanging rock. The Dotials made themselves comfortable in a little cave, but it was quite impossible to get a fire going. On the next day the Dotials departed for home, leaving the five explorers with provisions for thirty-five days. In front of them boiled the muddy glacier-torrent, and to the east stretched the most difficult part of the gorge, whose sides now rose perpendicularly from the river-bed. Just opposite the camp was a great rock, which provided a natural bridge across the stream and gave access to the northern side.

Since it was impossible to follow the river-bed, they began the final assault by a traverse along the southern cliffs at a height of over 1000 feet. Two hours zig-zagging brought them to a little spur, whence they were able to get a good view for two miles up the canyon. There they could see a gigantic black buttress, which swept down from the dizzy heights sheer to the water's edge, and which appeared to be impassable. They dubbed this formidable defence-work 'Pisgah,' for they were sure that, if once they could find the way round it, the route to the 'Promised Land' would be open. At first they tried to climb a gulley, but were brought up short by a menacing overhang; then they decided to try a terrace running steeply across the precipice. Two hundred yards farther along the terrace disappeared, where a recent landslide had caused a great scar. There was nothing for it but to climb the scar, and when the explorers reached the top they sighted a fault in the slabs, which led them on to another sloping terrace. So they clambered along from one dizzy ledge to the next, until they reached a point only a quarter of a mile from 'Pisgah.' At this point the ledge suddenly narrowed to a foot in width and actually overhung the river.

Having safely spanned this 'tight-rope' walk, they noticed that on the opposite side of the river was a little shore. So they climbed down and waded into the icy waters. Soon the little strip of shore petered out, and once again they had to cross the stream, which was so cold that it numbed the extremities. This process of crossing and recrossing was repeated six times, until they found a suitable camp-site. Tilman and Shipton then returned to camp and made preparations for bringing up supplies. At the most difficult places ropes were fixed to iron stakes, but even then it needed the balance of an acrobat for the Sherpas to carry the heavy bundles of stores along. In places the carriers removed their boots so that they might have a sure foothold on the slippery rocks, and elsewhere it was necessary to haul the loads up or down by means of ropes. On one ridge a load overbalanced and crashed down into a gulley two hundred feet below and then hung perilously on a ledge above the gaping gorge. The sack was retrieved, but valuable supplies had spilt down into the chasm.

Even Kusang, who had an incurable habit of chanting monotonously as he marched along, was hushed at one place, where, both above and below, the cliffs were smooth and sheer. The traverse had to be achieved twice so that all the loads could be brought along, and on the second journey it began to snow before they had reached the worst places. When they came to the ledge which had stilled Kusang, they found it covered with a thick blanket of snow. With great deliberation they edged along, clearing the snow from the ledge as they went. Then a wind started to blow down the gorge and dashed the snow into their faces. At last, however, they reached their camping-place and huddled down under the lea of the cliffs and tried to coax a few smoky, sodden pieces of driftwood into the semblance of a fire.

On the opposite shore there was a small clump of stunted birches and a cave, and as soon as the snowstorm had abated the party decided to make for this spot and establish a camp. By this time, however, the Rishi Ganga had been swollen by the storm, and crossing the raging torrent was no easy matter, especially with loads. The current was so fast that in midstream, where the water was waist-high, it was almost impossible to keep their feet, and all the time their legs were being bombarded by stones swept down by the stream. Passang, who was carrying a load of *satu* (toasted grain), and Angtharkay, with a load of clothes and bedding, had very narrow escapes, for their loads became waterlogged; but they just managed to haul themselves ashore by means of the rope which had been stretched across by the first-comers.

Soaked to the skin and tired out, they crept into the cave and planned a means of bridging the river for future occasions. A little downstream they saw a number of boulders, and soon they had linked these stepping-stones with a crazy bridge of twisted birches.

Now came the greatest problem of all—to find a practicable route past 'Pisgah.' Shipton and Passang followed a steep corridor along the northern cliffs, but it brought them to a little elevated platform beyond which it was impossible to go. High up on the opposite cliff they could see Tilman and Angtharkay climbing like tiny ants, until they reached a flaw in the mighty buttress where it seemed just possible that a way could be found. Soon they, too, had to turn aside, and they plunged into a steep gulley on the near side. Convinced that Tilman had failed to find a route, Shipton tried desperate measures to advance along his side of the river. But in the end he had to admit defeat and return disconsolately to camp. The hours drew on, and night began to fall. Still Tilman had not returned, and it seemed probable that an accident had occurred. Then suddenly they saw the wanderers scrambling precariously across the water, and evidently they were very excited. When they came into camp they brought the glad tidings that they had found at 1500 feet a gap in the defences, and from their vantage-point they had seen the way clearly into the inner sanctuary of Nanda Devi.

The next day, fully loaded, the whole party made their way up Tilman's gulley and came to a narrow chimney, which led to the crest of the buttress. A little farther on were two small caves and a bubbling spring, which provided an ideal camping-site. Moreover, they had a fore-taste of the surprises which lay beyond, for at their 'door-step' were quantities of wild rhubarb; this provided a pleasant change of diet. That evening, towards sunset, the clouds unfurled, and, as if to reward them for their struggles, Nanda Devi showed herself dazzling white, incredibly lofty, and majestically detached from the cloudy depths of the basin.

By noon on the next day they reached the junction of two streams which drain the glaciers of the southern and northern ends of the basin. Here there were gentle grassy slopes, never before trodden by man. A little above the junction of the streams was a little plateau where wild onions grew, and a mile and a half away the men could see the snout of a great glacier which swept down from the northern half of the basin. They could also see a small herd of *bharal* (mountain sheep) peacefully grazing on the gentle slopes of this highland paradise.

Like Balboa on his peak in Darien, the explorers climbed a spur which commanded a view over the northern glaciers, and away in the distance beyond the lateral moraine they could see an expanse of undulating meadows stretching for miles, a sanctuary for thousands of wild animals. Now began the task of mapping as much of the basin as they could, in the time at their disposal, before the monsoon came and their stores ran short. On the next day they crossed the snout of the glacier and mounted one of the lower buttresses of Nanda Devi—the first men to set foot on the peaks. Then they pushed on to the meadows they had seen, and walking over the soft, springy turf, they had a magnificent view of the inner side of the great encircling walls.

During the three weeks which ensued, one marvel followed quickly after another. Always in the centre of the landscape loomed the majestic peak of Nanda Devi, whose sides are so steep that even ice and snow can find little room to cling. There were mighty crevassed glaciers to be crossed, but there were also extensive areas of rich pasture-land, resplendent with wild flowers, and lakes deep blue and green. Here in the crystal waters the icy crests were mirrored. The

163

explorers saw large herds of *tar* and *bharal* and a considerable variety of birds. On the farther side of the great northern glacier, and not far from a beautiful little lake about eight acres in size, they made a camp, and from this point they climbed several peaks on the northern walls. From one peak of about 21,000 feet they had a clear view out of the basin over an inextricably confused mass of peaks round the Milam glacier. They climbed along a ridge with a mighty drop down to the Milam glacier, on the one hand, and an equally fearsome descent to the Nanda Devi basin, on the other. Then they cut steps in the ice and slowly went down to their camp.

Shortly afterwards, Shipton began to shiver violently and had to roll himself in his double sleeping-bag in spite of a scorching sun. For the next thirty-six hours he was in the grip of a fever, and was delirious. Then quite suddenly the fever went, and he was able to hobble back to the base-camp. Nearly a week later Tilman also was attacked by this strange malady. Once again they climbed the northern glaciers, and from a col of some 20,000 feet the men looked down a sickening cliff to the moraine-covered Bagini glacier, 5,000 feet below. Beyond, in the distance, over a maze of peaks they could see the untrodden glaciers of Hathi Parbat and the pinnacle of Mount Kamet. So far, however, they had seen no possible alternative exit, and so they had to return to their base-camp, since the swollen streams on the great North glacier were a sure indication that the monsoon was not far away. By this time the slopes about their base-camp, were carpeted with bright flowers and young grass, which straggled up the lower spurs of the mountains.

On June 24 the monsoon broke. Now the party had to plan a speedy retreat, because it was all too likely that the rushing glacier streams would be very swollen, and might cut off their retreat. Indeed, the stream issuing from the main glacier was a difficult proposition in itself, and it was only after an anxious period of rope-laying that they were able to cross even this obstacle. Two days later they entered the Rishi Ganga gorge again, pushing on at breakneck speed to avoid the full effects of the unexpected monsoon.

164

As they wound along the narrow ledges, the lightning flashed and the thunder echoed, and these phenomena added a theatrical atmosphere to the terrors of the passage. However, the way was known now, and so by June 28 they had reached their camp at the junction of the Rishi Ganga; from there they made their way to the flesh-pots of the nearest village, Joshimath.

During the period when snow and heavy rain made further work in the Nanda Devi basin impossible, Shipton proposed that they should investigate the mountain ranges to the north-west. Here they would be sheltered from the full effects of the monsoon. Some forty miles north-west of the ranges which they had been exploring lies the Badrinath range, where the sacred head-waters of the Ganges have their origin. Although Badrinath has for countless ages been the Mecca of devout Hindus, no one previously had crossed the ranges. On July 12 the explorers left Badrinath and made their way along the northern bank of the Alaknanda, one of the sacred head-waters. Before long they came to a rushing torrent, where Passang lost his footing and was swept away with his load. He managed to save himself from a severe buffeting on the rocks, but both he and Tilman lost their ice-axes in the process. Snow-conditions higher up were very bad, but they successfully reached the watershed and descended on the other side to the Gangotri glacier, and so reached Gaumukh. Here at the sacred 'Cow's Mouth' they saw the turbid thirty-foot stream which rushes out of a black-ice cave in the snout of the Gangotri glacier, to begin its journey of fifteen hundred miles of increasing girth to the Bay of Bengal.

When they returned to Badrinath, the men heard a legend that once, many hundred years ago, there was no high priest of the Kedarnath temple on the other side of the water-shed, and that the high priest of Badrinath used to hold services in the temples at both places on the same day. But the water-shed is so steep that to-day the shortest known route between the two shrines is by a roundabout route fully 100 miles long. Although it was now August and they were anxious to return to Nanda Devi, they decided to investigate this interesting story by climbing to the top of the range, *via* the Satopanth glacier, and from the top get a view towards Kedarnath. Although they little suspected it, this little side-excursion was to provide them with as many thrills as the ascent of the gorge of Rishi Ganga.

Soon they passed out of the ken of the little prayer-flags, which are planted by devout pilgrims all round this district, to the ice-fall which forms the head of the Satopanth glacier. Then, when they were barely 1000 feet from the col, they were held up by a huge crevasse, which spread from one side of the glacier to the other, forming an impassable barrier. They camped that night in driving snow on the brink of the chasm, and all night long they could hear the roar of ice-avalanches from the great cliff above. In the morning, determined not to be vanquished when they were so near the coveted view-point, they decided to try a way off the glacier on to the rocks at the side of the valley. There followed a difficult period of climbing over gulleys and crags, which brought them to an ice-ridge, up which they cut steps and mounted to the crest.

In front of them stretched a great ice-plateau, but the longed-for view was still denied them, since they were enveloped in a pea-soup fog. Early the next morning Tilman and Shipton went off to reconnoitre. Suddenly the fog rolled away, and they found themselves looking down into the immense depths of the Kedarnath valley-system. The glacier at their feet descended in a steep ice-fall for a thousand feet, and then flattened out for some distance, before taking a final plunge into a gloomy gorge some 6000 feet below. Although the descent looked full of difficulties, they felt that they had to make the attempt, and see where the gorge would lead them. So all that day they wormed their way down through the intricacies of the ice-fall, winding past seracs and ice-towers or across slender bridges spanning bottomless crevasses. At last they reached the level piece of the glacier; but then they found that the second ice-fall beyond was, if anything, even more fearsome than the ice-slope they had just descended.

Indeed, for a time they feared that they had ventured on

to that blind alley of the mountaineer—a hanging glacier. But the Sherpas, in spite of their mumbled imprecations to the demons of the icy regions, were keen to attempt the descent. They climbed over to the left side of the ice-fall, 200 feet below which they could see a steep gulley running down the margin of the glacier. Angtharkay volunteered to climb down the chasm. Then with a crash a huge chunk of ice hurtled down into the gulley, and for a moment they feared that the brave Sherpa had been dashed to his death. A few minutes later, however, he reappeared with a grin on his face and informed them that he had found a ledge from which it might be possible to lower the loads and themselves by means of ropes.

In the morning they dropped down the cold, sickly-green ice-walls to Angtharkay's ledge, and thence by means of the 180-feet Alpine rope they lowered themselves to the level glacier beneath. Then, as they raced along, they thought that at last all their troubles were over.

They were soon disillusioned. At the foot of the glacier they were confronted by a tangled mass of vegetation through which they had to hack their way blindly. It began to rain. There were treacherous, overgrown pot-holes and tearing brambles to pass. Then, late in the evening, they came to a formidable chasm where there was a sheer drop of over 1,000 feet to the bottom of the valley.

By this time their food-supplies were running short, and in view of this new difficulty they anxiously debated whether or not to turn back and return by the route they had followed. Even supposing that they could pass the 'cut-off,' every step forward now meant a step farther into unknown, thickly forested country. But the thought of the ice-slopes behind them made them decide to risk an advance, and so they set about the task of climbing up the side of the valley to round the precipice. At any moment it seemed probable that their bulky loads would pull them from the slender hand-holds of matted undergrowth. Soon they came to a bare vertical cliff and had to lower Angtharkay on a rope to a grassy ledge below. Then, doubling the rope over a juniper-root, the whole party shinned down to join him.

This process was repeated from ledge to ledge until they stood in the densely forested valley.

Once again they commenced their weary hacking with ice-axe and *kukri*. Meanwhile, the whole of the remaining stores had been thoroughly soaked in the sodden undergrowth, and the alarming prospect of starvation drew nearer. Fortunately the Sherpas found some young bamboo-shoots, which Tilman said reminded him of asparagus, and a little later on, not far from a bear's cave where they encamped, they found some forest-mushrooms.

That day the explorers advanced a mile and a half, and once more they were faced by a seemingly impassable obstacle—this time a raging mountain torrent. They wasted most of the next day climbing up a gulley to a place where it seemed that there was a natural bridge. This turned out to be a delusion and a snare, and they returned to the starting-point. Feeling very hungry on the vegetarian diet, they began to construct a bridge with some tree-trunks. While this was being done a great boulder came hurtling down and crushed Passang's left foot. Finally, after much straining and heaving, the men persuaded four poles to balance crazily on a slimy rock on the farther bank. Then, inch, by inch, Tilman edged his way along the swaying bridge, fixed up a rope hand-rail, and soon all the party had safely crossed.

Once more they hacked their way through thick forest, sometimes advancing only twenty-five yards in an hour. The sides of the valley were still so steep that they had to cut a platform with their ice-axes before they could pitch a tent. The rain fell in torrents, but they found that the friendly bamboos could be fashioned into a shelter, and, at the same time, provide them with food and fuel. For many miles more they found their way barred by gulley after gulley, chasm after chasm, and Passang suffered agonies with his injured foot. An advance of one mile meant a whole day's labour.

Lower down they found that they had rivals for the bamboo-shoots—the Himalayan bears. Once, when Angtharkay was making for a cave where they proposed to camp, a great black bear ambled out, gazed at the startled carrier, and then loped off into the forest. Two days later, when they were faint from lack of food, they suddenly emerged on an open grassy hillside, and a mile below them they spied two fields of standing crops. The great watershed had been crossed, and the Sherpas yelled with delight, for real food was in sight at last.

Once more they returned to Joshimath village, and after a few days' rest they prepared for a second attack on Nanda Devi. The terrors of the Rishi Ganga seemed to lessen with familiarity, and three days' steady climbing brought them once again into the inner basin. This time they explored the southern end of the valley and climbed to a height of over 20,000 feet up the south-eastern ridge of the twin peaks. Then they sought and found an alternative exit over the southern rim of the basin, and after many adventures on the precipitous icy slopes of the southern side, reached the valley below in safety. So in the space of four months the secret of Nanda Devi had been solved on two separate occasions, and eventually, in September, 1936, Tilman actually climbed Nanda Devi itself.

CHAPTER VIII

NEW LIGHT ON THE DARK CONTINENT

For the journey is done and the summit attained
  And the barriers fall,
Though a battle's to fight ere the guerdon be gained,
  The reward of it all.

BROWNING, *Prospice*

THE MOUNTAINS OF THE MOON

ONE day in 1876, when the Italian explorer, Gessi, stood
on the shores of the Albert Nyanza, he saw a strange vision
in the distant sky. He thought he could see, far above the
steaming valleys, a mighty snow-covered mountain range.
Naturally he dismissed the vision as a sort of hallucination.
What else could Alpine scenery on the Equator be?

Twelve years later, when Henry Stanley was passing
along the south-west bank of the same lake, a native boy
called his attention to a mountain which, he said, was
covered with salt. Stanley saw a peculiar-shaped cloud of a
most beautiful silver colour, which assumed the proportions
and appearance of a vast mountain covered with snow.
Following its form earthward, he noticed the deep blue-
black colour of its base and wondered if it portended a
tornado. Then, as his gaze descended the gap between two
ethereal plateaux, he became conscious for the first time
that what he was looking at was not the mere semblance of
a vast mountain, but the solid substance of a real one with
its summit covered with snow.

So was the existence of Ruwenzori, 'King of the Clouds,'
verified. Yet it is an extraordinary fact that this Alpine
range in the very heart of Africa was first reported by the
ancient Greeks. According to Ptolemy, the Nile rose in the
'Mountains of the Moon,' and Egypt was nurtured by the
snow from these silver peaks. For many years the natives
of the east coast had told explorers of snow-clad mountains
at the sources of the Nile, but Ruwenzori (which has been

170

identified with the 'Mountains of the Moon'), because of its position in the midst of low-lying forests, is nearly always surrounded by such thick palls of mist that explorers actually trod on the lower slopes of the range without dreaming that above their heads towered peaks and glaciers higher than any in Europe.

Stanley's amazing discovery prompted many mountaineers to attempt the exploration of the range, but the barriers of forested foothills, clouds of fog, and, higher up, of glaciers defeated them all. A few years before his death, the veteran explorer begged that some lover of mountains should choose Ruwenzori as his goal and explore its wild valleys and hidden gorges. The challenge was accepted by the late Duke of the Abruzzi, one of the greatest explorers of this century. As a young man of twenty he had been the first to climb the 18,000-foot peak of St Elias, in Alaska; two years later he had spent a winter in Franz Josef Land, when his ship the *Stella Polare* was crushed in the ice; and subsequently he sledged nearer to the North Pole than any of his predecessors.

It was in April, 1906, that the Duke began the expedition which was to lead to the conquest of Ruwenzori. With characteristic efficiency he had organized a great *safari*, which marched like a small army from the rail-head at Kisumu, on Lake Victoria, across Uganda towards Ruwenzori. The march across papyrus-swamps and through forests of elephant-grass was heavy and fatiguing. As they neared the mountains, the native porters clustered round the camp-fires, for there were numerous lions prowling about in the vicinity. One day, when the sky was clouded, but the air clear, they suddenly saw to the westward the snowy peaks of the great chain, about forty-five miles away. The glaciers looked as if they were suspended in the air, for the foot of the mountains was shrouded in thick mists. A few days later they left the forest behind and were soon struggling across the glacier-fed torrents which rush down the mountain gorges.

When they reached the main river, the Mobuku, the party found the current so violent that, although a rope was stretched across the ford, it was necessary to have a line of porters to help the loaded carriers across. Beyond the river the path steadily rose through thick ferns, heaths, and bamboos. Violent thunderstorms made the ground so slippery that the porters had difficulty in keeping their feet.

Before long an important tributary valley was discovered which appeared to lead into the very heart of the range, and which was subsequently fully explored by the Duke. At this stage a number of the local natives, called Bakonjo, were enlisted, because they were better acclimatized to the higher ground than the natives of Uganda. The Bakonjo were tall, robust men, with shaven heads and rough, sun-tanned skins. Some wore leopard-skins over their shoulders, or cloaks made of rabbit-pelts, with fur-pouches suspended from their necks for pipes and tobacco.

So the expedition was reorganized. The path forward was along the bottom of a valley, which was almost a mud-lake. The men sank up to their knees, and under the mud their feet were entangled in creepers or on fallen trunks. Sometimes they had to leap from one upstanding root to the next. Rain fell heavily, and from the heaths and tall ferns a chilly drip fell ceaselessly on the caravan. Soon the explorers were passing through a landscape so weird and unusual that they might have been travelling on some other planet. All the trunks and boughs were entirely smothered with thick layers of mosses, which hung like waving beards from everything and carpeted the innumerable dead trunks underfoot. When at last they passed out of the heath-forest they found themselves in a landscape totally different, yet equally strange. Here the ground was layered with springy moss and carpeted with most beautiful flowers; here there were pink, yellow, and silver-white everlasting-flowers, tall columns of lobelia, which looked like monster funeral-torches, and giant *senecios*, which look something like willow-trees with cactus-plants for leaves, and which recall the fantastic illustrations of the distant carboniferous ages.

Eventually a base-camp was set up at a height of 12,461 feet. Here there was a heap of blocks surrounded by tree-heaths and overhung by a high rock which served as a canopy. On this eyrie, where there was hardly any flat ground, were pitched six tents, and the porters burrowed under the pile of boulders to find caverns which would serve as shelters. To pass from one tent to another involved a good deal of acrobatic skill, but the place was the only spot which promised at least some protection from the terrible weather. The amenities of the base-camp were not improved by the near-by presence of a leopard's lair. The leopard was first seen devouring two sheep belonging to the expedition, and on the following night the Duke was sitting at the opening of his tent quietly writing when he looked up to find the leopard only a few paces off. When the Duke stood up the animal fled; but for many days afterwards the natives were very scared. Eventually the cook arranged a cunning snare with a piece of meat, and the terror of the base-camp was trapped and shot.

From the base-camp systematic expeditions were made to all parts of the range. The Ruwenzori chains covers an area of about eighty square miles, and the main range, about eleven miles long, is shaped like the letter 'G.' There are six main mountains—Gessi, Emin, Speke, Stanley, Baker, and Luigi di Savoia. Mount Stanley, which lies in the centre of the group, is crowned by two peaks which are the highest in the range. The Duke climbed up the Mobuku glacier to a peak on Mount Baker, from where he was able to see the chief features of the range. Far below him was a beautiful blue lake; but the way down to the lake and on to the highest peaks looked very difficult.

At length it was decided to establish a series of camps round the foot of Mount Baker, and to try a pass which led to the lake. For this work the natives were almost useless; even at the base-camp they had felt the cold severely. The Duke had provided them with blankets and warm clothing, and they made long and ludicrous attempts to squeeze their legs into the sleeves of some woollen vests which were issued. Sometimes they stripped themselves and clustered round the fires, so that they might get the full benefit of the heat. They huddled together in their smoky dens under the rocks, and when on the march, they carried some smouldering fungus so that at the first halt a fire could be lighted. Yet only a few of the Bakonjo deserted, and most of them marched as far as they could, even though suffering from frost-bite.

For the work of scaling the peaks the Duke had brought along two guides and two European porters from the Alps. With their help a way was found to the foot of the glaciers on Mount Stanley, and preparations were made for the final assault on the high peaks. As soon as day broke, two of the guides led the way up the glacier, and by 6.30 A.M. they had reached the ice-cap which crowns the mountains. A short distance away they caught sight of the twin peaks, which were joined by a rounded ice-col. The farther and higher peak appeared to be overhung by a gigantic cornice, supported on a colonnade of icicle-lacework. Before long, compact masses of cloud and mist belched up the valleys, completely shutting in the climbers. Silently they crunched along, cutting steps at the steepest points, and by 7.30 they had reached the top of the first peak, which they named Alexandra Peak (16,749 feet).

For the next hour and a half the mist was so thick that they were only allowed fleeting glimpses of the second peak. At last, tired of waiting, they set off along the col. They found that this was merely a narrow strip of ice bounded on either side by wide, unbridged crevasses. So they marched straight ahead on their icy tight-rope, until they could see an ice-wall looming ahead in the drifting mist.

Soon the slope grew steeper, and one of the guides went ahead, cutting steps, and showering ice and snow on the others. The mist closed in behind them, so that they seemed to be climbing a frosted staircase suspended over a bottomless abyss. Climbing almost vertically, they reached the bottom of the cornice, where ice stalactites and stalagmites stood as thick as trees in a forest. Upon these columns rested a heavy snowy-dome, extending upwards to the peak.

Like so many squirrels they scrambled round this fairyland colonnade until they came to a cleft in the cornice. Here there was a vertical gulley some six feet high. One of the guides planted himself firmly in a wide ice-step and thus served as a ladder for the second guide, who climbed first on his shoulders, and then on his head (in his heavy nailed

AIR-PHOTOGRAPH OF MOUNT STANLEY, RUWENZORI

Margherita and Alexandra peaks on left.

By courtesy of Dr Noel Humphreys

174

boots!), and stuck his ice-axe firmly in the snow above the cornice. In this way he hauled himself up, and soon the whole party stood on the highest peak of Ruwenzori.

Here, at a height of 16,815 feet, the little tricolour flag with its embroidered motto, '*Ardisci e Spere*' ('Dare and Hope'), was unfurled, and the spot was named after Queen Margherita. Subsequently all the other peaks in the Ruwenzori chain were climbed by one or other members of the expedition. A careful map was constructed, and when at length the party left for Lake Victoria again, most of the secrets of the 'Mountains of the Moon' had been revealed.

The final secrets were unveiled during the expeditions of Dr Noel Humphreys in 1926, 1931, and 1932. He made several flights across the range, discovered a number of lakes, and came to the conclusion that one stream—the Raumuli—is the 'Fountain of the Nile' of the ancients.

From July 1934 to August 1935 Dr Humphreys was in charge of the Oxford Univerity Ellesmere Land Expedition.

ROSITA FORBES AND THE SECRET OF THE SAHARA

Who has not been thrilled by the brave tales of the Foreign Legion, of lonely white forts in the midst of a blazing sea of sand, of sudden lightning raids by fanatical Bedouins? During the War the campaigns fought round the fringes of the Sahara were not noticed much in comparison with the struggles on other fronts. Yet those campaigns were none the less important; millions were spent on defences for western Egypt, and at one time the pro-German tribes had almost driven the Italians out of Libya. The secret of this endless hostility may be summed up in one word—*Senussi*.

The Senussi creed has been compared with that of the Cromwellian Puritans. The founder of the confraternity, Sidi Mohammed Ben Ali Es Senussi, was born in Algeria in 1787. He was something of a mystic—a kind of Mohammedan St Francis—and he preached a gospel of strict adherence to the Koran and the simple rules of the Prophet. His reform-movement slowly gathered impetus, until by 1882 there were about two million brothers, or *ekhwan*. These *ekhwan* travelled far and wide throughout Islam, founding *zawias* (combined colleges and markets) in every available oasis or wherever caravans met. By the beginning of the present century, the Senussi were the only really effective power throughout the length and breadth of the great Sahara desert. An area as large as the whole of Australia obeyed the rule of the *Sayeds*, and, like Tibet, it was practically a closed land to all foreign influence.

It has always been a characteristic of fanatical ascetic cults that they should seek out hiding-places far from the reach of the polluted herd. Just as the Pilgrim Fathers colonized New England, and the Cistercians the bleakest vales of Europe, so the chief strongholds of the Senussi were in far-off oases in the very heart of the desert. Kufara, their Holy of Holies, began to have a reputation second only to that of Mecca. It was known to be an important centre of trade and teaching, yet for decades no European ever succeeded in penetrating to the 'Secret of the Sahara.' In 1879 a German scientist called Rohlfs led a large and powerful expedition from Benghazi in an attempt to reach Kufara. Long before he reached the oasis his camp was attacked and looted, and although the adventurous German managed to reach the outskirts of the oases, he had to be secreted away by a friendly sheikh; and eventually he returned to civilization without any records or maps of his journey. He was indeed lucky to escape with his life, for the Senussi make it a rule to shoot all strangers on sight— especially if they are the hated *Nasrani* (Christians).

For forty years after the Rohlfs expedition no European even tried to reach the Kufara. Then, in 1920, Rosita Forbes, an English lady who has become famous for her adventurous travels in many parts of the world, decided to attempt what had been proved impossible for a male explorer. Possibly she thought that the fanaticism of the Senussi would not extend to the gracious 'Sitt Khadija,' as she called herself. She was fortunate in her choice of a companion explorer. Hassanein Bey, son of an Egyptian noble, and an Oxford 'Blue,' proved invaluable— in spite of a minor idiosyncrasy which made Balliol blazers, bottles of Eau de Cologne, bath-salts, and patent-leather shoes 'necessities' for travelling the waterless wilderness. Hassanein subsequently accomplished a notable exploratory journey on his own account when he discovered 'Uweinat.

Mrs Forbes was also fortunate in meeting at Benghazi, her landing-place in Cyrenaica, the ruling Emir of the Senussi. Idris Es Senussi had recently signed a peace with the Italians, and he proved to be a very charming and accomplished person. In her faltering Arabic Mrs Forbes explained her desire to make a journey into the deserts, and the Emir not only blessed the project but also wrote a casual letter of welcome, which was to act as a magic passport wherever it was shown to a Senussi *ekhwan*. In the interior the explorers found that the Emir enjoyed a prestige comparable with that of the Dalai-lama of Tibet. He was at once the head of the political and religious autocracies of the brotherhood.

Rosita Forbes did not, of course, express her intention of travelling to Kufara. The Senussi would have been shocked at such a proposal, and would at once have tried to convince her of the impossibility of the task. Kufara lies about 580 miles to the south of Benghazi, and although it is the trade-centre of the eastern Sahara, the journey from the sea is so difficult that none but the best-equipped caravans can attempt it. South of the oasis of Jalo a journey of seven hard, waterless days brings the caravan to Zeighen. Here there is water but no fodder or oasis. Another five waterless marches across the dunes leads to Hawari, on the outskirts of the Kufara group of oases; and then there is a chain of mountains to be crossed before the secret cities are reached. There is an alternative parallel route, which runs through the oases of Taiserbo, Buseima, and Ribiana; but this route is rendered even more difficult by the hostility of marauding bands of Zouias, who are reputed to wait in ambush for all strange caravans.

The initial difficulties arose at Benghazi. Hassanein Bey had previously been engaged in diplomatic work, and he was suspected by the Italians of deep pan-Islamic designs. Relays of kindly individuals took the utmost interest in the party's plans; soon the whole camp was full of spies, and the wildest rumours began to circulate. Nevertheless, the expedition safely reached Jedabia, 95 miles south of Benghazi, and was welcomed by the younger brother of the Emir. They were given a house, a cook, and servants, and invited to a feast of soup, chicken, mutton, tomatoes, marrow, rice, omelettes, and mint tea which lasted for three hours.

For some days they lived in what proved to be a fool's paradise at Jedabia, making their plans for a journey southward. They soon found themselves faced with innumerable difficulties. Almost all the servants were found to be spies in the pay of the Italians, and all plans had to be discussed furtively. They had considerable difficulty in hiring enough camels for their vague 'trip into the desert.' Rosita Forbes took care to correct the dangerous impression, which had gone the round of the bazaars, that she was a rich Christian woman ripe for plunder. She performed the obligatory Moslem prayers and frequently recited audibly verses of the Koran. Indeed, she so impressed one aged *ekhwan* that he promised to help her to reach Kufara, so that she might kiss the holy *qubba* and become a Moslem. The *ekhwan* also helped them to obtain an escort of ten black slave-soldiers under a commander called Abdul Rahim. It was also arranged that he should send a caravan to travel with the explorers as far as Kufara.

By this time, however, every one was becoming suspicious at the inexplicable desire of the white lady to stay for so long in the little mud village on the edge of civilization. In the end they had to plan a midnight flight, leaving instructions that the official caravan should catch them up as soon as possible. Two servants of the Emir's brother, Yusuf and Mohammed, were instructed to accompany the party as guides. Rosita Forbes adopted the Bedouin dress—tight white trousers, red gown, a *barracan*, and a *hezaam*, which is a strip of about twelve feet of red woollen material swathed round the hips. Under this she wore a revolver-belt with two fully loaded Colts and a prismatic compass in a case.

Late in the evening six heavy sacks of provisions were

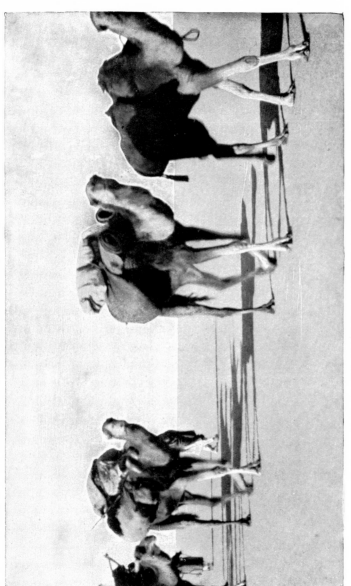

ROSITA FORBES ASLEEP ON A CAMEL

By permission of Rosita Forbes, from the "Secret of the Sahara" (Cassell)

surreptitiously dragged into the dark courtyard. There was a sudden knock on the door.

"Who's that?" asked Hassanein icily.

"Mabruk," answered the voice of the chief Italian spy! He began a long story about some clothes which were being prepared, but Hassanein managed to get rid of him without arousing any suspicions. Two hours later the provisions were spirited out of the courtyard by fellow-conspirators, and all was ready for the flight on the following night.

The Arabs were late, but at last stealthy footsteps approached. The explorers heard the faint grunts of protesting camels, and within twenty minutes they were off on the great adventure. The cold was intense. Yusuf, the guide, lost his way, and an hour before dawn they encamped on a sandy waste. To their amazement, when the dawn came, they found that they were within view of Jedabia. There was a hurried loading of camels, and away they went as fast as was possible, until they felt they were safely started. Rosita Forbes was suffering from a sprained ankle and suffered agonies as she swayed along on her huge blond camel.

On the second day out they reached the wadi Farig, where they saw a few scattered nomads' tents round the desert-well. Already the appalling dryness of the desert was cracking the lady 'Khadija's' skin, and her nails and hair were brittle and breaking. The caravan had not yet arrived, and it was agreed to push on to Aujela by forced marches. They made friends with a certain She-ib, a merchant whose caravan was going southward, and they joined his train and set off again.

The black soldiers proved to be troublesome and greedy. Owing to their carelessness the water-skins were almost empty before the Aujela oasis was reached. They were also held up by a *gibli*, the southerly gale which brings a dust-storm. Every package was finely dusted, both inside and out, and every meal had its seasoning of Sahara sand; the camels were blinded, and swung in circles. Fortunately, while they were encamped at Aujela the promised supporting caravan arrived—twelve camels and a dozen men under a famous guide, Abdullah.

At Jalo, the next oasis, they were given a rare welcome, as accredited friends of the Emir. Here there were two villages and miles of scattered palms. But it was beyond this point that the real difficulties began; the next stage, from Jalo to Taiserbo (or alternatively to Buseima), was a seven days' march across over 250 miles of waterless desert. The camels were already weak, and some were due to foal.

No sooner had they started than they ran into a violent *gibli*, which held them up until nightfall. The country here was a flat disc which stretched monotonously to the horizon on all sides. Abdullah, for all his reputation, proved to be a faulty guide. The Arabs and the black soldiers of the retinue were always quarrelling. On the sixth day it became quite evident that Abdullah was lost. The water-ration had to be cut down, and when Abdullah began to wander, the blacks wanted to beat him. At length, when all the fodder had gone, and there was only one day's water-supply left, the explorers decided to ignore Abdullah and to strike boldly south-east towards the reputed position of the notorious Buseima. The Bedouins were depressed and they related grim stories of desert tragedies on this route. The camels were famished and tried to eat the stuffing of the baggage-saddles; it was their ninth day without water.

Towards evening some high dunes appeared, and suddenly Yusuf flung himself on his face and embraced the earth. He had found a mound covered with a few dried sticks of brushwood. "Inshallah! There is more beyond," he said.

From the top of the ridge they could see a cluster of huge green bushes, but Abdullah soon quenched the burst of enthusiasm. "This place is El Atash (the Thirst)," he said. "There is an old well here, but its water will kill you."

So one more dry supper was eaten. The camels were given the straw stuffing out of their saddles, and the explorers ate a tin of spinach because it was at least moist. On the next afternoon they suddenly spied a few clustered palms. The blacks raced ahead and began to scoop madly in the sand; very slowly water began to ooze through the sand, and they soon had dug out a muddy pool and refreshed themselves.

Two days later the expedition reached Buseima. Instead of being massacred, as they had half expected, they were well received. The oasis only had a few inhabitants. After fourteen days in the unchanging sands, Buseima seemed a veritable Garden of Eden. There was a lovely blue lake, fringed by green rushes and palms, and ringed round by crimson hills. Before long, however, it became clear that the people of Buseima were not satisfied with their letters of credence. "Had we but a force equal to yours," said one, "you should not now depart."

By this time word of the approaching caravan had been carried to Kufara, and the story was being circulated that the Emir had sold Kufara to the Europeans and that the strangers were the advance guard of the conquerors.[1] But Rosita Forbes was determined not to be cheated of her prize now that she had come so far. They hurriedly packed and hastened southward. Four days' hard travelling brought them to Hawari, which is on the outskirts of the group. Here they met the full fury of the tribesmen for the first time; they were practically prisoners for a day or two. Then, when they attempted to move on, a wild, threatening group of Zouias surrounded them, shouting, "You shall not move from here till orders come from Jof! No strangers shall come to our country!"

Apparently the discredited guide, Abdullah, had turned traitor. Possibly he hoped to be avenged on the blacks, who had been so insulting when he had lost his way. He had gone ahead to Jof—one of the villages of Kufara—and had promised to send back news to the people of Hawari. Actually when he reached Jof he at once began to spread wild rumours about the explorers. He went to the Governor and warned him that two Christians from Italy were approaching the oases and learning all about the country.

"They have cheated the Emir," he said. "Ever since they

---

[1] The story was something of a prophecy. Ten years later the Italians occupied Kufara.

left they have been secretly making maps, and the *Sitt* held a watch (her compass) in her hand all the time."

He drew lurid pictures of the barometer which hung in the tent and the field-glasses "which make the country look big while it is far away." He succeeded almost too well in his plot, for the Governor ordered him to go back to Yusuf and Mohammed with orders to turn back.

Of course the whole plot was apparent when Abdullah presented this information to the faithful Yusuf. Mohammed swore that he would discover the truth, and post-haste he hurried away to Kufara to explain the true state of affairs. He came back at sunset, triumphant. He had exposed Abdullah's plot and brought with him a letter of welcome to the friends of the Emir.

So at last the caravan mounted the black hills until it came abruptly on a wonderful scene. Beyond the last black cliff was a beautiful hill-encircled *wadi*. On the edge of the cliff stood the Government headquarters, at a village called Taj. Here they could see a massive *zawia*—the holy place of the Senussi—rising above a group of dark square houses. Below stretched the wide, flat *wadi*, with mile upon mile of palms and green gardens surrounding a vivid blue lake. Eastward were more villages and a broad splash of emerald green round another lake. The whole scene was reminiscent of a lovely jewel in a setting of low, amethyst hills.

The magical letter of welcome from the Emir soon procured them friends among the stately *ekhwan* and officials. In spite of the fact that the common people were still distrustful, and even threatening at times, the explorers were permitted to visit almost every part of the oasis. Altogether they found that there were six large villages in the *wadi*. They saw carefully irrigated fields, where crops of many kinds were grown, besides palms, fig-trees, olives, and vines. They were also permitted to see the sacred places and the house of the Governor. This was a huge building of many courts and passages; the rooms were sumptuously furnished, and in one room there were no less than fifteen clocks!

When they had seen all that they wished to see, they

planned the homeward journey. Once again it had to be something in the nature of a flight, for Kufara had by no means been unanimous in its welcome. They decided to follow a route as yet unknown to Europeans; this route led through the mountains, and across difficult dune-country, to Jaghabub, on the Egyptian frontier. When they were two days out the party had a narrow escape from a band of marauders, who had doubtless followed them from Kufara. Once again they travelled for days on end without water, until the cry went up, "Land at last!" Far away on the north-east horizon they could see the long blue ridge of mountains between Jaghabub and Siwa—the outposts of civilization.

THE ADVENTURES OF HASSANEIN BEY

Two years later Hassanein Bey made another, and longer, expedition across the Libyan Desert. His object was to repeat the visit to Kufara and then to make a complete crossing of the desert from north to south. He started from Sollum, on the border of Egypt; but at the outset he had to change his plans, because he learned that the Bedouin from whom he had hired his camels was plotting to rob him on the way. So he had to arrange a fresh caravan, and set off for Siwa and Jaghabub on January 2, 1923.

Once again he was fortunate enough to meet Sayed Idris, who was travelling in the opposite direction—to Egypt. When the Bedouin saw that Hassanein and the Emir were friends, they at once became much more trustworthy. They insisted in following the revered footprints of the Emir all the way to Jaghabub. As before, the greatest trials were the *gibli*. The breeze would first show itself by raising whirling sand-devils, and then gradually increase in force until great dust-clouds veiled the sky. Frequently the traveller would be literally pelted with large stones picked up by the hurricane. Instead of waiting to be completely covered with sand-drift, Hassanein decided that the best plan was to march on with a cloth round his mouth to prevent the sand from choking him.

One night the gale reached such strength that the tent

183

was blown down and sand piled upon it. Hassanein, buried under the wreckage, was almost suffocated. For two hours he could not move, but he was able to crawl out when the storm moderated. The tents of the Arabs had also been blown down, and the camels had suffered badly. Three beasts died before they reached Kufara. All the fuel and all the fodder had been used up, but once in Kufara, the explorer was welcomed again by the chiefs of Senussi.

Hassanein stayed in the secret city for a fortnight, trying to learn something about the unknown desert to the south. He was told strange stories of two oases away to the south-east, which no white man, and few natives, had seen. He decided to seek out these oases, and then travel on to Darfur, in the Sudan. The Senussi told him that he would certainly die in the attempt, because, even if he succeeded in crossing the waterless stretches, he would encounter savage black tribesmen on the other side. It was eight years since a caravan had gone from Kufara in that direction, and it had been wiped out on the frontier of Darfur.

By this time Hassanein's curiosity was fully roused. On April 18 he left Kufara, and after six days' hard marching he reached Arkenu, the first of the two mysterious oases. There were no inhabitants to be seen, but there was herbage for the camels among the rocky hills. They could find no wells, but rain-water had collected in hollows in the rocks. The expedition stayed here for four days in order to recuperate, and then pushed on to the second oasis, named 'Uweinat. Here they found a small village built among the rocks; there were 150 inhabitants, and their nearest neighbours were 200 miles away! The country round is mountainous, and there are many caves. While exploring the district Hassanein made a remarkable discovery; on the side of some rocks he saw some deeply engraved carvings, depicting processions of giraffes, lions, gazelles, ostriches, and other animals. One significant omission was the camel, and Hassanein was driven to the conclusion that once upon a time 'Uweinat had been a fertile district where wild animals were plentiful, but camels did not exist. Later on, as we shall see, many other important archæological discoveries were made in this district.

Beyond 'Uweinat stretched a sand-sea, where for 270 miles there was no well. It was so scorching by day that the party travelled at night-time. Several times the guides lost their way in the maze of dunes and rocks, and soon they were very short of water. For weeks on end they saw nothing but miles of sand and rocks, and they struggled on, weary and footsore, until at last they reached a well, where they filled their water-skins and rested for a while. Then they marched on until they reached the hills of Erdi and Ennedi (4700 feet). In this hilly region they met the first human beings they had seen since leaving 'Uweinat; these were the blacks about which they had been warned. The natives were very suspicious about these strangers who had sprung like djinns out of the desert, but they did not attack them, and on June 2—forty-five days after leaving Kufara— Hassanein reached the first village in Darfur. They were short of food, and their clothes were in rags, but they had accomplished a wonderful journey from one end of the Libyan desert to the other. Hundreds of miles of unknown country had been explored, and the total distance travelled was about 2200 miles.

IN SEARCH OF ZERZURA

The Garamantians have four-horse chariots, in which they chase the Troglodyte Ethiopians. . . . The Troglodytes feed on serpents, lizards, and other similar reptiles. Their language is unlike that of any other people—it sounds like the screeching of bats.

HERODOTUS, *History, Book IV*

Ever since the days of old Herodotus the great Libyan desert has had its legends no less romantic than the fabled Atlantis of the Arabian sands or the myth of the Grand Pataiti. There is, for example, the story of the lost army of Cambyses. It is said that the Persian King once sent an expedition against the oasis of Jupiter Ammon. After some days of wandering across the desert, the column was overwhelmed by sand-storms and annihilated. Then the Arabs tell many legends of the oasis of Little Birds, or Zerzura.

Here they say is a white city, white as a dove; above the closed door there is a bird carved in stone, and beyond the door are many riches; and in the palace lie sleeping an enchanted king and queen, who must not be disturbed. The legends always say that Zerzura is a dangerous place to seek, and that from time to time black giants emerge from the lost oasis to attack the Nile-dwellers.

There is little wonder that such attractive legends have tempted many explorers to the 'Sea of Sand.' What a thrill it would be to find the remains of Cambyses' army—perhaps with the loot of many an ancient temple—lying beneath the preserving sands! That the stories of lost oases are not mere fiction has been shown by a number of travellers, and recent explorers even claim to have solved the age-old problem of Zerzura.

In the heart of the Libyan desert an advance-patrol during the Great War sighted a huge plateau, 3000 feet high, which was named the Gilf Kebir. The total area of the Gilf is roughly equal to that of Switzerland, and its centre lies about 450 miles west of the Nile. On the east and west sides there are precipitous escarpments, while on the north the highland slopes down until it is lost in the 'Sea of Sand.' Here there are thousands of square miles of sand, piled up in high parallel dunes—a formidable obstacle, which explains why the plateau was for so long undiscovered.

Some sixty miles to the south-west of the Gilf Kebir lies the mountain mass of 'Uweinat, which was discovered by Hassanein Bey in 1924. Here the natives told him that the djinns had lived round the wells in the olden days, and that they have left upon the rocks writings and drawings of all the animals in creation. Hassanein subsequently explored the valleys of 'Uweinat, and sure enough he found some drawings of animals deeply carved in the rocks. A few years later Patrick Clayton, another famous desert-traveller, reached the western side of the Gilf Kebir, where he found some rock-drawings.

Among those who had become fascinated with the old Zerzura problem was a Hungarian Count, Ladislaus de Almásy, who was one of the pioneers of motoring in the

Egyptian deserts. He read an old book by the first European who had ever heard the name Zerzura, and this led him to

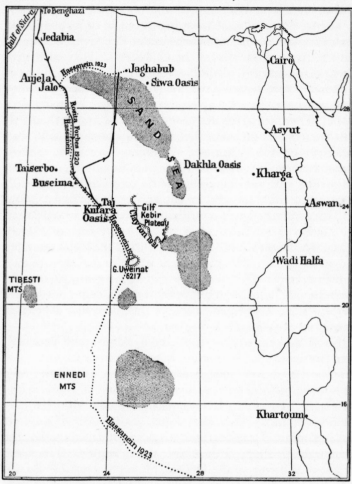

JOURNEYS IN SEARCH OF THE SECRETS OF THE SAHARA

believe that the mysterious oasis must lie somewhere in the newly discovered plateau—a belief which was strengthened by the news that rock-carvings had been found in the vicinity. Almásy argued that the heights of the Gilf would attract the tropical rain, and so create springs. If this were

187

true, then the campaign of King Cambyses could be explained, and also the mysterious raids by the Senussi Arabs during the Great War.

Eventually, in 1932, Almásy organized, in conjunction with Patrick Clayton and Squadron-leader Penderel, an expedition to the western side of the Gilf Kebir. They took with them three cars and a Moth aeroplane, in which they made a number of reconnaissance flights; but for a long time they were unable to find a way on the plateau or to see any signs of life. Then, when the petrol-supply was almost exhausted, as they were on their last flight over the northern Gilf, they suddenly sighted a long *wadi* with many trees in it. Unfortunately they were unable to find a landing-place, and when they tried with the remaining petrol to reach the *wadi* with a car, they could not find an entrance from the desert plain.

This thrilling, last-minute discovery led to the organization of a second expedition, which set off from Cairo in March, 1933. In the meantime Penderel, during the reconnaissance flights of the R.A.F. squadron to which he belonged, made a flight over the Gilf, during which he located a gap on the western side, which curved round until it came out on the eastern side. It seemed probable that here was a possible means of entry for exploring cars.

So the new expedition set off, led by Almásy and Penderel, and included Dr Bermann, a famous archæologist. For transport they took four Ford cars, which were fitted with enormous balloon tyres so that they would not sink in the soft sand. The first place they called at was Abu Ballas— 'Father of Jars.' Here they found, at the foot of a desert hill, a deposit of large earthen jars, some of which showed the unmistakable shape of the classic Greek *amphora*. This place is about half-way to the Gilf, and it seems probable that at one time it was used as a kind of relay-station for raiding parties from the notorious oasis of Kufara. On the rocks of Abu Ballas were some prehistoric rock-engravings, showing figures of men and animals. According to Herodotus, it had been the practice of the Persians, as soon as they became masters of Egypt, to take jars into the desert for storing water, so that the passage into Egypt should be fit for use.

Were the jars of Abu Ballas a clue to the solution of the campaign of Cambyses?

The Gilf Kebir lies half-way between Abu Ballas and Kufara, and Almásy thought that here, too, they would find some means of obtaining water. So they journeyed on to the eastern side of the Gilf. Soon they found the gap which had been seen from the air by Penderel, and successfully drove the cars through to the western side; thence they went to Kufara for supplies, and here they were told that Clayton had reached the *wadi* of the 1932 expedition. Almásy at once decided to visit this *wadi*, and also to search for the other two *wadis* associated with the Zerzura legend. In Kufara they found that the influence of the Senussi creed was still strong; there was still the old reluctance to reveal any of the secrets of the desert. However, they managed to find an old caravan-guide, a mysterious old man, who agreed to tell them something more about the Gilf. He said that, close by the *wadi* which had been discovered, there was a second *wadi*, called the *wadi* of Acacias, and told them of its approximate position.

So it was with high hopes that the expedition left Kufara for the Gilf again. Soon they found some old camel-tracks leading to the Gilf, and then a distinct man-made path. Near by were camel-bones and the skeleton of a cow, and camping-sites which had evidently been used by herdsmen. Then they tried to reach the promised *wadi* of the Acacias by climbing the precipitous western scarps of the Gilf; but although they successfully reached the top they still could not locate the *wadi*. Penderel then went on through his gap and continued the exploration of the eastern side of the plateau. His object was to circumnavigate the Gilf and so rejoin his companions, who were to make a second effort. When Penderel arrived at the eastern end of his gap, he found a message from Clayton, tied to an abandoned car, in which it was announced that he had driven all round the northern end of the plateau. Penderel promptly abandoned his plan to circumnavigate the plateau, and instead, managed to drive his car up an incline on to the top of the Gilf. Here he made an interesting discovery of a circle of stone pillars—yet another piece of evidence that in prehistoric times the region had been well populated.

Meanwhile Almásy and Bermann were continuing on foot the search on the western side. They discovered a cave with many pictures of giraffes and lions engraved on the rocks, and near it were many Stone-age implements. Examination of the surroundings suggested that at one time there had been a lake close by, amid tropical vegetation. Then the party struck northward into the *wadi* they had seen in 1932. They found it to be a long, dreary valley where hundreds of acacia-trees of different species were growing. They also found two rock-springs but with very little water. Here and there they found ample indications of Arab encampments; there were remains of grass huts, baskets, and camel-droppings, and many fresh tracks of Barbary sheep. They also observed large flocks of birds, and wondered if this could possibly be the famous oasis of Little Birds. Evidently the *wadi* would be a fertile spot after rains, but a long dry spell would dry it up to the condition in which they found it.

Following some old camel-tracks, the party drove into the bed of a dry mountain torrent and camped there. On the next day Almásy, accompanied by one of the native drivers, climbed the almost insurmountable stone walls of the Gilf, and when they reached the top of the plateau, they soon found a marked path. With increasing excitement they followed this along until, at last, they reached a broad *wadi* filled with luxuriant acacia-trees. So the second *wadi* of Zerzura was discovered.

A few days later they met the old caravan-guide again, and he told them that there was, indeed, a third *wadi*, called the Red *wadi*, which was the smallest of the three. Actually Clayton entered this *wadi* during the course of his expedition, and so at last all three of the fabled *wadis* were found. Of course it is by no means certain that these three are the oasis of Zerzura; in their present condition they can provide only occasional grazing for flocks. But there is strong presumptive evidence that at one time the region was thickly peopled, and probably the *wadis* had water in them.

Almásy had agreed to meet Penderel at 'Uweinat, and

so they went there. Here they had to take refuge from the hot sun in certain caves which surround one of the springs. The granite walls of the mountain are honey-combed with these grottoes, and one day the Count found some rock-paintings in one of them. This was the prelude to a remarkable series of discoveries. Rock-carvings had been found by several people in the district, but now for the first time a veritable Stone-age art-gallery was revealed. High up the mountain they discovered dozens of caves, all covered with beautiful rock-paintings in four colours. Here were flocks of domesticated animals and human beings, and dark-skinned archers with many ornaments and with plumes in their hair. One interesting picture represented a cave surrounded by a circle of granite boulders, and the two occupiers—a slender man and an enormous woman—who had decorated their home with their own portraits. Near the caves a considerable collection of Stone-age implements was made, and the question arose—had they stumbled upon the homes of the Troglodyte Egyptians mentioned by Herodotus?

Later on further rock-paintings were discovered near the Gilf, and Almásy actually found one cave near the three *wadis* where there were paintings which showed unmistakable swimmers—clear evidence that once there had been a lake in the district. The three *wadis* have not yet been searched for rock-paintings, but there is every reason to suppose that here, too, rock-paintings may be found. At least it is now clear that the Gilf Kebir was once a thickly populated and fertile area, and in consequence there is some foundation for the old stories of ancient cities and green oases in the midst of the Libyan desert.

CHAPTER IX

THE CONQUEST OF THE SOUTH POLE

The walls of the palace were formed of the driven snow, its doors and windows of the cutting winds. There were over a hundred halls, the largest of them many miles in extent, all illuminated by the Northern Lights, all alike vast, empty, icily cold and dazzlingly white.

HANS ANDERSEN, *The Palace of the Snow-queen*

AMUNDSEN'S JOURNEY TO THE POLE

THE news of the discovery of the North Pole in April, 1909, by Robert Peary led to a radical change in the plans of Roald Amundsen. He had intended to set out on a third voyage to the Arctic in the famous *Fram*, but now, in spite of the publication of the plans of Scott's Antarctic expedition, he decided to win fame by seeking the South Pole. In order to avoid newspaper-discussion and the possible criticism of 'shabby rivalry,' Amundsen made his plans in secret. When the *Fram* left Norway, in August, 1910, not even the crew knew her real destination. They had been mystified by the presence on board of ninety-seven Greenland sledge-dogs and a large sectional hut, but they were not told the truth until Madeira was reached. They were jubilant at the news.

Amundsen had made a close study of the previous expeditions of Scott and Shackleton; but he had drawn conclusions very different from those arrived at by Captain Scott. He decided, for example, that the Bay of Whales— an inlet on the Ross Barrier, which is nearly 100 miles nearer to the Pole than McMurdo Sound—was the best base. There was of course a risk that the base might 'calve' off the barrier and start off as a flat-topped iceberg towards the north, but Amundsen argued that in all probability this section of the barrier rested on the tops of submerged islands. In spite of Scott's decision to use Manchurian ponies as his draught-animals, Amundsen was so impressed by the success of Peary that he decided to follow his example and rely on dogs. Dogs suffer little damage if they fall into a crevasse, and they can always be rescued if their harness does not break. Then again, as a last resource, dog can be fed on dog, and the problem of making depôts of animal food is correspondingly less. Scott knew that he would have to kill his ponies when he arrived at the Beardmore glacier; but Amundsen had a reasonable hope that his draught-animals would travel all the way to the Pole. In order to avoid any question of 'poaching,' he decided to establish his base 350 miles away from Captain Scott's hut, and to strike due south from the Bay of Whales through the unknown, instead of following the route discovered by Shackleton.

The passage of the *Fram* through the pack-ice was a 'four days' pleasure trip.' On January 14, 1911, the Bay of Whales was reached. From the beginning Amundsen was favoured by good fortune. Instead of finding themselves confronted by a fearsome ice-cliff, the landing party discovered that the barrier at this spot was about twenty feet high, and the junction between it and the sea-ice was completely filled up with driven snow. "One, two, three, and a little jump, and the barrier was surmounted."

'Framheim,' the expedition hut, was soon erected; the foundations were dug into the solid ice, and the roof was anchored by hawsers. There were plenty of seals, and the dogs, who had increased their numbers to 116, soon had their fill of fresh meat; and the landing party quickly began to accumulate a vast store of blubber and seal-meat for the winter. By the end of the month the hut was ready, and 900 cases of stores had been landed from the *Fram*. Although a certain amount of scientific work was undertaken, the landing-party consisted of only eight men, and they had as their primary object the conquest of the Pole; Captain Scott, on the other hand, regarded the southern journey as merely incidental. The rival expeditions first met when the *Terra Nova*, on its way to explore King Edward VII Land, called at the Bay of Whales.

Six days later Amundsen, accompanied by three men, with three sledges and eighteen dogs, set off southward on a depôt-laying expedition. They went forward at a rattling pace over the level surface of the barrier and did seventeen miles on the first day without exertion. In the middle of the day they made a halt, and took a cup of scalding hot chocolate from thermos flasks. Latitude 80 degrees south was reached, and here a depôt was laid. On the way home the explorers rode on the sledges, and at intervals they stuck dried fish in the snow to act as guiding-marks, after the manner of a paper-chase. Incidentally, these original direction-posts provided many a meal for the hungry dogs on the next journey south. Amundsen had good reason to congratulate himself on his dogs, for on the return journey, pulling sledges with loads of 677 pounds, they actually did 62 miles on one day. Indeed, the barrier had proved to be such an easy sledging-route, that it was decided that lighter sledges should be constructed.

During the remainder of February and March two more depôts were laid, one at 81 degrees South, and another at 82 degrees South. On this trip the weather was not so good, and a number of the dogs succumbed; but a great many valuable lessons were learned about the conditions along the polar route. Then began the long winter night. Much time was spent in making adjustments to ski-boots and other details of equipment, so that everything should be ready for the dash southward in the spring. 'Framheim' proved to be rather cramped quarters, and so a number of chambers were excavated in a snow-drift round the hut; and in these 'crystal palaces' alterations were made to the sledges, provisions were packed, and scientific experiments were carried out. Above all, great care was taken to ensure that the dogs were comfortable and well fed.

When at last September came, Amundsen determined to make a trial trip, but he soon discovered that his dogs could not stand the intense cold. The temperatures reached 60 degrees below zero, and when the depôt at 80 degrees south was reached, Amundsen decided to unload the sledges and return. Two of the party suffered from severe frost-bites, and more than a month elapsed before a second start was made. By this time Amundsen had come to the conclusion that it would be better if two explorations were made—one to the Pole, and another to King Edward VII Land. The reduction in the numbers of the polar party would mean that the depôts would now contain more than sufficient for a prolonged trip.

A start was made on October 19. Amundsen was accompanied by Hanssen, Wisting, Hassel, and Bjaaland. They had four sledges, with thirteen dogs to each. On the second day out the expedition nearly came to grief, when Bjaaland's sledge sank into a crevasse. Bjaaland hung on convulsively, and the dogs, stretched out in the snow, dug their claws in and resisted with all their strength. Help came at the last moment. Hanssen and Hassel snatched an Alpine rope from a sledge and made the rope fast to a trace; then Hassel's sledge was placed across the crevasse to act as a bridge. The dogs were freed, and one sledge hung, suspended by ropes, from the 'bridge.' Wisting then went down the crevasse, and stood on a cornice a few inches wide so that he could unload the sledge. When at last the whole outfit had been hauled to the surface, Wisting came up again with the smiling comment that "it was nice and warm down there." A few minutes later Wisting fell into another bottomless crevasse, but he saved himself by spreading out his arms as he fell. A long detour was necessary to avoid this danger-spot, but when camp was pitched, the explorers were back on the line with a good surface before them.

Some of the dogs had to be killed, as they were unfit to go farther, and their remains were cached in snow-beacons to provide a reserve food-supply on the way home. At the depôt in 80 degrees south the party had a rest, and when they left, the weather was clear and mild. Amundsen made a rope fast to Wisting's sledge, and for the next 340 miles was pulled along on his ski towards the Pole. At the third depôt, at 82 degrees south, they rested for three days to give the dogs a good chance to reach their best form for the final dash. Snow-beacons were erected at frequent intervals, and for several days an average of 23 miles a day was maintained. On November 8, latitude 83 degrees south was reached, and they were in sight of land.

The explorers were able to distinguish the summits of

several mountains, and they decided that this must be an eastward continuation of the ranges in South Victoria Land. Here they made a depôt of hard blocks of snow, and placed therein provisions for five men and twelve dogs for four days. As they neared the mountains on the next day, they admired the blue-black peaks, which rose to heights of 15,000 feet. They could see an opening between Mounts Nansen and Pedro Christopherson, and this proved to be their gateway to the plateau. Another depôt was made at 84 degrees south, and here they made the interesting discovery of a chain of mountains running to the east. Instead of losing strength, the dogs seemed to become fitter and more active every day, and they were greatly attracted by the appearance of the black mountain-tops ahead.

On November 15 a depôt was made at 85 degrees south. The whole supply of provisions was overhauled; everything that was not absolutely necessary for the final assault was dumped. The distance still to be travelled was 683 miles. The plan was to take the forty-two remaining dogs up to the plateau with enough provisions for sixty days; then on the plateau twenty-four of the dogs were to be slaughtered, and the journey was to be continued with three sledges and eighteen dogs; thus when the day came to reduce their numbers to twelve there would only be two light sledges left.

Then the ascent up the glaciers was begun. With considerable difficulty the main ice-field—Axel Heiberg glacier —was reached. Here and there the trail was very steep and splintered with deep crevasses, but by dint of relaying, and by plentiful use of the all-important dog-whips, fair progress was made. The mountain-side along which they advanced gradually narrowed between vast fissures above and vaster fissures below, and finally the men gained access to the main ice-field across a snow bridge hardly wider than the sledges. There followed three days' hard pulling, and the great plateau was reached without mishap. Then at the camp called the 'Butcher's Shop' came a painful time, when the twenty-four dogs had to be shot. At first the surviving dogs seemed to have some scruples about the dog-cutlets which were placed before them, but soon ravenous hunger led them to participate in the meal.

Amundsen would have been glad to leave this horrid place on the next day, but a day's rest was needed for the re-arrangement of the stores on to the three remaining sledges; then the weather became unfavourable, and they were weatherbound for four days. At last the march was continued, but it was still blowing a blizzard. For some miles the way was downhill, and the fog was so thick that the view was impeded. As they were blindly advancing, one of the leaders suddenly called, "Hullo! Look there!" And to their amazement they could see a wild, dark summit rising high out of the mass of fog to the south-east. A few miles farther on they were able to make out a range of mountains —Helland Hansen's—running north and south on their right hand.

The explorers had not yet got out of the glacier-region, and they were soon floundering among dangerous crevasses again. Indeed, the ice beneath the high mountains to the east was so chaotic that it looked as if some giants had been battling with blocks of ice for ammunition. They agreed to call this terrible place the 'Devil's Glacier.' Before this obstacle had been passed, they saw a mighty range of mountains extending far to the south on their left hand. Massive peaks were named after the members of the party, and they found that the highest—Mount Thorvald Nilsen—was 15,500 feet above sea-level. Even so, the atmosphere was so misty that on their return-journey they found that they had seen barely half of this mighty polar range. Chasm after chasm, hummock after hummock barred their further progress, until they found a narrow bridge which reminded one of a tight rope crossing the Niagara falls.

Eventually the party reached the 'Devil's Ballroom,' where dogs and men frequently sank through the treacherous surface. It was like walking across the glass roof of a railway station, and at any moment there was the frightful possibility of a sudden rapid descent into the 'cellar.'

The 'Devil's Ballroom' proved to be the last serious obstacle, however, and from that point to the Pole the surface was good, and the dogs made good progress. Shackleton's 'farthest south' was passed, and near by the explorers made their last depôt. Like many of the others, it was marked by improvised flags at right angles to their course. By this time the explorers were suffering from frost-bitten faces, and as they neared the Pole they were in a fever of anxiety to learn their fate. "What shall we see when we get there? Shall we be first?"

At three o'clock in the afternoon of December 14 a simultaneous "Halt!" rang out from the sledge-drivers. The goal was reached; the journey was ended. The men took great care with their observations, and to preclude the possibility of error, encircled the Pole about a radius of several miles. Eventually, on December 16, a small tent was erected as near as possible to the exact Pole, and five frost-bitten hands raised the Norwegian Flag simultaneously. Bjaaland astonished his comrades by making a fine oration, and to celebrate the occasion he produced a cigar-case full of cigars from some mysterious private cache.

On the next day began the long journey home. The going was good; a mild, summer-like wind was their last greeting from the Pole. Now and again they lost the trail and had to steer by compass, but the snow-beacons which they had erected with such care served them in good stead. On December 26 they passed 88 degrees, going well, and were amazed to see their new range of mountains looming up in the east. Amundsen thought that this range possibly extends right across the continent. By January 1 they had reached the 'Devil's Ballroom,' and with incredible luck they managed to steer clear of the bad ice. Unfortunately they missed a depôt, and a party had to go off to find it. They were not, however, worried about food-supplies, and all the dogs seemed to be fit and well.

Soon the party arrived at the 'Butcher's Shop' again, and the dogs seemed to derive great benefit from the change to fresh meat. On the Heiberg glacier the men saw immense avalanches, and they found it necessary to put brakes on the sledges to prevent collisions. In spite of frequent snowstorms, good progress was made once the barrier was reached. Here, to their unspeakable astonishment, they saw two great skua-gulls. These were the first messengers of the living world far to the north. At one of the depôts they found that the stores had been plundered by runaway dogs, but by that time they knew that they had plenty of supplies to see them through. Between 81 and 82 degrees they were surprised to see the appearance of land to the north-east, and this land—Carmen Land—they decided must be the east coast of Ross Sea.

On January 25 they reached 'Framheim' again and found all well. All the polar party and the surviving eleven dogs were hale and hearty. Moreover, to their great joy they learned that the *Fram* was in the bay. Within a few days everything had been packed, and they were sailing away for Hobart, in Tasmania. So ended a brave and happy adventure.

THE TRAGEDY OF CAPTAIN SCOTT

Although he was mainly interested in the scientific aspects of polar exploration, in order to raise the large sums necessary to fit out another expedition Scott undertook to reach the South Pole, if it were humanly possible. In June, 1910, the *Terra Nova* sailed for New Zealand, and thence south to the Antarctic. The ship carried heavy supplies of food, scientific impedimenta, huts, sledges, thirty-three Siberian dogs, seventeen ponies, and three motor-sledges. The overloaded ship nearly foundered in a plunging sea; loose coal-bags swung against the lashed cases on the deck like battering-rams. Then the pumps choked, and the water began to rise rapidly in the engine-room. For a night and a day a string of buckets was plied, until it became evident the baling was gaining on the flood down below.

On December 9 the *Terra Nova* entered the pack-ice. Sometimes they steamed through acres of sludgy, sodden ice, while at other periods they were enclosed by ice-sheets for days on end. Huge icebergs crept silently past them. Long before land was sighted, on the last day of the old year, numerous penguins, sea-leopards, seals, and birds had been encountered. When the ship reached Cape Crozier an attempt was made to land, but this was found to be impossible, owing to the swell and the high cliffs. Eventually a base was made at Cape Evans, so named in honour of the second-in-command.

The process of unloading was not without its excitements. Ponting, the camera-man, had a thrilling escape from six 'killer' whales, which dived under the floe on which he happened to be standing and struck the underside with their mighty backs. The next moment the whole floe heaved up and split into fragments. Ponting fled for safety to the next floe, but he records how their huge, hideous heads shot vertically into the air through the cracks which they had made. As they reared them to a height of six or eight feet, it was possible to see their tawny head-markings, their small, glistening eyes, and their terrible arrays of teeth—by far the largest and most terrifying in the world.

Although one of the motor-sledges fell through the ice, before long the majority of the stores had been landed, and a house of considerable size had been erected. Scott described it in these words:

> Our residence is really a house of considerable size, in every respect the finest that has ever been erected in the polar regions; 50 feet long by 25 feet wide and 9 feet to the eaves. If you can picture our house nestling below this small hill on a long stretch of black sand, with many tons of provision cases ranged in neat blocks in front of it and the sea lapping the ice-foot below, you will have some idea of our immediate vicinity. As for our wider surroundings, it would be difficult to describe their beauty in sufficiently glowing terms. Cape Evans is one of the many spurs of Erebus and the one that stands closest under the mountain, so that always towering above us we have the grand snowy peak with its smoking summit. North and south of us are deep bays, beyond which great glaciers come rippling over the lower slopes to thrust high blue-walled snouts into the sea.

On January 21 the *Terra Nova* had to leave her berth alongside the ice-edge, and almost immediately ran ashore. For a few hours the expedition was faced with disaster, and

THE "TERRA NOVA" ICE-BOUND

From the "Great White South" (Duckworth)

200

only by clever manœuvring were Pennell and his crew able to refloat the vessel.

On January 25, 1911, came the real beginning of the southward journey. A party of twelve men went off with ponies and dogs to lay depôts of food and supplies along the route to the Pole. The most important depôt was laid at 'One Ton Camp,' where over a ton of provisions were cached. On the way back, Scott's dog-team suddenly disappeared into a crevasse. As soon as the men had grasped what had happened, the sledge was hauled clear of the gap and anchored. The dogs were hanging in all sorts of queer positions by their harness. Two of them had dropped out of the traces and had fallen on a snow bridge far below. After the expenditure of much effort, eleven of the dogs were hauled to the surface, and then Scott volunteered to be lowered down the crevasse on an Alpine rope to rescue the remaining two, which he did.

Owing to the fact that the sea-ice had melted, the party had to make an enforced rest of several weeks in the old *Discovery* hut, since the only alternative route lay across the dangerous outlying ridges of Mount Erebus. When the leader did eventually arrive back at his headquarters, he found that a good deal had been done to make the house more comfortable and to arrange scientific laboratories and so on. Soon afterwards, too, he learned the fateful news that Amundsen was at Whale Bay. During the long winter, a number of lectures were given by various members of the scientific staff, and there was a good deal of discussion about the details of the sledge-journeys. It is rather curious that one of the chief problems which faced explorers of the period was that of scurvy—nothing was known then about vitamins. From time to time the men were entranced by the ethereal beauty of the Aurora; now there would be masses of arches, bands, and curtains of light, and then waving curtains of palish-green colour, which were suffused with rosy blushes.

The sun returned in August, and on October 24 the advance-guard, consisting of the two motor-sledges, set off pulling heavy cargoes. Even at the outset Scott realized that Amundsen had a good chance of reaching the Pole first, since "he is bound to travel fast with dogs and pretty certain to start early." The motor-sledges made fairly good progress for a few days, until the cylinders cracked, and they had to be abandoned. Scott had staked everything on his ponies, but it soon became clear that they were going to suffer dreadfully in the blizzards. Scott, with the main party, started off on November 1, in cold, chilly conditions and with much snow. By November 15 One Ton Camp was reached, and the expedition was averaging thirteen miles a day. The chief obstacles to rapid progress were the frequent patches of *sastrugi*, or frozen snow-waves. According to the plan which had been arranged, at intervals ponies were shot to provide food, and at fixed points certain members of the supporting parties were told to return to the base. Towards the end of the November the going was very hard, because for long stretches men and ponies were sinking through a soft top-surface of snow on to a harder layer beneath. There were snowstorms and blizzards, and by that time all the remaining twelve explorers had taken to horse-meat. On December 5 they could see clearly before them the ice-rounded Mount Hope and the gateway to the Beardmore glacier; this mighty ice-floe, which is over a hundred miles long, sprawls down from the great central plateau to the Ross barrier. Then came a miserable four days' delay in a raging, howling blizzard, and after that a sudden warm spell which melted the snow, and which prompted Kerhane to remark that, "If this goes on much longer we shall have to turn the tent upside down and use it as a boat."

At Camp 31 all the ponies were shot, and from that time on the expedition became a man-hauling party. The long pull up the glacier soon showed the difficulties of this form of traction. In the occasional periods of high temperatures the haulers were soaked with perspiration and quite breathless. Nevertheless, Scott was very pleased with the progress which had been made up to this point. On December 21 the supporting party led by Atkinson returned, and the journey across the summit plateau began. On January 4, 1912, when latitude 87 degrees 32 had been reached, the last supporting party—Evans, Lashly, and Crean—returned.

So the final assault-party consisted of five persons—Captain Scott, Doctor Wilson, Bowers, of the Indian Marine, Captain Oates, of the 6th Inniskilling Dragoons, and Petty-officer Evans. They were now 140 miles from the Pole, and they began the final dash with a good heart. Five days later Shackleton's 'farthest south' was passed, but by this time Scott realized that it was "going to be a stiff pull both ways." On January 16 it happened that, during the course of the second hour of the march, Bowers's sharp eyes detected what he thought was a cairn. But when they reached the spot they found that it was a black flag tied to a sledge-bearer. Near by were the remains of a camp and clear signs of many dogs.

> This told the whole story. The Norwegians have forestalled us and are first at the Pole. . . . To-morrow we must march on to the Pole and then hasten home with all the speed we can compass. All the day-dreams must go; it will be a wearisome return.

The Pole was reached on January 16. Scott's comment was "Great God! This is an awful place!" They found Amundsen's tent with a record that five Norwegians had been there.

So, deeply disappointed, they began the return-journey—800 miles of solid dragging. At first they made good progress since, although Evans and Oates were frost-bitten, the tracks still showed quite clearly. Then came the usual obstacle—*sastrugi*. Hard, torturing pulling brought them to the depôt at the top of the Beardmore glacier. Since the way now lay downhill Scott was more cheerful, and he began to collect geological specimens. Then, on the middle of the glacier, an unlucky decision to change their course led them into a terrible mess of crevasses and confused ice. There were huge chasms to be crossed or circumvented, and all the time their stores of food were running out. Then, at the last minute, they struck the next depôt and were saved for the time. Evans, however, could not stand the terrible privations, and after some days of slow decline, he collapsed and died—possibly as the result of a fall.

Next day the barrier-surface was reached at last, but once again the tide of misfortune began to flow. The surface was bad, and it grew desperately cold. March 2 was a bad day. To their surprise and mortification the explorers discovered that there was a shortage of oil at the Middle Barrier Depôt—and this at a time when Oates's feet were badly frost-bitten and they were faced with an exhausting pull over rough ice.

Then came one of the most heroic episodes in the whole history of exploration. Oates realized that he was desperately ill and therefore a serious handicap, since he had to delay the march every morning while he struggled into his foot-gear. Incidentally, he knew that these delays would mean that the supporting party of dogs, which was waiting at One Ton Camp, would have to return to the base owing to shortage of food.

> He [Oates] slept through the night before last, hoping not to wake, but he woke in the morning—yesterday. It was blowing a blizzard. He said, "I am just going outside and may be some time." He went out into the blizzard, and we have not seen him since. . . . We knew that poor Oates was walking to his death, but though we tried to dissuade him, we knew that it was the act of a brave man and an English gentleman. We all hope to meet the end with a similar spirit, and assuredly the end is not far.

The stricken survivors struggled painfully on until, on March 19, when only eleven miles from One Ton Camp, there came a fearful blizzard. They had no fuel, and but one or two days' food. In the last hours Scott still kept his diary. The last entry was dated Thursday, March 29, and records that for the last eight days the gale had been so ferocious that they had not been able to leave the tent.

Eight months later their bodies were found and among the various papers recovered was this message to the public.

> Had we lived, I should have had a tale to tell of the hardihood, endurance, and courage of my companions which would have stirred the heart of every Englishman. These rough notes and our dead bodies must tell the tale.

AT THE SOUTH POLE

Left to right: Capt. Oates, Lieut. Bowers, Capt. Scott, Dr Wilson, P. O. Evans. (Photo by Lieut. Bowers.)

By courtesy of Messrs Duckworth

To turn from the story of this tragedy to the records of the other exploring parties of Scott's expedition might seem to be something of an anti-climax, but these too were not without their heroisms. For example, the supporting party led by Lieutenant (now Admiral) Evans had a perilous journey back to their base. They were held up by blizzards before reaching the head of the glacier, and soon afterwards Evans began to show signs of scurvy. Realizing that any slackening would mean the forfeit of his life, Evans continued to pull, and he even went so far as to advance his watch one hour so that the 'turning out' signal was early. However soon after 'One Ton Camp' had been reached, Evans could pull no more, and he asked that he should be left in his sleeping-bag. Crean and Lashly, his heroic companions, insisted on pulling their comrade for four days until Corner Camp was reached. Then came a heavy snowfall, and further progress in this fashion became impossible. On the next day Crean set off alone on the terrible march of thirty miles across the ice, to fetch help from Hut Point. Lashly stayed behind to nurse Evans. Fortunately when, after a march of eighteen hours, Crean reached the hut, he found that dog-teams were available, and these were rapidly sent to the rescue.

The adventures of the northern party were no less remarkable. This party, which was led by Commander Campbell, had been sent to make surveys in the region of Cape Adare and near Evans Coves. Since a stay of only six weeks was intended, only a small depôt was arranged. The six men had between them seven boxes of biscuits, fourteen tins of oil one box of cocoa, one of sugar, one of chocolate, and a supply of pemmican. But on the day when the *Terra Nova* was due to arrive and pick them up, a blizzard sprang up, and the tents were split. As it happened the ship was unable to reach them, and eventually they realized that they were doomed to winter in their present post. They were lucky enough to find a good supply of seals and penguins, which were killed and cached.

Since the tents were soon pierced with holes, the marooned explorers built an 'igloo,' or rather excavated a cave in an ice-bank which had a roof of hard snow. They had enough cocoa to give them a mug of very thin cocoa five nights of the week; enough tea for a mug of equally thin tea once a week; and for the seventh day they had to manage with the reboiled tea-leaves. On Saturday every man had a stick of chocolate, and on special days and birthdays a bag of raisins. All sorts of efforts were made to vary the monotonous diet of seal-hoosh. Even the medicine-chest was raided for ginger tabloids and mustard plasters. The position of the party was rendered all the more serious when one of the men developed dysentery. They were, however, quite snug in their ice-cave, which was ventilated by means of a funnel through the roof.

One night in May the snow-drifts blocked this funnel, and the men had great difficulty in keeping their blubber-lamps alight. Then they suddenly realized that there was no air, and only in the nick of time was the air-way cleared. Thenceforth the funnel was kept free by means of a bamboo-stick. It was not until September that the horrid dirt and squalor of the igloo could be safely left, and the march back along the coast to headquarters begun. The march was difficult because Browning was still suffering from dysentery, and there were some terrifying crevasses to be crossed. However, fresh stores were found at Butter Point, and eventually the whole party reached Cape Evans in safety.

ADMIRAL BYRD AND THE 'LITTLE AMERICA' EXPEDITION

Immediately after completing his flight to the North Pole, Richard Byrd told Amundsen that his next objective would be the South Pole. During the next few years he began to accumulate funds for the largest Antarctic expedition ever organized. His aims were to make a flight to the South Pole, and then to explore as much of the unknown territory as possible. A wireless-station was to be set up, and no less than five engineers went with him. He also had three aeroplanes and a full complement of mechanics, meteorologists, scientists, ski-experts, and so on—a total landing party of forty-two men. In order to avoid scurvy—the dread disease which had ruined so many polar expeditions—a supply of dried fruit-powder (which contained the vital vitamin C) was taken. The result was that not one member of the expedition suffered from scurvy.

On January 1, 1929, after the usual battle with the ice-pack, a base was selected on the Bay of Whales not far from Amundsen's 'Framheim.' The base was promptly christened 'Little America.' Since the ships could not approach within nine miles of the selected base, the work of transporting the hundreds of tons of supplies and machines was a formidable one. However, ten dog-teams were available, and by January 15 a hut was erected, and one of the aeroplanes had already made trial flights over the barrier. The advantage of such a form of reconnaissance was immediately proved by the fact that, within a few hours, 1,200 miles of unknown areas had been surveyed. It would have taken sledging-parties weeks to see so much.

A few days later Byrd and a small party took an outboard motor-boat for a cruise along the edge of the Great Barrier. They had just reached an open lead when they saw some 'killer' whales porpoising, about a quarter of a mile ahead. The ugly black fins drew closer, and thinking that discretion was the better part of valour on such an occasion, Byrd began to edge the boat towards firm ice, where it would be possible to make an emergency landing. The affair soon developed into a race. The 'killers' seemed to be travelling twice as fast as the flimsy boat, and they gained rapidly; each dive brought them nearer. Now the men could see their ugly heads, and the sickly yellow patch under the terrible jaws. That short dash to firm ice seemed to take a very long time. Then, with a bang, the boat came alongside and was abandoned with a hustle; a second later the 'killers' rose only fifteen feet away. It had been a sharp reminder that cruising in the Ross Sea is no pleasure-trip!

On January 27 an important exploratory flight was made over King Edward VII Land. The party carried with them 700 pounds of emergency equipment—sledges, sleeping-bags, a tent, and enough food for three months; a forced landing in that mystery-land would have meant a long walk to the nearest supply-store. Just over an hour's flying brought them to Scott's Nunatak, a rocky hill sighted by the Englishman in 1902, and visited by Prestrud, one of the Amundsen party. A little later they caught a glimpse of new mountains to the east and south, and then quite suddenly they found themselves flying in 'a bowl of milk' caused by a snowstorm. They had to fly out over the Ross Sea for a time, and when they returned they once again saw the strange mountains. Then petrol-supplies were getting low, so they had to return to 'Little America.' The new range was given the name Rockefeller Mountains, in honour of one of the chief benefactors of the expedition.

Three days later an alarming accident almost caused a disaster. The two expeditionary ships were unloading alongside the barrier, when a huge portion of the ice broke away. Byrd said that a new glacier was born almost on their decks. The *Bolling* heeled over almost on to her beam-ends, and then rolled back again. Her captain, who had been on the other ship, took a flying leap from the rail to his own bridge. The sea was boiling from the impact of the rocketing ice-blocks. Two men were thrown into the water, and another was clinging to a thread of rope over the edge of the barrier, with his feet dangling in space. One of the men in the water, named Roth, who could not swim, had grabbed a piece of ice, but since this was round and slippery it kept spinning continually. A boat was lowered rapidly. Too many men jumped into it, but one of them, realizing that there was a danger of capsizing, pluckily dropped overboard into the freezing water and told the others to carry on. By this time poor Roth had grabbed another small cake of ice, and he now had one piece under each arm. But his strength was ebbing. Then it was observed that yet another man had been thrown into the water by the avalanche. This one, named De Ganahl, came paddling past the ship astride a plank, headed in the direction of the unfortunate Roth. When De Ganahl saw that he would be beaten by the lifeboat, he calmly scrambled on to a floe and awaited rescue himself. Meanwhile, the fellow who had been hanging over the edge of the barrier had been rescued by means of a looped rope.

Two further flights were made before the long winter closed down. On the first two new mountains were seen, and the name of Scott Land was given to the area south of the Rockefeller Mountains. The second flight was made by a geological party to the newly discovered mountains. They made a safe landing, and for some days were in constant wireless communication with the base. Then came an ominous silence. The silence was all the more mysterious because the wireless-transmission sets on the 'plane could not have been put out of action, unless there had been a crash. Yet strict orders had been issued that the 'plane was not to attempt a return flight until favourable weather-reports were issued from the base. The weather was, however, so bad that not only had no such instructions been issued, but for some days it was impossible to arrange for a relief-flight. Eventually, just after sledging relief-parties had been dispatched, the 'plane got away.

A search of four and a half hours among the mountains brought the explanation of the mysterious silence. Down below Byrd suddenly caught sight of the three men and a tent; about three quarters of a mile away were the grotesque outlines of a wrecked 'plane. Byrd's aeroplane made a daring landing on the bumpy ice, and soon the whole story was told. A series of blizzards had stricken the camp, and finally, in a gust which was estimated to have reached 150 miles an hour, the 'plane had been torn away from her anchorage and actually flew backward for half a mile before crashing, a hopeless wreck, on the ice. Fortunately nobody had been hurt, and the whole party was soon back at 'Little America' making preparations for the long winter.

'Little America' became a most interesting village. Several huts had been erected, and in case of fire they had been placed some distance apart. Now communicating-tunnels were made through the snow, until it was possible to move from one end of the base to the other without once going above ground. For example, it was decided to arrange a gymnasium. A pit was dug in the snow, and a tarpaulin roof (which soon became snow-covered) was thrown over it. Then another tunnel was made, so that there was yet another addition to this strange troglodyte village. Even the dogs had a cave and a tunnel. Above ground the site of the colony was marked by three tall radio-masts, and on the top of one of these was a powerful electric beacon. Telephones were installed, and electric lighting was arranged; altogether, 'Little America' was the most elaborately organized winter quarters which had been known in the Antarctic.

There was plenty of work to keep everybody busy during the winter. Some were making sledges, others were attending to the 'planes in the special snow-hangars, while the photographers and scientists had a full programme. It was not all work, however. Wireless-concerts were frequent, and these were sometimes varied by amateur performances, when burly members of the expedition tried to ape chorus-girls. A regular programme of films was provided, although sometimes the shows were a trifle out of the ordinary, owing to the practice adopted by the photographers of grafting extraneous portions of another film into the parts where pieces were missing! There were lectures, card-parties, musical concerts, discussions, and arguments without end. The practical jokers were not above arousing the whole village early in the morning, with the false alarm that the barrier was splitting. There was, of course, always a chance that the portion of the barrier on which the base stood would 'calve' away from the land.

At last spring came, and everything was made ready for the departure of the southern sledge-parties, and for the flight to the South Pole. After many struggles among badly crevassed areas on the barrier, the geological party finally reached its goal, and brought back specimens from the mountains at the head of the Ross Sea. All parties were in constant wireless communication with the base, and this precaution not only increased the safety-factor, but also meant that extra supplies could be sent out and dropped from one of the aeroplanes. The preparations for the main flight included the establishment of a base at the foot of the Axel Heiberg glacier. The aeroplane had to carry such a heavy load of petrol and emergency supplies that there was always the possibility that they would have to land before the journey could be completed. The greatest problem which arose was to calculate whether the Ford 'plane would be able to climb high enough, with a full load, to cross the 10,000-foot

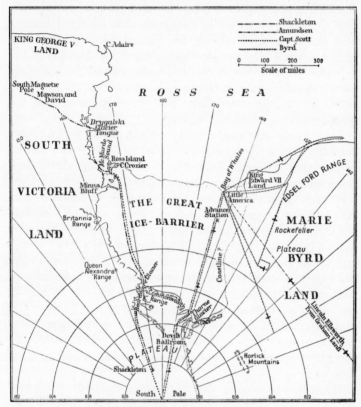

THE CONQUEST OF THE SOUTH POLE

pass between the mountains, and so reach the inland plateau.

Soon after three o'clock on November 25, the 'plane took off. The total weight was approximately 15,000 pounds. The course followed the thin trail made by the various sledging parties which had gone south. When this guiding line was invisible, the navigators had to rely on a sun-compass; an ordinary compass is of course almost useless in these regions. June, the wireless-operator, was constantly sending out messages, and McKinley was busy with the mapping-camera. The cabin was cluttered up with gear; there was a small sledge, sleeping-bags for four men, mounds of clothing and heavy food-sacks, and rows of petrol-cans. The three masts of 'Little America' soon dropped behind, and at about eight o'clock the Queen Maud Range was visible. A few minutes afterwards the geological party was in sight—looking like a cluster of ants round the two dark tents. A parachute carrying some promised photographs taken on the previous flight was dropped, and then the 'plane sped on, climbing steadily.

Now came the most critical period of the flight. After some discussion, it was decided to fly up Liv's glacier instead of the Axel Heiberg. According to Amundsen, the highest point of these passes was about 10,000 feet above sea-level. The crew set about putting the aeroplane in fighting trim. The main tank was refilled, and the empty cans were thrown overboard; soon the 'plane had reached an altitude of over 9000 feet. Now they had a clear view of the glacier sweeping down between mighty bastions 15,000 feet high. The floor of the glacier rose steeply in a series of falls and terraces, and some of the glacier 'waterfalls' were 400 feet high. The air began to roughen, and the wings shivered. At the top of the pass was a snow-covered rock, for which the 'plane appeared to be aiming like a rifle. As yet the explorers were not high enough, and the Ford had evidently almost reached her 'ceiling.'

They had to make a swift decision; something would have to be dumped overboard. Should it be petrol or food?

"Harold, a bag of food overboard," said Byrd to June. The brown bag, weighing 125 pounds, fell spinning through the trap-door and crashed on the glacier below. The 'plane climbed higher, but still not high enough. On either hand were the grim ice-walls of Mount Nansen and Mount Ruth Gade, towering high above the struggling aeroplane.

Another bag of food was sacrified. They had now truly burned their boats behind them; but the 'plane rose again, and it was now obvious that they would be able to clear the top of the pass, with about 500 feet to spare.

Soon they were flying over the floor of the great plateau. The way to the Pole, three hundred miles ahead, was clear. Soon after one o'clock June sent a wireless-message to 'Little America': "My calculations indicate that we have reached the South Pole. Byrd." The flag of the United States was dropped over the Pole, and then the aeroplane turned for home. A favourable wind sprang up, and for some way the 'plane travelled at 125 miles an hour. Before four o'clock they were passing down the glaciers again— this time they followed the Axel Heiberg. At the foot of the glacier the 'plane came down on the level barrier, at the point where the refuelling base had been laid. Fresh petrol-supplies were taken aboard, and by six they were off again on the last leg of the trip. At ten o'clock the wireless-masts of 'Little America' came in sight, and a few minutes later the Ford's skis touched snow. The great flight had been accomplished.

A week later an important extended flight was made eastward. A little over an hour's flying brought the party to the Rockefeller Mountains, and ahead they were looking into the great blank space on the chart which had aroused so much speculation. Forty minutes later Byrd realized he had made a first-class discovery. A mighty chain of mountains began to open up along the horizon. Flying at the rate of 100 miles an hour, they soon passed the 150th meridian, the eastern boundary of the British claims in Antarctica. By this time the new range of mountains stretched from one end of the horizon to the other, and there was evidently a high plateau beyond. Byrd was delighted with his discovery; he thought that some of the new peaks were at least 10,000 feet high, and McKinley was able to photograph 200 miles of the new range. When the 'plane finally returned to 'Little America,' it was decided that the new range should be named the Edsel Ford Range, and the new land was appropriately named Marie Byrd Land, after Byrd's wife. A vast new area had been placed on the map, and the United States had gained a great new possession.

The second expedition organized by Admiral Byrd was probably the most elaborately equipped Antarctic expedition which ever set out. They had two aeroplanes, an auto-gyro, four tractors, a large number of dogs, and a complete wireless-transmitting station. In the way of mechanical equipment they had everything from tiny watch-screws to bolts more than eight feet long. They had two ships, the steel *Jacob Rupert* and the old polar ship, the *Bear of Oakland*. During the period from January 17, 1934, to February 6, 1935, a most comprehensive series of observations was carried out, including research in meteorology, biology, geophysics, botany, and cosmic rays. In comparison with Amundsen's expedition, this was like the invasion of an opulent army.

Instead of heading for the Bay of Whales, the *Jacob Rupert* steered for the unknown pack-ice sector between 'Little America' and South America. In order to ease the task, an aeroplane was mounted on pontoons, so that reconnaissance flights could be made. No one had explored farther south in this sector than Captain Cook, but his record was passed, and the aeroplane flew to 69 degrees south. Hereabouts there were many icebergs which are specially dangerous to steel ships, and eventually the *Jacob Rupert* reached the 'Devil's Graveyard,' which has the reputation of being the greatest iceberg-producing region in the world. Actually the crew counted about 8000 icebergs in twenty-four hours. Enormous, ghostly ice-castles would suddenly loom ominously in the grey mist, and every hundred yards gained by the *Jacob Rupert* raised a new flotilla, with spray dashing up their icy, green bulwarks.

Soon afterwards the ship once again entered the pack-ice, steering south, and the aeroplane flew forward far into the unknown. No islands were seen, but the explorers observed one iceberg which was at least twenty-three miles long. Eventually the ship found an opening where there was no ice at all, and they reached the Bay of Whales without trouble.

There was some speculation, when the expedition reached the Bay of Whales, as to whether 'Little America' had been buried by the drifting snows. From the mast-head of the *Jacob Rupert* they could just see the poles of the wireless-station sticking up, and near by a few stove-pipes and the wing-tips of the Floyd-Bennett 'plane. When they arrived, they found a four years' growth of ice-crystals festooning the tunnel to the administration building like so many stalactites in a cave. Part of the roof had collapsed under the accumulated weight of ice, but the electric light and telephone still functioned! The seal and whale-meat and beef which hung in the tunnel had been perfectly preserved in this inexpensive cold store.

The transference of the stores from the *Jacob Rupert* to the huts presented many difficulties, since pressure-ridges made it necessary to anchor the ship six miles away, and more than 400 tons had to be hauled over that distance. An attempt was made to berth the ship along the edge of the barrier, but as she cruised along, a huge section of the barrier, a quarter of a mile long, broke off, and several hundred thousand tons of ice spread fanwise in the water. It was thought safer to return to the anchorage in the bay-ice!

Eventually, however, the stores were transferred to the 'village,' which was equipped with electric light and power, wireless and meteorological stations, repair-shops, an emergency hospital, a library, a science-hall, a dairy with three cows and a young bull, a mess-hall which could be converted into a cinema, and a United States Post-office. Some thousands of letters had been brought out so that they could be stamped with the mark of the most southerly post-office, and these stamps helped to defray the cost of the operations. Regular broadcasts were also made to the wireless-stations in America.

'Little America' was not really so safe as it sounds, since it had been built on the barrier, and there was always a chance that a huge block of ice might break away and carry the whole expedition with it. On several occasions fresh cracks appeared, and the ice beneath the huts began to move up and down with the swell. In order to make certain of safety, a retreat-camp on the high barrier was stocked with the bare essentials for survival, and the four tractors did useful work in laying a trail of depôts as far as 80 degrees south.

Admiral Byrd was anxious to establish an inland weather-station for winter observation. The observatory was planned for three men, but owing to the arduous task of unloading, only enough stores were taken to the advanced post for one man; and Byrd himself decided to undertake the lonely vigil. His hut was to be fitted with wireless so that he could keep in contact with the base. He flew to his winter home on March 25, and at once began to collect observations on wind-velocities, temperatures, barometer-readings, and aurora, at a point 100 miles away from 'Little America.'

All went well for the first three months; then the fumes from a faulty burner in an oil-stove began to make him ill. On May 30 he was prostrated by the fumes from the engine of his wireless generating set. Moreover, the thermograph recorded an unprecedented cold spell—reaching 80 degrees below zero. Byrd was placed in an awkward dilemma; a lapse in communication by wireless would have been tanta-mount to an S.O.S. call, and this would involve a terribly dangerous mid-winter rescue-trip. So with dauntless courage he continued to crawl to the wireless to transmit messages. Eventually, however, he hurt his arm, and this made it so painful to operate the hand-generated wireless set that he was obliged to ask for relief. He promised to hang a light on a pole and to fly an illuminated kite to guide the relief-party to his hut.

Dr Poulter, who had been in charge at 'Little America,' at once set out by tractor through the Arctic night. With the greatest difficulty his party of five men managed to get half-way to the hut, but since the temperatures were ranging about the 70's, and there were dangerous crevasses ahead, they were forced to turn back. Then another message was received from Byrd, saying that his receiving set was now out of order. Dr Poulter set out again, with only two men and a tractor, hauling two months' provisions. Having travelled twenty-three miles a fan-belt broke, and they had to return again for a fresh tractor. Finally they covered the hundred miles of crevasses and blizzards in complete darkness and reached the leader. They found Byrd so weak that they were all obliged to stay in the tiny observation-hut for

LITTLE AMERICA

The camp is entirely snowed under, and only the radio-towers, flag, and smoke-stack show above the snow.

From Byrd's "Little America" (Putnam)

another two months before he could return. Finally, early in October, an aeroplane was sent out, and they all came back to the base. The rescue-expedition had proved that tractors can be used successfully in the Antarctic, provided that they are fitted with square cabins and folding bunks.

During the summer months which followed, a number of important land and aerial explorations were carried out; temperatures of the upper air were frequently recorded by means of the autogyro, which unfortunately crashed. Dr Poulter found that much of the barrier is aground, and he gave the name of Roosevelt Island to the immediate vicinity of 'Little America.' He came to the conclusion that the reason why the Bay of Whales keeps its shape is because the barrier-ice is anchored on rocks for large distances.

Towards the end of September, a four-man tractor set out to lay depôts as far as Mount Grace McKinley. On the way there they discovered that the land rose slowly, until they were on a plateau 4500 feet high. Another party, which was mainly concerned with biology and geology, went to Marie Byrd Land. At places in the Edsel Ford Range they found the rocks daubed with scarlet lichens, which looked like red paint. Two southern parties were arranged, but one, equipped with tractors, found so many crevasses that they had to turn to the east, and explored in the newly found plateau. The other southern party, which was mainly a geological expedition, pushed on up the glaciers, in spite of the crevasses. At one spot the fissures were enormous in size, and they had to thread their way along narrow ice-ridges which fell away to bottomless pits on either side. They explored several mountains—only 200 miles away from the pole—and they discovered, among other things, plant-fossils, impressions of leaves and stems, coal, and fossilized wood, which indicate that the climate of Antarctica was once sub-tropical. Just south of 86 degrees they found the most southerly recorded plant-life—tiny primitive lichens growing on the northern face of a mountain. On the return-journey they made the discovery that the land to the east of the Thorne glacier is a great plateau, and altogether they travelled more than 1380 miles by dog-team. Meanwhile, the tractors, in spite of many crevasses, had explored the eastern plateau by describing a wide loop, and they completed a journey of 920 miles in two and a half months.

The flying parties were chiefly concerned with the old problem about the supposed strait which connects the Ross and Weddel Seas. They skimmed along the surface of the ice, measuring heights by their altimeters, and discovered that the long-sought strait was non-existent. Other flying parties found that the Edsel Ford Range ran east to west, parallel with the coast-line, for about 150 miles. A new range was called the Horlick Mountains.

Thus a vast new plateau was added to the map. Hundreds of new peaks in the Edsel Ford and Queen Maud Ranges were sighted, and it was definitely shown that Antarctica is one continent.

LINCOLN ELLSWORTH'S TRANS-ANTARCTIC FLIGHT

Although 'Little America' was abandoned to the elements after Byrd's second expedition, the village was destined to provide a useful home for an explorer who reached there overland. Accompanied by a Canadian, Hollick-Kenyon, the aviator Lincoln Ellsworth took off from Dundee Island in the north of Graham Land on November 23, 1935. His objective was the Bay of Whales, and the route was over an immense tract of unexplored country. The aeroplane was a Northrop, and it carried full rations for sixty-one days. The ship of the expedition was the *Wyatt Earp*, under the command of Sir Hubert Wilkins, and it was hoped that wireless communications would be kept up with the ship. For a few hours the messages came through, and then there was a sudden silence when the 'plane was scarcely half-way across.

Days passed, and there was still no news of the aviators. At last, on December 3, it was decided to send the *Discovery II* to the Bay of Whales to seek information. This wonderful research-ship has for many years been engaged in scientific work in the Antarctic, and it was equipped with two aeroplanes. The rescue-ship was hurriedly fitted out, and it left Melbourne on December 23. The *Wyatt Earp* was also struggling towards the Bay of Whales, but the British

218

ship arrived first, on January 15, 1936. The Moth aeroplane was sent out on a reconnaissance flight, and it came back with the news that there was a tent with an orange-coloured streamer on the barrier, and that one man had been sighted. A rocket was fired from the ship, but there was no answer. On the next day a landing party went ashore and met Kenyon, who reported that Ellsworth was alive but suffering from a slight cold. While the whole world was wondering anxiously about their fate, the two aviators had been living in moderate comfort at 'Little America.'

The flight was not accomplished in one hop. Some five hours after wireless communications had ceased, the 'plane came down between Hearst Land and Marie Byrd Land. On the next day they took off again, but landed after thirty minutes' flying. Two days later they flew on for another fifty minutes, and then they found that their position was approximately 650 miles from 'Little America.' Two more hops brought them to within sixteen miles of Byrd's base, and then they ran out of fuel and had to sledge in. Having reached the barrier-edge they found they had over-shot the mark, but they finally reached 'Little America' on December 15.

So ended the first flight across the Antarctic continent. A huge segment between 80° and 120 W° was given the name of James W. Ellsworth Land, and a high plateau in the heart of the continent was named after Ellsworth's co-pilot. Several new mountains were sighted, the most important being in the 'Eternity' and 'Sentinel' ranges.

In 1939 Ellsworth made another important flight from a base on his ship into the interior of the Antarctic continent behind Enderby Land, and claimed a large area for the U.S.A.

CHAPTER X

GREENLAND'S ICY MOUNTAINS

One crowded hour of glorious life
Is worth an age without a name.

SCOTT. *Old Mortality*

MAROONED ON THE ICE-CAP

GREENLAND looms so vast and blankly virgin on the Mercator maps that to many people it suggests comparison with the empty silences of unexplored Antarctica. However, although it is about ten times the size of Great Britain, it is only one-sixth the size of Antarctica; moreover, it has a population of 16,000, mainly Eskimos. Greenland may be compared with an upturned plate over which salt is being constantly shaken. The raised rim represents the mountains and the salt the snow, which spills itself over the edge, wherever it can, in the form of glaciers. Along the southern coasts in the summer the barren mountains slope down to fresh-water lakes and little fertile valleys, where musk-ox graze in meadows carpeted with bright saxifrages, azaleas, harebells, and Arctic poppies. But beyond the coastal belt are the eternal glaciers—the great ice-cap, which in places is thousands of feet thick.

Before the present century, few men had travelled on the ice-cap, and it had been crossed only twice (by Nansen and Peary). But the last thirty years have seen a number of brilliant exploratory journeys into the interior, and although some parts of the north-east remained untouched, the general configuration of Greenland is now fairly well known. The island is a dependency of Denmark, and the Danes have done a good deal to open up the interior. In 1906 Mylius Erichsen and Captain Koch established a base, about 700 miles north of the Arctic circle, in a bay called Danmark's Harbour. From this point they travelled along the sea-ice to the extreme north of Greenland and found Danmark's Fjord. Erichsen decided to do some further exploration to the west

220

before returning to his ship, and he set off with one companion and an Eskimo. Koch safely reached the base again, but Erichsen's party disappeared. Relief-expeditions were organized, and eventually, in the spring of 1908, the dead body of the Eskimo sledge-driver was found. Beside him was a message which told of a brave struggle to reach the base.

> Perished on fjord, latitude 79 deg. north, after attempt to return over inland ice in month of November. Arrived here by light of waning moon. Cannot go on, because of frozen feet and darkness. Bodies of comrades in middle of fjord below glacier. Hagen died on November 15, Erichsen about ten days later—Jorgen Bronlund.

When this news reached Denmark a new expedition was arranged, with the object of finding the bodies and diaries of Erichsen and Hagen. Captain Einar Mikkelsen, a sea-captain who had had experience in the Arctic, was given the command, and in 1909 his ship, the *Alabama*, reached a base at Shannon Island, 100 miles south of Danmark's Harbour. As soon as the young ice was thick enough for sledging, Mikkelsen led a small party northward to where Bronlund was buried; there he searched, unsuccessfully, for traces of the lost explorers. In the following spring the party set off again towards Danmark's Fjord, and began to ascend the ice-cap from a bay to the west of Danmark's Harbour. There were many storms, and soon Mikkelsen sent back all but one of his companions, the ship's engineer, a man named Iversen.

It was the middle of April, and they had fifteen dogs and provisions for 100 days. As they toiled on up the steep slope of the ice-cap, they had many narrow escapes from crevasses, and when they did reach Danmark's Fjord, they had to descend an ice-cliff 100 feet high before they could reach solid earth again. Here they found a little Arctic oasis with moss and heather and little stunted willow trees; but as they journeyed along down the fjord the vegetation became scarce again, and the scenery more and more wild. Once, for a day and a half, they sledged past a perpendicular wall of rock at least 1500 feet high.

At last they reached their goal, and found messages left by Erichsen at places where he had camped. Erichsen had made the discovery that Peary Land was not cut off from the rest of Greenland, and that the so-called Peary Channel was nothing more than a steep-sided fjord. Mikkelsen decided to return to his ship, keeping close to the coast. It was now the end of May, and a number of accidents had reduced their outfit to seven dogs and one sledge. The sun was melting the snow, and this caused the sledge to drag. Worst of all, Mikkelsen was suffering from scurvy and grew easily tired, while his legs were stiff and painful.

On Midsummer's Day they had to call a halt, because great pools of water from the melted snow were forming in all directions. Game was scarce, and a whole day's hunting rarely produced more than a couple of gulls. Then they found a food-depôt left by Erichsen, and although the chocolate had turned green and the oatmeal was mouldy, they welcomed the addition to their stores. Mikkelsen by this time was in desperate straits. For three weeks he was unable to stand on his feet without help, and his limbs had grown black and very swollen. The diet of fresh meat and porridge seemed to do him good, however, and one day, when it was necessary to shift camp, he staggered to his feet and, with the help of two sticks, tried to walk. At first he felt dizzy, but then he found that he could manage with only one stick. He took a few more paces, and then threw away the other stick and walked alone. All that night he lay awake whispering to himself, "I can walk, I can walk— not going to die this time—get well again soon and do my share."

When at last they were able to march again, they found that a broad channel had melted along the coast, and from this channel branched out smaller channels across the course of the travellers. They had to make long detours, and sometimes had to raft the sledge across on floating ice-cakes. On one occasion they had chosen a big floe to serve as a raft and had driven the dogs on to it. Then the dogs took fright at the open water before them, and stopped pulling when only half the sledge had crossed on to the floe. At the critical moment the floe began to drift; the rear part of the sledge hung suspended and slowly began to sink into the water, until the sledge was almost vertical. Heaving frantically, they saw all their possessions slipping gradually down into the depths. Then, with feverish haste, they slashed the ropes on the sledge and pulled the packages on to the floe. By good fortune they were able to save not only the greater part of the provisions, but also the sledge, although the survey-instruments and other things went to the bottom.

After this terrifying experience the explorers so arranged the stores that the sledge would float and could be punted across the open water-lanes. The dogs were all sick or dying, and progress was very slow; but soon they managed to find a few supplies in one of the Erichsen depôts. Now the summer was passing quickly. The explorers were so hungry that they ate the livers of the dead dogs, although they knew that such meat would have a narcotic effect. In September they reached one of the depôts, to find that all the stores had gone. Here there was so much water that they had to abandon the sledge and make their way to land over young ice, which was so thin that seals could poke their heads through. With sixty miles to go to Danmark's Harbour, they had only three pounds of food left, and they were racing against death.

On they staggered until they reached a fjord, where there was open water, and they had to make a long detour. A snowstorm came on, and for forty hours they had to take what shelter they could among some rocks. When they were able to travel again, they were possessed by strange delusions, for they thought they could see packets of sandwiches on the ground; but when they stood to pick them up they found that they were merely stones. At the last moment they found another depôt, and so were able to reach Danmark's Harbour.

By now the winter was fast approaching, and they still had a hundred miles to go before they reached the winter quarters of the *Alabama* at Shannon Island. So, somewhat refreshed, they set off again through foul weather, and when at last they did reach the promised haven of rest, came the greatest disappointment of all. Instead of the trim *Alabama*, all they could see was a hut built from its timbers. Their ship had been wrecked, and the members of the crew had been taken home in another vessel!

Mikkelsen and Iversen passed the winter in the hut, and when at long last the sun came back again, they made a trip to the north to recover their left belongings. All that summer the two castaways waited in vain for the expected relief, and finally they realized that they must have been given up as lost or dead.

The sun declined, and once more they had to prepare for a lonely winter in the hut. Their only visitors were Arctic foxes and polar bears. One day when they looked out of the door they saw a big polar bear gazing at them. The bear was curious and began to come after them. They quickly barred the door, but the bear refused to go away and began to tear at the wood. The situation was truly alarming, for they had allowed their rifles to get frozen, and the only available weapon was an axe. Frantically they struggled with the rifles to make them work, and Iversen just succeeded when, with a final crashing blow, the bear burst open the door and sent him spinning across the room. For a split second the bear hesitated with surprise, and then Iversen's rifle rang out, and the shaggy beast fell dead.

Life in the hut was one long struggle against frost-bite. Even with their stove alight, the temperature was never more than two degrees above freezing-point, and if they spilt water on the floor it froze immediately. In order to avoid frost-bite it was necessary for them to take off their foot-gear a dozen times a day and put their feet in the stove. The sun returned in February, and the two forgotten explorers made a journey to Bass Rock. Here they waited patiently for week after week, until one morning in July they awakened to see a small steamer lying off the rock. So at last, after an ordeal such as few travellers in the Arctic have survived, they were picked up and taken home to Denmark.

GREENLAND'S ICY MOUNTAINS

The career of Roald Amundsen has been called an epitome of Arctic exploration. He alone has visited both Poles *and* sailed through both the famous northern passages. It was in July, 1918, that Amundsen set sail in the *Maud* with ten Norwegians, hoping to achieve what Nansen had once tried to do—to drift over the North Pole.

At the outset there was some danger of being torpedoed by German submarines, which at this period were at their venomous tricks of sinking all and sundry without warning. But the trip was uneventful until Cape Chelyuskin, the most northerly point of Asia, was passed. Then they encountered heavy drift-ice, and had to prepare for the winter. Unfortunately there was no good harbour near by, and eventually the *Maud* took refuge between two little islands, on one of which a base was arranged.

A gang-plank was set up from the ship to the shore and fitted with a rope hand-rail. One day the *Maud's* watchdog, Jacob, was so enthusiastic in her greeting that she knocked Amundsen's feet from under him, and the explorer fell headlong down the slope and severely damaged his shoulder. A few days later Amundsen was up and about again, but he had his arm in a sling. One day Amundsen set off for an early morning walk, accompanied by Jacob, and suddenly he heard a noise like the soughing of a gentle wind. The wind seemed to strengthen, and then through the half-light Amundsen saw the dog racing for the ship at full speed, with a great polar bear panting in pursuit. Apparently Jacob had disturbed the polar bear's cub, and was suffering the penalty.

However, when the bear saw Amundsen it turned its attention to this larger-looking meal. Amundsen was almost helpless, with his arm in the sling, and so he began to run for the ship. Just before he reached the gangway the bear struck him a heavy blow on the back, which felled him to the ground. The explorer was sure that his last moment had come, and then Jacob suddenly appeared again and diverted the bear's attention. The next moment Wisting, who had heard the noise, came on deck with a rifle, and the bear was soon shot. Amundsen always said that this incident was one of the narrowest escapes of his life.

For some time afterwards, however, Amundsen was more or less an invalid, and it was only with great difficulty that he regained the use of his arm. His condition was not improved by yet a third accident. One day he went into the observatory, which was a small, windowless room, to take observations, when he suddenly felt ill. Just before losing consciousness he managed to struggle to the door and fresh air. Apparently the kerosene-lamp had exhausted all the oxygen in the room, and Amundsen was badly poisoned.

Spring came, and the ship still held fast. When summer came, and conditions were not better, Amundsen decided to employ a trick he had seen used when he went to the Antarctic with the *Belgica* expedition. Half a mile away, beyond the packed land-ice, they could see clear water. Some fifty holes were bored along a line leading to the clear water, and dynamite was inserted. The electric charge was switched on, and there was a deafening explosion; but to the amazement of the crew nothing appeared to have happened to the ice. A few nights later, when there was a high tide, the effects of the explosion were seen at last, for a cracking sound began to come along the dynamited path, and soon the massive ice-sheet began to break up.

Once again the *Maud* turned her bow eastwards and passed to the south of the New Siberian Islands. There was a great deal of pack-ice, and progress was very slow. In September the *Maud* was fast again, and a second winter had to be spent at an island near Cape Chelasky. One of the party, Dr Sverdrup, made important investigations among the Siberian aborigines who lived in this district. In the next summer the *Maud* continued her voyage, but by this time she was in such need of repairs that Amundsen decided to sail for Nome, in Alaska. Thus in August, 1920, the Norwegians completed the north-east passage.

THE STORY OF GINO WATKINS

Undoubtedly the most brilliant of the younger generation of Arctic explorers was Henry George (Gino) Watkins. One day, in the spring of 1932, a cable was delivered to a smiling young man in a small room at the Royal Geographical Society. It bore the laconic address, "Watkins, explorer, England." Gino was then only twenty-five years old, but his fame had already reached the ends of the earth. When still an undergraduate at Cambridge he had organized a successful expedition to Edge Island, an uninhabited island, 2500 square miles in extent, which lies to the south-east of Spitsbergen. He had been intrigued by the fact that parts of the coast-line of Edge Island were shown only by dotted lines, and during the course of some important survey-work he made a crossing of the central ice-cap. When he reached the farther side, with his companion, Forbes, he could not find his ship, the *Heimen*, and he was already short of supplies. It was characteristic of his humour that he could write in his diary at this juncture:

> We are feeling very empty and have only got food for two more days. As a matter of fact, I think one could live on some of the moss round here, as it looks quite good; anyhow, Forbes's socks look meaty enough to last us for some time!

Fortunately they were not reduced to this extremity, for later on the same day they were picked up by the *Heimen*.

Gino Watkins had been fond of adventure from his school-days. He had made mountaineering-trips up the tower of his school, and on one occasion he persuaded a pilot to take him up in an aeroplane and 'stunt' above the cricket-field, where he was supposed to be playing. On another occasion he tried to climb the spire of Salisbury Cathedral; he was getting on very well until it started to rain, and he had great difficulty in descending the slippery stones. He spent many holidays ski-ing and climbing in the Alps and in the Tyrol. Once he crashed down a 150-foot slope when out hunting chamois. Although he was terribly battered, and only semi-conscious, he had a shot at a chamois while he was waiting to be rescued by the guides.

At the age of twenty-one Watkins went with his friend, Scott, to Labrador to make exploratory surveys on the boundary of Labrador and Canada. They planned a tributary of the Hamilton river, and then went off to explore the

mysterious Lake Snegamook, about which some Indians
had talked to them. Their map consisted of a few pencil-
lines drawn by an Indian, but they pushed on across lakes
and through forests and marshy valleys until they came
across a tribe of Indians who were almost starving. Watkins
was always optimistic about his food-supplies, and he gave
a good deal of his remaining stores to the Indians. Eventually he found Lake Snegamook, which proved to be about
twenty-five miles long; then he set off for a settlement called
Hopedale, on the coast some seventy miles away. The
country became more difficult, and the explorers began to
run out of supplies, until they had only half a candle left.
When things were getting really serious, they found a
snow-shoe trail which led them on to Hopedale and safety.
After Christmas Watkins explored the 'Unknown River,'
and he found four large waterfalls, potentially of great
industrial value.

On returning to England—already a famous man—
Watkins began to plan the most audacious expeditions. He
once suggested, for example, that he and his friends should
make a sledging-trip across Antarctica from the Weddell
Sea to the Ross Sea, making a side-excursion on the way to
climb Mount Everest! The industrial slump of the period,
however, made it impossible to raise ample funds, and he
had to be content with another idea which had some claims
to be a commercial proposition. From his early years he
had been interested in flying, and he now began to advocate
an Arctic air-route between Europe and America. The
route proposed would cross the Faroes, Iceland, Greenland,
Baffin Island, and Hudson Bay. The advantages were that
this was the shortest way to the centre of America, and the
sea-crossings are nowhere very long. The disadvantages
were that the route ran for a long way along the Arctic
circle, and for a great distance, especially on the Greenland
ice-cap, was unsurveyed and practically unknown.

Watkins proposed to set up a base at the Eskimo village
of Angmagssalik, and from there seek out a suitable landing-
ground. In order to learn something about the meteorological
conditions on the ice-cap, a camp was to be established

228

about 140 miles inland, where observations could be taken for a whole year. Also a number of sledging-trips would be made across the ice-cap, and a survey of the mountains along the east coast. Gino took a great deal of trouble to ascertain what was the best sledging-ration for his expeditions. Having worked out a diet, which included large quantities of fat, he decided to try it out for a week in London, doing his best to create Arctic conditions. He slept by a window with practically nothing on, and skated at the Hammersmith ice-rink before he had his breakfast of porridge, pemmican, and margarine. Even when invited out to dinner he took with him his little paper bag of greasy rations!

One fine day in July, the *Quest* nosed her way through the pack-ice to the Eskimo settlement at Angmagssalik. The natives welcomed her with an energetic dance. Two days later a base had been found about thirty miles west of the village, where there was a suitable beach for sea-planes and a good position for the wireless-masts. The heavy work of transporting stores completed, the *Quest* went off to survey the coast for 200 miles to the north, in the hope of finding a really good station for flying-boats. Watkins accompanied the ship with an aeroplane, and eventually they found a small fjord with a fresh-water lake at its head. This fateful spot they called Lake Fjord, and it proved to be an excellent flying-base.

Meanwhile the central ice-cap station had been established by five men, who had marched 250 miles across the lifeless desert of ice. Watkins had hoped to be able to make a number of sledge-trips along the axis of the ice-cap from this weather-station; but he found that the climb up the crevassed slopes to the summit was such a lengthy and exhausting proceeding that it would be possible to arrange only a small southern expedition.

Scott and Watkins, with four others, arrived at the ice-cap station to find the two occupants well and in good spirits. Bingham and D'Aeth now took charge of the station, while Watkins and Scott set off southward down the middle of the ice-cap. They hoped to find a transverse valley, which would be easy for aeroplanes to follow, and then they planned to return to the base *via* the coastal mountains. During the first three days they travelled at the rate of just over one mile an hour. The men and their fourteen dogs were eating twenty pounds of food a day, and they had reasonable hopes that, since the loads would soon become lighter, they would be able to travel three or four hundred miles. On the fourth day they crawled out of the tent into a miniature blizzard. This was followed by a warm, snowy day, and then a sudden drop of 60 degrees in the night. The sudden change made the dogs listless and miserable, and Gino suggested that they should be given extra food. So that evening they slit open a seven-pound tin of margarine to add to the dogs' supper and prepared for their own feast.

The night was still and cold, and the tent was well secured. The paraffin-stove was fuming, as it often did at those high altitudes, and Gino, whose eyes were sensitive to smoke, was lying on his face by the tent-wall while Scott stirred the bowl of pemmican and poured in porridge-oats and pea-flour to make it more appetizing. Suddenly everything went black; and when Scott woke up he found himself with his head and body in the snow outside and his feet still in the tent. He crawled back into the tent, to find Gino squatting in the midst of disordered kit, and wringing the pemmican-soup out of his sleeping-bag.

"Are you all right?" asked Gino quietly.

"What happened?" asked Scott, his head still full of noises.

"You suddenly blew your nose into the butter," replied Gino. "I thought that a bad sign; but when I protested mildly, you started throwing your arms about and knocking everything over. So I turned off the primus and hauled you outside."

Apparently Scott had been knocked completely out by the carbon monoxide which had formed above the stove, and but for Watkins's prompt action he might have been seriously ill.

They travelled on slowly. The dogs seemed to be listless,

and after they had journeyed about a hundred miles in a southward direction they turned eastward for the mountains. Then came a blizzard, which kept them in the tent for fifty hours. The snow was still drifting when they started again, but they travelled steadily onward over a snow crust that was not quite firm enough to bear a man without snow-shoes. Towards evening one of Scott's shoe-bindings worked loose, and when he stopped to fix it, the dogs suddenly started off at a trot. Gino set off in pursuit with quick, short steps, breaking through the crust every four or five yards; several times he almost reached the handle-bars, and then stumbled. It was growing dark, and there was a distinct prospect that the explorers would be left with only one sleeping-bag and half the provisions. Gino made a final effort, dived for the sledge, caught it, and held on; the dogs, having thoroughly enjoyed the game, promptly lay down. Watkins later admitted that this had been one of the most anxious occasions of his life.

In the next six days, they travelled only fourteen miles, and for the rest of the time they were in their sleeping-bags while the wind howled and thrashed the little tent. Outside there were gusts of hundred miles an hour, which bellied the canvas and made the bamboo-poles creak and bend under the pressure.

One night there came a sudden calm. "We had better get on," said Gino. By this time they were getting short of provisions, so they abandoned one sledge and harnessed all the dogs to the other and travelled fast most of that night. Two days later they caught sight of a broken black line, which turned out to be Chapman's sledge-party, which was on its way to relieve Bingham and D'Aeth at the ice-station. They had experienced terrible weather, and had taken a fortnight to come as far as this. They now proposed to send back half their party, and the remaining three, Courtauld, Chapman, and Wager, were to push on with heavy supplies of food to the station.

Five weeks later Chapman and Wager came back, after a gruelling journey. They had brought back Bingham and D'Aeth, but Courtauld had insisted that he should be left to carry on the work at the station, although he would have to be alone owing to the shortage of food-supplies.

During the winter months Watkins kept open house for the Eskimos, and they in return taught him how to hunt seals with a long harpoon at the breathing-holes. He also learned a good deal of the Eskimo language, for it was his objective to learn how to live the Eskimo life as well, or better than, the Eskimos. There were frequent storms, when the wind-gauge registered gusts of over a hundred miles an hour. Once a wireless mast was blown down, and Gino was soon anxiously inquiring how long it would take before they could be listening to the Savoy Band again!

Meanwhile they were beginning to be anxious about Courtauld. He had with him sufficient food to last until May, but on the two days when flying was possible, and an aeroplane was sent up to the station with food, it returned with the report that the station (which was a bell-shaped tent) could not be located. On March 9, after two previous attempts had been made to reach the ice-cap, Scott led a party to relieve Courtauld. The relief-party spent forty days on the ice-cap, but they failed to locate the station. Actually what had happened was that Courtauld's tent had been snowed under, and his only connexion with the outside world was *via* a snow-tunnel, which by this time had got blocked. So, almost dropping with fatigue and anxiety, Scott's party had to return to the base unsuccessful.

Watkins at once organized a second relief-party, and this time he went as leader. The course was plotted with as much care as if they were navigating a ship, until on May 4 they knew they must be near. Then each man took a dog and started out to search. They advanced in a long line, until they suddenly saw a dark speck a half a mile away. They raced to it, and as they came nearer they saw that the dark spot was a very tattered Union Jack, the top of a wind-gauge, and a spade. Everything else was entirely hidden beneath a huge snow-drift, and there was no sign of life. Now came the anxious moment. Was Courtauld still alive down below? Watkins caught sight of an inch or two of a brass ventilating-pipe sticking up above the drift; he knelt over it and shouted, and at once he heard Courtauld reply. The snow was dug away, until the apex of the dome-tent appeared. Then Watkins slit a hole in the canvas, and gazed down at a very dirty, bearded hermit in the midst of a squalid, frozen ice-cave, some nine feet in diameter. Six days later the whole party had safely returned to the base, and Courtauld, the hero of this strange adventure, was modestly apologizing for the inconvenience he had caused!

To round off the expedition, Watkins now organized a number of journeys for various members. One party went to Mount Forel and climbed to a record height for the Arctic; another party crossed the ice-cap to Ivigtut; and another crossed to Holsteinborg. Watkins himself, accompanied by Lemon and Courtauld, planned to join his comrades by sailing round the south coast of Greenland in an open boat.

This plan at first sounded suicidal, because in the small outboard motor-boat, if they carried enough fuel for the engine to carry them the 600 miles to the nearest West Greenland village, they would have practically no room for food. Watkins, however, had been busy learning how to use a *kayak*, and he was confident that he could provide enough food by hunting as they went along.

Unlike the clumsy seal-skin *umyak*, the Eskimo *kayak* is a thing of grace and beauty. The framework is made of cunningly spliced driftwood, and over this skeleton is stretched a half-cured seal-skin, neatly sewn with sinews. Places are provided for the harpoon and its seal-skin float, and for the white screen and gun-case. The cockpit is just wide enough to take a man, and it is fitted with a waterproof skirt which tucks round the *kayak* so as to make it watertight. Such craft are, of course, very unstable and will turn turtle at the slightest awkward movement. The huntsman, therefore, has to be expert at the tricky game of turning somersaults in the water, and by a skilful thrust of the paddle to make the boat upright again. Watkins and many others of the expedition practised this difficult art until many of them were really expert. Indeed, Gino was able to do such tricks as rolling over the *kayak* without the aid of a paddle—an accomplishment which makes his ultimate fate all the more mysterious. Then for days on end he went watching the seals, so that he would know how each species would behave in any given set of circumstances. He learned the art of stealing up to his prey, while crouching behind the white screen on the front of the *kayak*, and then how to make the seals dazed with a charge of gunshot in the head, and how to harpoon them before they died and sank.

Eventually Watkins decided to take two boats instead of one, since this would allow him to carry a certain amount of supplies to eke out the proceeds of the hunting. They also had three *kayaks* and three hand-sledges, a wireless-transmitter, and tools for building in case they had to winter. For the first ten days they had good weather, and were able to make their way slowly along the coast, threading their way between the icebergs and rocky islets. At night a tent was pitched on a mossy beach, and the boats were tied up in a cranny. Gino was successful with his hunting, and usually he came back with a seal or some gulls or ducks. They made several landings and surveyed a good deal of the coast-line, which had never before been mapped.

Beyond the half-way mark the weather was less favourable, and the sea often had a nasty swell. The engines were soaked with rain, and more than once suddenly cut out, so that the boats began to drift against the icebergs. Once, when the boat was being swamped in the heavy swell, Courtauld jumped up to get a bucket, and the outboard motor kicked overboard. Courtauld just caught it as it went under, but the wetting put it completely out of action. The others quickly got out the oars, and in the nick of time they were able to get enough way on to pass between two icebergs.

From this point onward they had so much trouble with the engines that they decided to abandon one of the boats with all the wireless-gear. Then, having persuaded the other engine to work, they kept it going continually, filling up with petrol from a teapot as they went along. On September 19 they reached the most critical stage of the whole journey. They had gone too far to risk turning back, the coastal mountains were so high that there was no possibility of

WATKINS HUNTING IN HIS KAYAK

The harpoon lies by his right hand ; its line, coiled in front, passes to the bladder behind. His paddle steadies him while he fires. The black belt seals the cockpit-rim.

From "Gino Watkins," by J. M. Scott (Hodder and Stoughton). By courtesy of the author

making a crossing of the ice-cap from this region, and before them stretched the thirty miles of the dreaded Puisortok glacier-front. This glacier is a great iceberg-manufactory. It frequently 'calves' huge masses of ice, which shoot down under the water like submarines and emerge again offshore to deal destruction to any boat in the vicinity. The first attempt to pass was foiled by bad weather and 'brash' ice. Then the engine refused to work, and the boat, which had been bumped about a good deal by rocks and ice-floes, was leaking like a sieve. For ten days following either the weather was too bad or some accident held up the start; and it really began to look as if they would be compelled to winter in this bleak spot. At last the explorers got the engine to limp along shakily, and so they chugged along at about the rate of one knot past the frowning glacier, every moment fearing that a mighty crash would herald the birth of a devastating ice-torpedo. Slowly they drew in behind some islands and found a place where they could camp.

By this time the engine seemed to be almost hopeless. They took it to pieces as far as they could, but found they had not all the necessary tools. Then some one suggested that they should disconnect the silencer. Immediately the engine went full speed, and that trouble was cured. The next day they travelled fifty miles, but by this time the sea was freezing harder every night, and the boat was leaking so badly that one man had to be constantly baling. Luckily they encountered a party of Norwegian fox-hunters, who fixed them up with provisions and materials for making the boat almost water-tight again. So they entered the fjord which cuts off Cape Farewell from the rest of Greenland, and soon came to an Eskimo village on the western coast.

Watkins then returned to England and tried to raise funds for an expedition to cross Antarctica; but finding this impossible, he decided to return once more to East Greenland and make further investigations round Lake Fjord, which he had decided was the best air-base on the coast.

He proposed to live like an Eskimo for a year, to explore the region around Mount Forel, and possibly to cross the ice-cap in the spring. Watkins had succumbed to the 'call of the North.' "It is queer how it gets hold of one," he wrote. "The first time a man comes to the Arctic he probably comes half for adventure, half in pursuit of some scientific object. On his first visit he is either scared, and never comes again, or he gets the Arctic in him and returns again and again."

On August 4, 1932, Watkins, with his companions Rymill, Chapman, and Riley, arrived once more at Angmagssalik. A week later they had settled in their base at Lake Fjord. This fjord is Y-shaped, the northern arm being somewhat short and broad. On either side of this arm there are high mountains, and at the head is a 100-foot wall of ice, which marks the end of a glacier. As is usual in such circumstances, the ice-wall frequently 'calves'

SOUTH GREENLAND, SHOWING THE JOURNEYS OF WATKINS, SCOTT, AND LINDSAY

and sends new-born icebergs shooting down into the fjord, and incidentally creates a considerable 'tidal' wave. The other arm of the fjord is, however, quite safe and ends in a flat expanse of marshy ground, through which meanders a little river flowing from a lake.

The base was set up near the mouth of this river, and the party began to lay in stores of seal, fish, and birds for the winter. Gino, as usual, did most of the hunting, and, in spite of the risks, preferred to hunt alone. This meant that there would be no chance that a less skilled companion would disturb the seals at the critical moment. On August 14 he had a very narrow escape from disaster. He paddled up to within 100 yards of the ice-wall, saw a seal, and harpooned it. He towed it out of the danger-zone, and then climbed out on to an ice-floe with his *kayak* and started to inflate the seal. Suddenly a large piece broke off the glacier. In a flash a great wave came rolling down and dashed the floe against the cliffs. Watkins clung on to a ledge; the *kayak* was overturned, and all the hunting-gear carried away. Luckily he managed to collect everything again, and he reached the base without further incident.

A week later, while Rymill and Chapman were surveying the fjord by motor-boat, Watkins went into the danger-zone again. Actually the surveyors did not see Gino pass beyond them because of the ice-floes, and so when, about 11 o'clock, they heard the crash of a big ice-fall from the glacier two miles away, they took no particular notice. Early in the afternoon, when they had crossed into the northern arm of the fjord, they suddenly saw a *kayak* drifting low in the water. The harpoon was in its place, but the throwing-stick and the gun were missing. With fear in their hearts they began to search the ice-floes, and in the middle they found Gino's trousers and *kayak*-belt soaking wet on a flat, irregular floe. Clearly there had been an accident of some sort, but they still hoped that Gino had managed to swim ashore, although this was half a mile away. The wet clothes on the floe remained a mystery, for in spite of a lengthy search, nothing more was seen. They searched till midnight, and all the next day, but Gino Watkins had gone as perhaps he would have wished to go, quietly and bravely to his icy grave in the Arctic.

CHAPTER XI

ADVENTURES IN NORTHERNMOST AMERICA

But howling Winter fled afar
To hills that prop the polar star;
And loves on deer-borne car to ride
With barren darkness by his side.

CAMPBELL. *Ode to Winter*

WILKINS'S ARCTIC FLIGHTS

SINCE the attempt made by Andrée, in 1897, to fly from Spitsbergen to the Pole in a balloon, much attention has been given to the possibilities of Arctic exploration and travel by air. The North Pole has been visited three times by air—twice in airships and once in an aeroplane—and a considerable number of exploratory flights have been made over the Arctic Ocean. There are plenty of emergency landing-grounds on the level parts of the ice-sheet, and there is a surprising absence of air-pockets and other dangers. Nevertheless, the risks involved in a forced landing are obvious.

One of the most daring pioneers during the present century has been George Wilkins. During 1926, with Carl Eielson as pilot, he flew four times from Fairbanks, Alaska, to Point Barrow, on the north coast, to arrange a flying-base. On the first trip, after missing Barrow in the fog, they flew out over the Arctic Ocean for 120 miles. The interior of Alaska is only vaguely known, and on more than one occasion they were lost among the mountains. On one trip, when they had scarcely sufficient gas left to carry them back to Fairbanks, they saw a village which was not marked on their chart. Eielson flew low over the houses, while Wilkins dropped a note asking the inhabitants to spell the name of the village in the snow. The natives soon began stamping large letters in the snow, but these spelled a village not mentioned on the maps. This was all the more confusing. Wilkins dropped a second note asking the people to stamp

238

out an arrow pointing in the direction of Fairbanks. The villagers immediately lined themselves up into the shape of an arrow, and thanks to this novel sign-post, the airmen were able to reach the Fairbanks aerodrome.

On the third flight across Alaska, conditions were very bad as they approached the mountains. The valleys were filled with dense fog, and high clouds wreathed the mountain-tops. The machine was so heavily laden that they had no hope of rising above the peaks, and Eielson flew on, hoping to find a gap. In order to give the 'plane a better chance of climbing, Wilkins began to move some loose cases of petrol near the pilot's cockpit. As he was doing this, they reached a very bumpy area. The aeroplane was tossed about like a cork on the ocean, so that he lost his balance and fell against the cabin-wall, fracturing his arm. But there was no time to attend to this. Looming up on the left, Wilkins caught sight of a sharp mountain peak. He hurriedly signalled to Eielson to keep to the right to avoid a crash; but the pilot indicated that there was a mountain peak on that side also. There was no time or space to turn; they had to keep straight on, trusting to luck that they could get sufficient height to scrape through the narrow pass. Slowly the gap narrowed, until there was only a foot or two between the wing-tips and the jagged walls of rock. On the topmost ridge the wheels actually touched the snow and started to spin, just as they do after a take-off. But they were through —and by a margin so small that it seemed a miracle.

In the following year Wilkins flew again into the Arctic regions. This time he had a 73-foot Fokker, a commercial biplane, and two Stinson cabin-biplanes. Early in the morning on March 29 Wilkins and Eielson set out in one of the Stinsons, intending to land, take soundings through the ice, and look for any signs of land. For the first four hours they flew smoothly along over the ice-sheet, observing many cracks and a few open leads of water. Then the engine began to show signs of trouble. By eleven o'clock the coughing and spluttering had become so bad that they decided to land on a flat expanse of ice. They made a good landing, although the ice-crystals cut deep into the duralumin skis.

While Eielson examined the engine, Wilkins picked two holes in the ice for his Sonic sounding-apparatus. This apparatus consists of a cartridge and an accurate timing-device fitted with head-phones. A charge is detonated, and the time which elapses before the echo returns from the ocean-bed indicates the depth. Here they found the depth to be over 5400 metres. Then for two hours both men fiddled with the engine in the icy wind, trying to locate the cause of the trouble. The cowling and carburettor had to be removed, and eventually, after five attempts the 'plane rose again and headed for Barrow. Ten minutes later the engine was stalling and kicking again, and soon they were once more on the ice. This time the ignition had to be overhauled. A bitter wind had arisen, and the temperature was thirty degrees below zero. Eielson worked on with four of his finger-tips frozen solid, a misfortune which involved amputation later on at Barrow. An hour's painful work produced a steady, reassuring roar from the engine, but by this time it was snowing, and the surface had become so sticky that at the first attempt they could not rise. However, by following their tracks they managed to get greater speed on the second attempt, and unstuck from the ice on the very brink of a bad patch of ridges.

The forced landings and lengthy delays had used up a great deal of petrol, and it was now doubtful whether enough fuel remained to carry them back to Barrow. But there was nothing to do but to push on, and by 9 P.M. they had crossed a particularly dangerous area, where a forced landing might have been fatal. Then, quite suddenly, the engine cut out completely. They could feel the sag of the falling 'plane. Eielson steadied the machine into an easy glide, but near the ground the 'plane swerved, pitched, and then plunged into the swirling snowdrift. The 'plane struck a pressure-ridge, bounced, and then landed. It still rested on the skis, but they had been twisted, and the stanchions were broken. The explorers were stranded on the Arctic Ocean with no hope of flying back to their base.

Since it was dusky, and the snowdrift was too thick to permit closer examination, the aviators climbed back into the cabin and made themselves comfortable for the night. As a forlorn hope they sent out the following message from their wireless installation: "Went out 550 miles. Landed out of gas 65 miles N.W. of Barrow." Apparently the apparatus had been damaged in the crash, for this message was never received. On the following morning they ascertained that they were drifting to the north-east at a speed of five or six miles an hour, so that now they were about 100 miles north-east of Barrow, and steadily receding from their base. For emergency supplies they had ten pounds of biscuit, twenty pounds of chocolate, five pounds of Army rations, and about three pounds of mixed food-stuffs. Fuel-shortage was the greatest danger. By draining the five tanks they collected about half a gallon of petrol; in order to save this, they improvised an oil-burner with a gallon-can, and in this they burned engine-lubricating oil, using two slats of wood from the cabin-roof as wicks.

For four days they were unable to move owing to a blizzard, and they passed the time making sleds with parts of the 'plane. Then off they started for a trading-post at Beechey Point, 100 miles away, dragging their improvised sleds. Eielson's frozen hands were now giving much trouble, and this meant that Wilkins had to do practically all the work in connexion with building the snow-houses in which they spent their nights. For the next five days they made slow progress over rough pack-ice, and when at last they reached land-locked ice, they found that it was easier to abandon the sleds and carry their loads, Indian fashion, on their backs.

Progress was more rapid now, although at times they were halted by leads of water or thin ice, where they had to crawl along, sometimes on all fours. On two occasions, when Wilkins was attempting to cross thin ice, he went through into the water. At one place soft snow had fallen and hidden the character of the ice. Wilkins had almost crossed a doubtful patch when the ice beneath him gave way, and he went into the water up to his waist. Eielson stood transfixed with horror. Wilkins flung out his ice-pick, and by throwing his weight on his arms, he found that he could draw his feet out, and he rolled over and over to the thicker ice where his companion stood.

Wilkins's clothing was soaking wet. The outside of his clothes froze almost immediately, and his feet and legs were slowly stiffening. The men grabbed their packs and hurried away to take shelter beside some rough ice. Then Eielson pulled off the frozen boots and socks, which stood up stiff and solid as he threw them aside. As quickly as possible Wilkins put on dry foot gear and then marched for two hours without stopping, so as to give his fur clothes a chance to dry.

Undoubtedly the explorers would not have risked such accidents in normal circumstances, but it was increasingly evident that Eielson's fingers required immediate attention. So they plodded along, and on the eighteenth day after landing on the ice, they sighted the low tundra of the Arctic coast-line, and dimly, away to the east, they could see the trading-settlement for which they were making. Three hours later they were eating their first hot meal for a fortnight, and an Eskimo was speeding away with his dog-team to fetch help from the base at Barrow.

One morning, when he was sitting at the window of his hotel in San Francisco meditating how to sell the aeroplanes he had used on his previous Arctic expeditions, Wilkins suddenly had a fleeting glimpse of the most efficient-looking monoplane he had ever seen. It was beautifully streamlined, there were no flying wires, no controls exposed, nothing but a flying wing. In a flash Wilkins realized that here was a 'plane which could carry him to the successful culmination of his dream of a flight right across the Arctic Ocean. Wilkins promptly 'phoned to all the neighbouring flying-fields, but none of them could give him any information about his wonder 'plane. Then he began to tour round the flying-fields, and at last he saw the monoplane on the ground. It was the first *Lockheed Vega*. Arriving at Los Angeles, Wilkins went to the small factory and was soon busy making plans to have a similar machine for a new expedition.

Once again he arranged that Eielson should be the pilot,

but this time diminished funds meant that he had to be his own mechanic, business-manager, and news-correspondent. Carefully he watched over the making of the 'plane, and suggested various modifications which would make it suitable for Arctic flying. Then came the tedious period of test-flights; at last all was ready, and the 'plane went north to Barrow.

The course Wilkins proposed to follow was from Barrow across the unexplored Arctic Ocean to the north of Grant Land, and then across to the north-west corner of Spits-bergen. With considerable difficulty a run-way was made through the snow, and everything was prepared for the great flight. At the first effort the 'plane bounced off the end of the run-way and damaged one of the metal skis. New wooden skis were fitted, and once again they tried to get off in the heavily loaded machine. The run-way was length-ended but even then they had not risen when they reached the end, and on they went, careering over the bumpy, snow-covered tundra. Wilkins then decided to harness dog-teams to the aeroplane and haul it to a near-by lagoon, where it was possible to get a very long run-way.

At last, late in the morning of April 15, 1928, all was ready again; and this time, although the tail-planes swayed into one side of the snow-banked run-way, they managed to take the air. For the first hour or so Wilkins was very busy arranging things in the cabin, for as usual he had taken ample stores and equipment in case they should be forced down on the ice and have to walk back to civilization. From time to time he took observations or made notes about the condition of the ice. The two men saw no indications of new land throughout the whole of the flight; for hundreds of miles they flew over floes, ridged ice, and pack-ice. Then they ran into a belt of clouds, but Eielson cleverly sought out the lanes between the clouds, without deviating too far from the plotted course. After about twelve hours' flying, as they ploughed through the clouds, Eielson suddenly shouted and away to the right they glimpsed the rugged mountain-tops of Grant Land. Hereabouts there was a storm, and Wilkins asked the pilot whether he would prefer to land there or to fly on to Spitsbergen—with the possibility that they would never find the island. Eielson replied, "I'm willing to go on and chance it."

They had now been thirteen hours in the air, and below them they could see Peary's celebrated *Big Lead*, which stretched away to disappear in the distant haze. For two hundred miles after they had left Greenland behind the weather was good. Then they could see before them high, curling rain-clouds. Just before they entered the clouds Wilkins was able to take a sun-observation, which showed that they were now approximately two hundred miles northwest of Spitsbergen. By this time they had enough petrol to last them for only four more hours, and they had to make a landing. Southward the clouds seemed lower, and having turned in that direction, they soon caught sight of two sharp, needle-pointed peaks. Down they swooped, in an effort to find their position. The air was very bumpy, and since the 'plane was now light she bucked like a broncho. Like a flash they swept past a patch of smooth, snow-covered land, and then dead ahead they saw a mountain looming up. Eielson swerved adroitly, and they stood out to sea again. The machine went back into the whirling drift, only to be faced again by steep mountains; there was no choice left but to try to locate the small plain again. They swooped about this way and that, until at last they reached the spot again, and down came the 'plane into the whirling snow.

Once on the ground, they could see no more than a few feet on either side. Wilkins jumped out and emptied the oil-tanks, so that they should not freeze; then he and Eielson stamped snow about the skis so that the 'plane would be prevented from turning turtle in the hurricane. Wearily they climbed back into the cabin, realizing that they had triumphantly crossed 2200 miles of frozen seas and reached Spitsbergen; but they also realized that the adventure was not over yet. As far as they had been able to gather, they were on a small island, which according to their calculations ought to be somewhere near King's Bay. But there was no island shown on their chart, and so until the sun shone again, they would have no idea where they were exactly, or in which direction to walk or fly to the nearest houses.

On the next day they plodded through deep snow and surveyed their immediate surroundings, without getting any very definite clue. An observation of the sun showed that they were somewhere on the west coast of Spitsbergen, and between the settlements at King's Bay and Green Harbour. If they could find enough petrol for an hour's flying, they were reasonably certain of reaching some habitation. On the next day they carefully measured their petrol into a can; they got five gallons from each of the wing-tanks, and this meant that if they had any trouble in taking off that there was scarcely enough to take them into the air.

They still had a hope that there would be some left in the cabin-tanks. Warily they placed the can beneath, and Wilkins pulled the rip-cord. A full stream of petrol came flowing out, and the five gallon can was soon filled. Now came a problem; they only had one can, and every drop of petrol was precious. Some soft obstruction was needed to block up the pipe. Wilkins tore off his mitten and shoved his palm against the pipe; the petrol ran down his shirt-sleeve, and by evaporating, decreased the temperature still further, so that before Eielson could empty the can and bring it back, Wilkins was suffering agonies from frost-bite. Still, it was worth it, since altogether they collected twenty gallons, and that would take them to anywhere in Spitsbergen.

For five days the weather was so bad that they had no chance to move. Then, in the afternoon of Saturday, April 22, the storm ceased, and the two explorers spent six hours shovelling snowdrifts to clear the machine and prepare a hundred foot run-way. The oil was heated up, and every-thing made ready for a start. But now the machine was so light that, in spite of a downhill run-way, they could not get her to budge. Wilkins climbed out and gave the tail a push. Then the 'plane began to move, but it was no easy task jumping into the moving machine. Actually this diffi-culty had been foreseen, and they had started out with a special block and tackle which could be operated from the cabin. Unfortunately this tackle had been stolen at Fairbanks, and they had brought with them a rope ladder in its place.

Wilkins once more pushed on the tail, and as she started, he clung to the step and tried to climb in, but soon fell off again. The pilot, unable to see what was happening, took off, circled round, and seeing his companion forlorn on the ice, landed. When the 'plane took off again, Wilkins tried to use the rope ladder. They started again, and as the machine gathered speed, Wilkins clambered on to the tail and struggled desperately to reach the cockpit. He had thrown off his mittens in order to get a good grip of the rope, but his hands were soon so numbed that he had to hang on to the rope with his teeth. Just before the 'plane left the ground, Wilkins realized that he could not reach the cockpit, and he slithered off the fuselage into a deep bank of snow. The tail struck him and left him half stunned. So once more Eielson circled round, to find Wilkins alone on the run-way, and had to land again. By this time about half the remainder of the petrol had been used up, and it began to look as if one of the men would have to walk to civilization after all. Then they had a third attempt. This time Wilkins hooked one leg in the cockpit-opening, and with his foot against the fuselage, pushed with all his might on a log of driftwood placed in position to act as a lever. Then suddenly, with a slight lurch, the 'plane swung free. Wilkins dropped the log and fell headlong into the cabin. Hardly had he had time to collect his wits when Eielson shouted, "What's that over in the bay to the left?"

Wilkins peered out, and away in the distance he could see two tall wireless masts and a group of houses. This must be Green Harbour, he decided. They crossed over about five miles of open water, and then planed down, close to the feet of the wireless-masts. The flight from Alaska to a town in Spitsbergen was safely accomplished at last.

THE CONQUEST OF THE NORTH-WEST PASSAGE

One day, in the summer of 1900, a nervous young man was ushered into the presence of a famous Professor, who was at that time the greatest authority on terrestrial magnetism. The young man was Roald Amundsen, a budding explorer, who had recently returned from a voyage to the Antarctic. At first the Professor was only mildly interested in his visitor, but when Amundsen announced that it was his ambition to sail through the north-west passage and locate the North Magnetic Pole, the great Professor became keenly enthusiastic. "Young man," he said, "if you do that, you will be the benefactor of mankind for ages to come. *That* is the great adventure."

However, it was not until three years later that the young explorer was able to find enough supporters to fit out a small fishing-smack of forty-seven tons, the *Gjöa*, for his expedition. Indeed, even at the last moment, it seemed probable that the ship would never leave the wharf at Christiania, for one truculent creditor was demanding payment within twenty-four hours for goods supplied. Therefore, at midnight on June 16, 1903, in the midst of a deluge of rain, Amundsen and his six fellow 'conspirators' cast off the hawsers and sailed for the Arctic Ocean.

A month's battling through pack-ice and fog brought them to Godhavn, on the west coast of Greenland, and thence they passed through the dreaded Melville Bay to Dalrymple Rock, in northern Greenland. Here they picked up supplies, which had been left there by a Scottish whaler. By this time the *Gjöa* was so overloaded that she looked like a floating pantechnicon. The hold could not contain all the barrels and cases, and the deck was littered with high piles of boxes. Although this meant that the quarters were very cramped, Amundsen did not wish to run out of supplies on what might be a five years' battle with the frozen north.

Fog and sleet hindered progress at the start, and before they reached Beechy Island, where they proposed to make magnetic observations, the *Gjöa* grounded on a low island; fortunately she floated off undamaged. The voyage from Beechy Island to their wintering-base at Gjöahavn, King William Land, was full of perilous adventures.

One evening, when Amundsen was quietly writing in his journal, he was startled by a terrific shout. In a moment he had rushed on deck, where he saw thick clouds of smoke

247

belching through the engine-room skylight; the engine-room was ablaze. Moreover, close to the fire were several tanks holding more than 2000 gallons of petrol. The situation was critical; if the fire reached the tanks there would be a terrific explosion, and the survivors would be shipwrecked in the icy wastes, with a long winter facing them.

The ship's engineer bravely stuck to his post, and the others began pumping water for their lives. The fire was quickly extinguished, and then they discovered that one tank had actually been affected by the fire. By a lucky chance, however, a few hours before it had been noticed that this particular tank was leaking. Amundsen had ordered that the tank should be emptied, and it was the prompt attention to duty of Ristvedt, the first engineer, which had saved them from a frightful catastrophe.

Shortly afterwards the *Gjöa* ran aground on a large submerged reef, which ramified in all directions and held the ship in a grip of iron. In order to lighten the vessel, twenty-five cases of supplies were thrown overboard. Night fell; high tide came and went, but still the *Gjöa* held fast. At daybreak a gale was blowing, and Amundsen ordered that the boats should be made ready to abandon ship.

Then desperate measures were tried. The sails were set, and they began to bump their way along over the rocks, half afloat, half ashore, and every moment expecting a jagged spur to rip through the keel. Then the first mate suggested that the remainder of the deck-cargo should be sacrificed. The cases were heaved overboard; the ship was lifted up high by a gust, and then flung bodily on to the rocks again. Then, with a last shattering crash, the *Gjöa* made her supreme effort and slid off into deep waters.

Even then their battle was not won. For the next five days it blew a gale, and there was an imminent danger that the anchors would drag and that the ship would be driven ashore. At last, however, the gale moderated, and the little fishing-smack sailed into a natural harbour, which was to be her anchorage for two winters and a summer.

For the next month they worked hard, building observatories, huts, and kennels, and then settled down for the winter. Before long the *Gjöa* was beautifully decorated with icicles, and the ice in the bay had frozen twelve feet thick. The explorers had shot a number of reindeer and spent some time trying to cure the skins. One day reindeer were reported on a near-by hillside, and preparations for a hunt began. Then Hansen began to laugh. "I am not going to shoot that sort of reindeer," he chuckled, "they walk on two legs."

So they made their first contact with the Eskimos, and in the year which followed they were to be valuable allies. The natives laughed heartily at Amundsen's skin-curing methods, and soon returned with a number of fine dressed skins which they were prepared to barter for a sewing-needle each. Amundsen made an intensive study of the Eskimo mode of life, and he could soon erect igloos with the dexterity of an expert. The Eskimos were anxious to barter large quantities of surplus furs for hunting-knives or scrap-iron. Indeed, when the time for departing drew near, Amundsen found that there was so much rivalry for their huge dump of empty tins that he had to organize a sort of 'gold-rush.' The women were ranged round the heap in a circle, and then at a given signal they rushed in to grab their bargains. When the heap was reached, a jostling 'scrum' was formed, and the women soon proved adept at 'heeling' and throwing the tins through their legs to the men folk standing behind them, like so many scrum-halves! It must have been a hilarious sight, and there was no referee to spoil the fun by whistling for infringements!

The Eskimos were also useful helpers on the many sledge-trips which were made from Gjöahavn. Many blanks on the map of northernmost Canada were filled in, and important magnetic observations were completed.

At last, in July, 1905, the time came to continue the voyage in search of a north-west passage. This search had begun with the Cabots and Frobisher, and had lured many a brave man to an icy grave. On one of the trips from the base Hansen had found two skeletons, which were a grim reminder of the tragedy which had overtaken Franklin's expedition sixty years before. Now the Norwegian flag was hoisted at the mast-head, and the battle with the ice-floes was on again.

There were many shallows, and it was necessary to creep along, using the lead continually. More than once the explorers were in danger of being held up by drifting ice. At one place, where they were delayed by fog, friendly Eskimos came out in *kayaks*, and provisions of reindeer and salmon were obtained. In the shallow sounds, which cut off Wollaston Land and Bank's Land from Canada, they had many narrow escapes. They frequently bumped over rocky reefs, and Amundsen said it was like sailing through a ploughed field! The water was so shallow that a boat had to be lowered to take soundings ahead, so that the *Gjöa* could follow with some chance of safety. Once, in Simpson Strait, they had just one inch of water to spare beneath the keel. But seventeen days of almost continuous toil brought them to the farthermost point ever reached by a ship from the western end of the passage.

On the morning of August 26 Amundsen was roused from sleep by sounds of excitement on deck, and a moment afterwards Hansen rushed into the cabin. "Vessel in sight, sir!" he shouted; and sure enough, away in the west, could be seen the dim outlines of an American whaling-ship. "All doubts of our success in making the north-west passage were at an end," wrote Amundsen. "Victory was ours!"

Before very long, Captain James McKenna of the whaling-ship was congratulating Amundsen on his magnificent success. But the jubilations which followed were not the end of the adventure. As the *Gjöa* slowly nosed her way along, the ice became thicker, and within a week she was held up off King Point. Here they had to winter, for the third time, near the winter quarters of the American whaling-fleet, a dozen units of which had been trapped along with the *Gjöa*. It is an interesting sidelight on the adequate preparations which Amundsen had made for his expedition to read that he was actually able to give over a ton of flour to the whalers, who were on short rations.

During the winter Amundsen accompanied the captain of one of the whalers on a sledging-trip to the nearest telegraph-office, at Eagle City, in Alaska. This involved a journey of 500 miles and the crossing of a little-known range of mountains, 9000 feet high. The captain was short and fat, and since he objected to pemmican, they had to take a number of heavy sacks of cooked beans. Since he paid the expenses, he expected to be treated as commander, and while Amundsen and an Eskimo broke the trail, he was pulled along on a sledge. The inadequate food-supplies (beans are a poor substitute for pemmican) soon began to tell, and eventually Amundsen flatly refused to continue unless the captain agreed to more meals a day. Since the latter had no idea how to manage a dog-team, he had to give way; and so they reached Eagle City, where Amundsen at once received his due as a triumphant explorer.

In the following July the ice had broken sufficiently to allow the *Gjöa* to proceed. Even then fog and drifting floes were a constant hindrance. Then the propeller struck a submerged reef, and the men had to rely on sails alone; this involved the danger of becoming becalmed and freezing into the ice. All sails were set, and the *Gjöa* battered her way along until at last she reached open water.

On the last day of August, 1906, the *Gjöa*'s gaff was smashed, and she dropped anchor off Nome. A launch promptly appeared and took Amundsen and Hansen ashore. Deeply moved, they heard the strains of the Norwegian national anthem; and then they knew that they were faced with a dreaded 'reception fit for heroes.'

STEFANSSON'S ARCTIC EXPLORATIONS

The tragic stories of Hudson, Franklin, and of many more northern explorers have led many people to imagine that all Arctic lands are covered with eternal ice, like the Greenland ice-cap; that the winter is depressingly dark and intensely cold; and that the country is a lifeless waste of eternal silence. It has been one of the main objects of Vilhjalmur Stefansson to dispel this gloomy picture. In the introductory chapters of his book, *The Friendly Arctic*, he shows that the minimum temperatures for the heart of Montana are actually lower than those experienced in the vicinity of the North Pole. During the Arctic summer, temperatures of 90 degrees in the shade are not unknown. Then, too, the general conception of a 'lifeless waste' is incorrect. The Arctic grasslands support herds of caribou and musk-oxen, numbering sometimes hundreds of thousands in a single band. Banks Island, for example, in the summer is white with millions of geese and resplendent with beautiful Arctic flowers.

Five years (1908–1912) spent among the Eskimos of the northern coasts of America taught Stefansson how to live happily in the Arctic. The secret was to adopt the old maxim, "When in Rome, do as the Romans do." He learned the Eskimo language and lived the life of the Eskimo—the only mode of life which is practicable for continuous existence in the Arctic. The startling originality of his methods of 'living off the country' has brought a rich reward: he has completed a number of exploratory journeys which had been condemned as 'impossible' or 'suicidal'; he has learned many things about the flora and fauna of the Arctic; and he has discovered, among other interesting things, a tribe of blond Eskimos. During the important expedition of 1913–1918 his obituary was actually published; but to everybody's surprise he returned safely, having explored 100,000 square miles of the Beaufort Sea and the Arctic Ocean. He had also added three large and several small islands to the maps of the region north of Melville Island.

The expedition was organized for the Canadian Government. At Nome, in Alaska, three ships, the *Karluk*, the *Mary Sachs*, and the *Alaska*, were fitted out with an elaborate equipment of stores and scientific instruments. Stefansson sailed in the *Karluk*, which was the largest of the fleet. The first objective was Herschel Island, which is a little to the east of the boundary-line between Alaska and Canada.

Unfortunately the *Karluk*, which followed a course twenty miles off shore, was trapped in the sea-ice and began to drift backward towards Point Barrow. Off the mouth of the Colville River the *Karluk* came to rest, firmly beset, about ten miles offshore. Since there was a hunting-ground on the mainland, Stefansson decided to set out across the ice on a week's hunting-trip. His party was lightly equipped and consisted of four white men and two Eskimos.

The next day they reached a small island four miles off the coast. Beyond that point the sea-ice was rotten, and a camp had to be made. The next morning brought an ominous change in the weather; a fierce gale sprang up, and the sea-ice was soon adrift. For most of the time the *Karluk* was hidden by snow-squalls and drifting clouds of mist; then, to Stefansson's amazement, he saw the ship slowly begin to move eastward. For three days the hunting-party was marooned on the little island, and when the weather finally cleared, the *Karluk* had disappeared.

When he had reached the mainland, Stefansson began to sledge along the coast in search of information about his other two ships. He found that a number of whaling-boats had been frozen in, and one of them had been wrecked. As for the *Alaska* and the *Mary Sachs*, they were both safe at Collinson Point.

Then the news of the *Karluk* began to come in. The ship had drifted steadily westward with the ice and had been sighted ten miles off Point Barrow. At this time Stefansson was not particularly anxious about the misadventure, because he had no doubt that in the event of shipwreck the crew, led by Captain Bartlett, Peary's companion, would be able to reach the inhabited coasts of Alaska or Siberia.

Eventually Stefansson joined the other boats at Collinson Point, where he arranged a modified programme for the remaining ships. The necessary extra supplies were obtained from the whalers or from Canada overland, and a comprehensive survey of the delta of the Mackenzie river was undertaken. One important result of this scheme was that a practicable route for steamships was discovered.

Stefansson himself proposed to make a trip across the sea-ice to the unexplored regions of the Beaufort Sea. His plans were so unorthodox that he was accused of being a 'crazy theorist,' and his two companions were described as 'deluded.' Dr Anderson, the second-in-command, went so far as to refuse any assistance; and indeed, adopting the attitude that Stefansson was only in charge of the lost *Karluk*, he accused the explorer of wasting Government money on a mere 'stunt' which was bound to end in tragedy. After a great deal of argument and difficulty, Stefansson managed to get enough equipment to make a start.

Contrary to the expressed opinion of all previous Arctic explorers, whalers, and even Eskimos, Stefansson believed that it was possible to live on the ice without taking enough food-supplies to ensure a safe return to his base. The Eskimos said that there were no seals ten miles away from land; Nansen and Peary had been of the opinion that all food-supplies would have to be carried on the sledges, and would have to be carefully rationed to last out; but Stefansson argued that marine science had shown that there is always plenty of life in cold sea-water, and that if there are fish there must be seals. If he found land he was confident that he would find caribou or polar oxen or polar bears enough to keep him well supplied.

So the 'madman' set off with two companions, Storkerson and Andeasen, six dogs, and enough food in the sledges to last only thirty days, to try out his original theory of living out of the so-called Arctic waste. Stefansson was adept at the difficult art of seal-hunting, and his prowess with the rifle meant that, unlike Peary, they were always able to keep warm in camp, because they had abundant supplies of blubber. He had also taken the trouble to learn how to build a snow-house on the Eskimo pattern. The igloo has many obvious advantages over the usual silk tents, and an experienced team can construct one in about an hour. The snow-blocks are built up spirally, the walls being inclined at an angle so that they meet at the top of the dome. Stefansson always built his snow-houses on a bank, and the entrance was so excavated that it entered the house at floor-level. This meant that the warm air inside the house could not escape, except out of the ventilation-hole in the roof. Once the house is completed, a stove is lighted, and the walls begin to melt; then the stove or fire is put out, and the water on the walls freezes into a firm layer of ice. After this treatment the house is so strong that it will support the weight of

three or four men. The snow-houses were so snug that
Stefansson and his party always undressed before they got
into their sleeping-bags.

Stefansson's originality was not confined to houses or
food-supplies. He had formed the opinion that the Eskimo
dog is not the ideal type it is so often assumed to be. His
six dogs were half St Bernard and half Eskimo. They were,
of course, larger and stronger than the usual type; they
would require more food—but here again the explorer was
confident that there would be no shortage. His theories
about transport were vindicated, since he kept all his dogs
in good condition for years on end.

The journey over the ice was full of adventures. There
were bad gales which split the ice and caused wide leads or
created terrible pressure-ridges, which threatened to overwhelm the camp. Occasionally a polar bear would wander
into camp, being attracted by the smell of the seal-meat.
After they had travelled about 100 miles there came a
crucial time when it seemed that the great experiment was
doomed to failure. For days on end they saw no signs of life.
It almost seemed that the Eskimo prophecy was coming
true. Stefansson, however, came to the conclusion that they
had been unlucky enough to strike an 'ice-desert'—*i.e.*, a
region where the ice is so thick that it is impossible for seals
to find breathing-holes. He was confident that once they
reached broken ice again they would find food. So they
'crossed the Rubicon,' and instead of turning back to the
coast of Alaska, as everybody said they would have to do,
they struck eastward towards Banks Island.

Five weeks after they had left the coast they were camped
on the edge of a wide lead when Stefansson caught sight of
a seal. The seal was so far away from firm ice that it was
impossible to catch it; but here was proof that his theory
was sensible. Food-supplies by this time were very low—
partly because Stefansson was so confident in his theories
that the men and the dogs had been eating their fill almost
the whole of the time since they started. Now that they were
obliged to feed the dogs on bedding and skin-boots had
come the crucial test. During the next few days several

seals were seen, but the two which they shot promptly sank. This was both disconcerting and unusual. A seal will usually float, except in the summer time, when melting snow causes the salinity of the water to become less. Two more days passed before Stefansson shot a seal which floated. Storkerson was delighted. "It floats," he yelled. He knew now that the faith he had reposed in his leader was well-founded.

Now that they had passed out of the confines of the 'ice-desert' they found increasing signs of life. Seals were so abundant that instead of starving, as the Eskimos said they would, they were living in comfort, and they actually suffered indigestion from over-eating! The solution of the problem of supplies of food and fuel (the seal provides almost all the elements for living in the Arctic) did not end their struggles, however. They were still adrift on ice-floes in the middle of the ocean. By swathing a sledge in a tarpaulin Stefansson made a sled-boat, which was a satisfactory method of crossing narrow, open leads. But when they were still many miles away from Banks Island, the explorers reached a lead which was many miles wide; for several days they were marooned on an island of ice and drifted westward. They were not short of food-supplies, but they did not relish the prospect of spending a whole year on their floating home.

Polar bears were frequent visitors; while the men were encamped on the floe, no less than five bears strolled into camp. The second brute made a dramatic interlude. The six dogs were tied near the tent, while the men were about a quarter of a mile away. Storkerson, who was in the sled-boat paddling along a lead, suddenly spotted a bear about a hundred yards away from the dogs, steadily advancing. The bear had not been seen by the dogs. It slunk behind an ice-hummock, and then, with legs bent, began to slide forward. Just as the bear was making ready for a final dash over the last twenty yards, Stefansson, who had come running to the rescue, managed to hit it with a lucky shot. The bear sank to the ice, and Stefansson took up a position between it and the open water. The bear, however, was not dead and suddenly launched forward. Stefansson

256

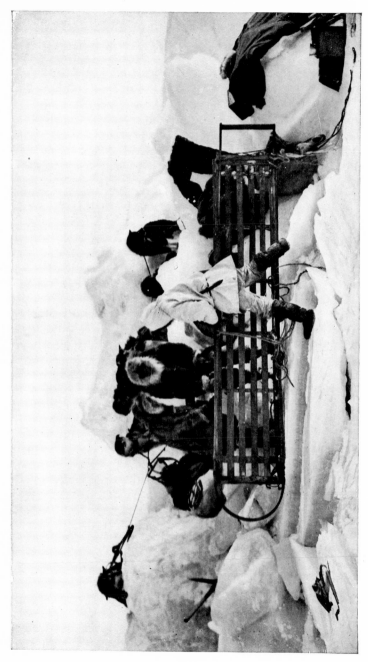

STEFANSSON REPAIRING A BROKEN SLED

From Stefansson's "The Friendly Arctic" (Macmillan & Co.). By courtesy of the author

256

luckily had his finger on the trigger, and he shot the brute through the brain when it was only two yards away.

Some days later the lead began to close, and at last it was possible to ferry the party across on to fast ice in the sled-boat. After drifting for ninety-three days on the ice, the party safely reached the western coast of Banks Island. Here they had hoped to be picked up by the *Northern Star*—a vessel which Stefansson had chartered to replace the *Karluk* —but it was not in evidence. Actually Anderson and the remaining members of the expedition had been so convinced of the folly of the ice-trip that the whole party had been presumed dead for some time. Stefansson, however, soon found plenty of geese and caribou. He also found a new island, which was given the name of Bernard Island, and then he made the first trip into the interior of Banks Island. Here there were beautiful meadows, and plenty of fuel in the shape of a special kind of heather. So the three adventurers spent summer in comparative ease and comfort.

When all hopes of the *Northern Star* had been given up, it was decided to journey towards the southern end of Banks Island. Stefansson always led the way, hunting for caribou. When they had almost reached the southern end of the island, Stefansson one day came across fresh footprints. Four miles farther on he saw the tips of two masts, and then, when he got a clear view of the beach, he was amazed to see the *Mary Sachs* pulled up on the beach, and a camp close by. Captain Bernard, her commander, took no notice of the approaching explorer, because he thought it was one of his own crew returning from a hunting-trip. Then came a sudden shout from one of the men: "Stefansson is alive! He's here!"

The crew of the *Sachs* could hardly believe their eyes. So sure had Anderson been that Stefansson's party had per-ished that he had ordered the *Northern Star* to go south. Captain Bernard, of the *Sachs*, had gone to Banks Island believing that he was carrying out the orders of a leader who must have died months before. There was great jubilation in the camp that night.

Captain Bernard had met with misfortune on his way northward. The *Sachs* was not really fitted for travelling among rough ice-floes, and one of her propellers had struck an ice-cake and was broken off. She was, moreover, leaking so badly that the crew had been obliged to haul the boat ashore and prepare to spend the winter on the island. The finding of the *Sachs* meant for Stefansson that he could renew his supplies of ammunition and equipment, and would be able to continue his explorations to the north in the following season. During the winter the whole party never ran short of food; plenty of caribou meat was available, and they were lucky enough to find a stranded whale-carcass. Besides providing plenty of oil and dog-meat, this carcass also served as a bait for wolves and polar bears. Some of the men managed to collect a fine store of pelts.

In the spring of 1915, Stefansson made another ice-trip as far as Prince Patrick Island. This island had been partly explored by McClintock, and at the northern end of the island Stefansson found a document left by McClintock when he was searching for Franklin sixty-two years before. Having completed as far as possible the survey of the western coast of the island, Stefansson sledged northward beyond McClintock's farthest point. A few days later a discovery of first-class importance was made. From one of the small reefs which they discovered, Storkerson spied a big new land some miles away to the north-east. Ultimately this was explored and found to consist of two new islands (called Borden Island and Brock Island). When they reached the shores of the new land they found plentiful traces of lemmings and caribou, and fifty miles away could see a chain of mountains. Stefansson took possession of the land in the name of the King.

Unfortunately the lateness of the season made it impossible to make a complete exploration, and the party returned to their base *via* Melville Island and made the first crossing of Banks Island from north to south.

Soon after the party had safely reached the crew of the *Sachs* again, a ship called the *Polar Bear* was sighted. A little later the crew of the *Polar Bear* were expressing their astonishment that Stefansson's party were actually alive and well. Incidentally they made casual references to the War. "What war?" asked Stefansson.

There was a chorus of replies, which informed the explorer that since he had been away from civilization the greatest war in all history had been raging for the last year. Captain Lane, of the *Polar Bear*, also brought sad news of the *Karluk*.

Soon after Stefansson had left the *Karluk* a gale sprang up, and the ship began to drift. Three months later she landed up against the Siberian shore-ice, far to the west of Point Barrow. Sleds were made, and canoes and provisions were placed on the ice. The men also attempted to make deer-skin clothes, but without much success. A few days later Wrangel Island was sighted. There were plenty of seals about, and there was no shortage of fresh meat.

On January 10, 1914, came the last fatal 'squeeze'; there was a loud cracking of timbers, the ship heeled to starboard, and water began to pour into the engine-room. On the ice two large houses were built out of boxes of bread, sacks of coal, and sails, and here the whole party lived until 'Shipwreck Camp' was deserted some weeks later.

The next day the *Karluk* sank, and preparations were hurried along for the fifty-mile march to Wrangel Island. Captain Bartlett ordered a line of depôts to be established in the direction of the shore at distances of a day's travel apart. The mate went off with a party to form a base, and to build a house on Wrangel Island for the remainder. Several days later some of his men returned with the news that the mate had been held up by a lead three miles wide. He had lost all his dogs, and one of his men had badly frozen feet. The following day the ship's doctor and a band of friends decided to go landward on their own account. They had no desire to spend the winter on Wrangel Island as Bartlett proposed, and were planning to march all the way to St Petersburg.

A relief-party set out to assist the mate returned with the alarming news that he and his men had disappeared. The ice was adrift, and it is probable that the mate was carried away on a drifting floe. The relief-party also reported that the doctor and his companions were faring badly; one man had his hands and feet frozen solid. Nothing more was ever heard of the mate and the doctor and their men.

The remainder of the crew managed to reach Wrangel Island in safety. Hadley, one of the most resourceful of the men, rescued supplies of pemmican from 'Shipwreck Camp,' although on the way he was attacked by three polar bears on the same day. Then, on March 18, Captain Bartlett set off for the mainland with one Eskimo as a companion. The distance from Wrangel Island to the coast of Siberia is 110 miles. Since three of the men were injured, and there was still a chance that the mate and the doctor would arrive, he decided to leave the crew on the island.

He was held up from time to time by open leads, but he reached the mainland seventeen days later. His Eskimo companion was rather afraid that the people of Siberia would be hostile, but actually when they did come to a house, the people were very hospitable. Bartlett made his way eastward, and at the end of each day's travelling he was able to find a native house, where he was welcomed. Slowly he began to develop signs of nephritis—a disease caused by living on a diet of pemmican alone. Fortunately he managed to reach the house of a Russian trader where he met Baron Kleist, a Russian official. Bartlett was assisted to Alaska and sent a message to the Canadian Government explaining the plight of his men on Wrangel Island. Immediately rescue-operations were commenced.

Meanwhile, on Wrangel Island all had not been going well. One party which went off to look for the mate returned after falling through the ice, having lost everything with which they had started—dogs, sleds, guns and ammunition. The loss of the ammunition was serious, because the only chance of survival for the remainder was that the hunting should be successful. Before long several of the men developed nephritis, and some died. The men who preferred fresh seal-meat or bear-meat remained fit; but those who were prejudiced against 'blubber.' and lived on pemmican,

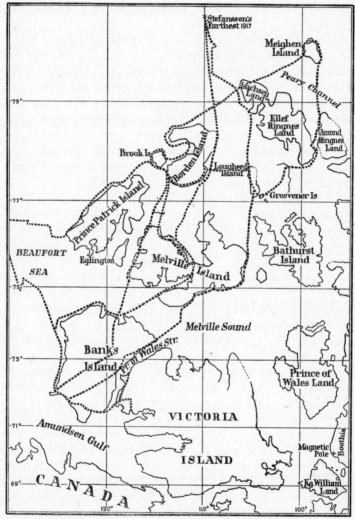

THE EXPLORATORY JOURNEYS OF STEFANSSON, 1914–1918

died. The summer of 1914 came and went, and the stricken crew were still marooned on the island because they had no boat. Then, on September 8, 1914, one of the Eskimos sang out, "I think I see a ship." It proved to be the *King and Winge*, of Seattle, and a few hours later the haggard

261

survivors of the *Karluk* were headed for Nome and comfort.

Although Stefansson was deeply saddened by this tragic story, the work of his expedition went on. A new ship was chartered, and a winter base set up on Victoria Island. Stefansson paid another visit to the blond Eskimos. The Eskimos attached to the expedition feared this tribe and tried to impress them by telling them that Stefansson was a magician. By a strange coincidence, shortly after some of the blond Eskimos had stolen some stores, the tribe was visited by an epidemic of colds. They were quite convinced thereafter of the efficacy of Stefansson's spells!

In January, 1916, the expedition started northward, up the coast of Banks Island, for the lands which had been seen on the previous trip. Crossing Melville Island, they reached Brock Island, and then followed the coast of the newly found Borden Island. An ice-trip into the unknown beyond the Ringnes Islands resulted in the discovery of Meighen Island. This island was the nearest approach to a barren land which they had so far seen. Even here, however, there were great flocks of geese.

On the way back to the base considerable alterations to the charts of King Christian Land were made. It was discovered that a large land called Findlay Island was mythical, and a third important island (Lougheed Island) was located. This land was forty-five miles long, and it had an average width of twelve miles. The country was rolling hills, well covered with vegetation, and there were plenty of caribou. The winter of 1916 was spent on Melville Island, and then in the next spring another journey to the new lands was undertaken. When Stefansson finally returned to civilization in the spring of 1918, he was suffering from the after-effects of an attack of typhoid fever. He had spent five and a half years continuously in the Arctic regions, and had conclusively shown that far from being a frozen waste, the Arctic is indeed 'friendly' to the explorer who has the courage and skill to adopt the Eskimo mode of life and live off the country.

CHAPTER XII

THE SUMMIT OF THE EARTH

While far below men crawl in clay and clod,
Sublimely I shall stand alone with God.

LEITCH, *The Summit, Mount Everest*

THE EARLY EVEREST EXPEDITIONS

A VISITOR to the famous Rongbuk monastery, which lies almost under the shadow of the highest peak in the world, might be shown some crude frescos painted by a holy lama. One particularly striking scene depicts the ice-demons of Mount Everest pushing a white man down off the mountain. The fresco is symbolical of the general attitude of the Tibetans to the numerous assaults which have been made on their holy mountains. For a long time after it had been discovered that Mount Everest was the highest mountain in the world (1852), the lamas of Tibet would not countenance any intrusion by white men into the 'Bird Country of the South,' as they call the region round Everest. They could not understand why any man should want to risk his life trying to climb the mountains, and they were reasonably sure that the gods of the snows would be so angry that some disaster would befall them.

However, in 1920 a representative of the Royal Geographical Society obtained permission for an expedition to enter Tibet and go to Everest. In the next year a reconnaissance party went out, and they succeeded in learning a great deal about the approach to the mountain. Mount Everest (29,002 feet) is capped by a triangular pyramid on the western end of the whole mountain. The southern slopes are not only terrifyingly steep, but since they are exposed to the full effect of the monsoon, they are usually covered with mighty ice-fields and precipitous glaciers, which are quite unclimbable. The northern slopes, which look towards the highlands of Tibet, are rather a different proposition. During the period which follows the monsoon, the west

263

winds from the highlands sweep down with hurricane force and scour the sides of the mountain, so that much of the snow is carried away. It is this factor alone which makes it possible to climb Mount Everest, since, although the slopes are very steep, the great variations in temperature make the ice and snow of such plastic consistency that they cling to the scarps at almost impossible angles, until the fierce drying winds of Tibet approach.

From the towering, final pyramid a mighty ridge runs down to the north-west at a steep angle, and this is practically unclimbable. In the opposite direction (north-east) there is another ridge which slopes at a much easier angle, and which leads down to a narrow neck of ice called the North Col, which can be reached *via* the glaciers sweeping down from the foot of Everest. Apart from the incidental difficulties due to the physical and psychological effects of high altitude and lack of oxygen, there are four major difficulties which confront those who would reach the final pinnacle. In the first place, having ascended the East Rongbuk glacier, the eastern slopes of the North Col must be climbed; here a way has to be found up a steep hill of ice some 1,200 feet high, which is seamed by crevasses and broken into terrible ice-cliffs. Secondly, above the North Col the strata have an outward and downward dip, something like the tiles on a sharply pointed roof; a slip here would mean a headlong plunge to the glacier 6000 feet below, and when there is any snow on this section, it is a veritable death-trap. Thirdly, if a way is sought *via* the north-east ridge, the main obstacles are two steps formed by the ends of two horizontal bands of dark-grey rock, which are so precipitous that they are probably unclimbable. The alternative is to make a traverse some hundreds of feet below the crest of the ridge. This will lead the climber to the fourth major obstacle—a gigantic snow couloir, or gulley, which sweeps down from the final pyramid almost to the foot of the mountain. The snow here is often something like castor-sugar, and it is hard to get a foothold in it. The passage of the couloir alone would be too difficult for any but the most determined and skilful mountaineers.

ICE-PINNACLES ON RONGBUK GLACIER

By permission of the Mount Everest Committee

The discoveries made by the reconnaissance party led to an expedition in 1922, led by General Bruce. The party included a number of proved climbers, and since some scientists were of the opinion that nobody could reach higher than 25,000 feet owing to the lack of oxygen in the attenuated air, a supply of oxygen-cylinders was taken. Everest was approached *via* the highlands of Tibet from Darjeeling, in India, and a base-camp was set up at the foot of the East Rongbuk glacier. Unlike most of the peaks in the Alps, it is not possible to climb a Himalayan mountain in the course of one or two days. It is necessary to establish a series of camps, each one some thousands of feet above the next; and altogether it may take weeks before any party has reached a point from which the final attack on the pyramid is possible in one day.

Thus Bruce's party had to place three camps on the East Rongbuk glacier, a fourth near the crest of the North Col, and a fifth on the north ridge, at a height of about 25,000 feet. From this point Mallory, Norton, and Somervell, without the help of oxygen, reached a point almost 27,000 feet high, and Finch and Bruce, using a heavy oxygen-apparatus, climbed 300 feet higher. In the first week of June the monsoon broke. The warm winds softened the snow slopes on the North Col, and a disastrous avalanche occurred, which resulted in the death of seven of the brave porters. A number of valuable lessons had been learned, however, since something had been learned about the need for acclimatization and about equipment and food-supplies.

Two years later came the third expedition. The oxygen-apparatus had been improved, and most of the climbers were already partly acclimatized. This time a series of accidents and misfortunes culminated in final tragedy, which was all the more heart-breaking because it came on the very eve of success. The leader, Bruce, was stricken with fever, and Norton had to carry on; then dysentery attacked one of the climbers. However, the base-camp was established with commendable speed, and before long Camp 3 at 21,000 feet, had been established. Then came a time of biting blizzards and very low temperatures, which strained the endurance of the Sherpa porters to breaking-point. A retreat had to be made to the base-camp for a short rest. Then, when the glacier-camps were once more occupied, Norton, Mallory, and Somervell had to undertake an exhausting rescue-expedition to fetch down four porters who had marooned themselves on the North Col. Again they had to retreat to the base-camp, and when they returned to the assault, after being blessed by the lama of the Rongbuk monastery, only fifteen of the porters could be persuaded to go to the high camps. After fighting their way against a terrible north-west hurricane, a Camp 5 was established at 25,200 feet. Beyond this point the porters refused to go.

On the next day Norton and Somervell reached the same place, and then Norton stood for four hours in the biting wind outside the porters' little tent, trying to persuade them to continue. Finally he succeeded, and so was established the first Camp 6, at 26,800 feet. On June 4 Norton and Somervell began an attack on the summit by traversing across the north face, keeping some 300 feet below the crest. Before long it became evident that Somervell had suffered in condition from his heroic exertions on the glacier, and he collapsed at 28,000 feet, near to the second 'step.' Norton had removed his snow-goggles so that he could see foot-holds better, and before long he began to suffer from snow-blindness. Nevertheless, with wonderful pluck he struggled on alone, although he was seeing double almost all the time. He passed beneath the second 'step' and crossed the couloir with its treacherous slippery snow, only to be brought to a halt by steeply sloping slabs at 28,100 feet. One slip here would have meant a headlong plunge to the main Rongbuk glacier 10,000 feet below. So Norton reached the 'highest ever,' and luckily both he and Somervell regained the North Col in safety.

Then followed the much-debated climb of Mallory and Irvine. Mallory was of the opinion that the best approach to the summit was to climb to the top of the ridge and then follow it along, trusting that he would be able to climb the two formidable 'steps.' This time oxygen was taken.

Mallory sent down a note to Odell, who was in support at Camp 5, which indicated that the weather was good and all was well. Then followed the tragedy. Nobody will ever know whether Mallory and Irvine actually reached the summit. Odell reported that as he was climbing from Camp 5 in support, he had just reached a little crag when there was a sudden clearing of the atmosphere above him, and the whole summit-ridge was unveiled. He noticed far away, on a snow-slope leading up to what appeared to be the last 'step' but one from the base of the final pyramid, a tiny object moving towards the 'step.' A second tiny dot appeared, and then the first climbed to the top of the 'step.' Then the curtain of cloud fell again. Odell was surprised to see the climbers at the second 'step' at such a late hour, and indeed it is probable that what he saw was not the actual climbers, but a kind of illusion caused by looking at the rocky steps across the snow. The 1933 expedition found an important clue, which seemed to throw some light on the mystery; but even now it is not certain whether the disaster occurred when they were approaching or returning from the summit.

When he realized that an accident had happened, Odell put up a marvellous performance in support. Twice he ascended alone to a height of 27,000 feet, and he visited Camp 6 to make quite sure that Mallory and Irvine had not returned. Then, numbed with the cold, and aware that a storm was approaching, he closed the little tent at Camp 6 and signalled the tragic news to his companions below.

For the next eight years the Tibetan authorities would not grant permission for another attempt. Some of the 'Everesters' went off to climb Kamet and Kanchenjunga. Then, in the summer of 1932, permission was granted, and Hugh Ruttledge organized the fourth Everest expedition. Most of the veterans were now too old to undertake a further ordeal on the mountain, but Ruttledge gathered together a wonderful team of climbers, including F. S. Smythe, Eric Shipton, and Captain Birnie, who had climbed Kamet; Wyn Harris, a Cambridge running 'blue,' who had twice ascended Mount Kenya; T. A. Brocklebank, who had stroked Cambridge to victory in three boat-races; and a number of other experienced stalwarts—a total of fourteen Britishers and about ninety porters. Many of the porters, who are such a vital factor in an Everest expedition, had already had experience of climbing in the Himalayas, and they were all Sherpas or Bhutias, members of the hardy mountain races who inhabit the borders of Nepal and Tibet. It was their wonderful efforts in carrying heavy loads at heights where each step forward makes a man pant with exhaustion that made it possible to establish camps in places 12,000 feet higher than the summit of Mont Blanc.

The 1933 expedition left Darjeeling in March and began the 350-mile march across Tibet to Everest. In each Tibetan province through which they passed they had to change their transport of yaks and local porters. Although a good deal of the equipment was lost during the march owing to pilfering, the members of the party managed to keep on good terms with the Tibetans, and even played football and boxing with the natives of Tinkye Dzong. On April 16, after marching for hours along a desolate valley, they suddenly rounded a corner and came in view of the Rongbuk monastery. On the next day a base-camp was set up, four miles away from the monastery, at a height of 16,800 feet. Then came the slow process of finding a way along the troughs in the glacier, and the establishment of three camps, which led to the base of the North Col. The climbers were slowly acclimatizing—a complicated business, which means that the heart must become accustomed to lack of oxygen and to exertion at high altitudes.

Then came the task of climbing the wall of ice leading to the North Col. Steps were cut in the ice to a point where there was a vertical wall 40 feet high. Smythe made a tremendous effort here. Supported by Shipton, with the head of an axe he hammered an ice-piton into the wall, as high up as he could reach. Then, having cut hand- and foot-holds, he managed to get one foot on the piton. His foot slipped, but he just saved himself by clinging to the slippery hand-hold. Smythe tried again, and this time he succeeded in cutting enough steps to plant a piton on the top of the wall. Then a rope ladder was hitched on to the piton, and henceforth the porters were able to use this staircase with some ease.

During the next few days there was a violent gale, and the Arctic tents shook furiously, as if anxious to free themselves from the stone ballast round the guy-ropes. Then preparations were made for establishing a Camp 5, well above the North Col, at about 25,700 feet. Camp 4, 3000 feet lower, was pitched in a spot on the lower side of a crevasse; above it towered the upper side of the crevasse, and below stretched a slippery ice-slope. Two steps to the right from the Arctic tent meant a plunge into the crevasse, and two steps to the left meant a fall down the ice-hill. All the water for drinking-purposes had to be obtained by melting chunks of ice over a Primus stove.

By a cleverly arranged system of relays, Camp 5 was provisioned; but on the afternoon of May 23 snow fell heavily, and on the next day the mountain was a terrible sight, with a howling gale throwing up clouds of spindrift across the North Col. Smythe, Shipton, and Birnie, who were at Camp 5, had to ride the storm out, and then on the next day had to retreat for a time, as food-supplies were running out. The wind on the north ridge is torturing; even goggles cannot protect the eyes from its acid sting, and fingers clasping an ice-axe have to be prised open and beaten to restore circulation. Panting lungs seem to be scoured by each icy breath, and the climber becomes no more than a plodding, semi-conscious automaton. Birnie nearly came to grief on the way down by trying a *glissade*; in a second he was flying head downward for a precipice, when one of the porters dived at him from behind a rock and pulled him into a patch of soft snow. Every one of the eight porters had been frost-bitten, and one of the famous 'tigers' lost two fingers.

A promise of fine weather on May 28 led to a renewal of the attack, and after a five hours' climb Camp 5 was re-occupied. On the next day Wyn Harris, Wager, and Longland, with eight 'tigers,' set off to make a Camp 6. They began the traverse along the north ridge, across downward-sloping slabs where only the friction of their boot-nails saved them from a sensational death. Here it was useless to use a rope, because if one man slipped he would pull down all the others. Above 27,000 feet the angle grew steeper, and it was necessary to seek a camp-site, as some of the porters were beginning to show signs of exhaustion. At last the party reached a snow-clogged ledge three feet wide, and here a tent was pitched. The floor sloped precariously, and about a quarter of the tent projected unsupported over the outward edge. But this three-foot platform was the only possible camp-site, and so Camp 6 it had to be. The height was 27,400 feet—that is, about 600 feet higher than any previous camp on the mountain.

Harris and Wager were left in possession, and Longland had the difficult task of piloting the tired porters down to safety on the North Col. They had just completed the traverse across the evil slabs of the face when down came one of the sudden, violent, unheralded storms which are such a menace on Everest. In a few seconds the screaming wind tore past, blotting out the landscape in blinding snow-sheets. Goggles were iced up, and when they were discarded, eye-lashes froze together so that it was difficult to see at all. Now began a desperate fight for life. Longland kept his head, collected his men in close order, and staggered on, peering for a glimpse of the ridge which would lead them to safety. They stumbled on the remains of Mallory's Camp 6, and then for a time Longland feared that he had missed the way. Painfully they scrambled along, leaning against the wind to keep their balance. So for two nightmare hours the fight went on, until at last over a little crag appeared the green tent of Camp 5. Longland by this time was a walking snowman. His face, his nose, and his beard were festooned with icicles. After a warm drink and a short rest, Longland went down to his post at Camp 4.

Meanwhile Harris and Wager, at Camp 6, were trying to sleep on the sloping ledge. At 5.40 A.M. the next morning they began their great effort to reach the summit. Traversing diagonally across the face of the north ridge, for the first hour they suffered severely from the intense cold. Then they made a dramatic discovery. At a place where the smooth brown slabs were inclined at an easy angle, but just above a steep drop, Harris suddenly saw an ice-axe. The name of the Swiss maker was still clearly stamped on the polished head.

There could be only two solutions of this mystery. The axe had belonged to either Mallory or Irvine. Since it is most unlikely that either would have abandoned his precious ice-axe from choice, it seems probable that hereabouts the unfortunate climbers began a fatal slip on the slabs. If Odell really saw Mallory and Irvine on the second 'step,' then the axe must have been dropped on the return-journey. So the problem whether they reached the summit will remain unsolved unless—who knows?—when Everest is finally conquered, some relic of one or the other is found planted on the topmost pinnacle.

Harris and Wager continued their horizontal traverse over snow-covered slabs and rounded the first step. Soon they were under the second step, and at once they realized that further progress along this line was going to be very difficult. The dark-grey precipice was so smooth that they could see no hand-holds. They tried to surmount a shallow scoop which looked like a gulley, but found it impossible to climb. Eventually they continued to traverse well below the ridge-crest, and cautiously climbed along until they rounded a a corner and looked on the great snow couloir which sweeps down from the pyramid.

The fifty feet of powdered snow which had to be crossed before the farther side of the couloir could be gained were the most sensational of the whole climb. The couloir ribboned precipitously below them—down, down, down to the main Rongbuk glacier, 10,000 feet below. Creeping carefully along, the two roped adventurers reached a point about 150 feet beyond the couloir. It was now past noon, and there still remained 1000 feet to the summit. The going above looked possible, provided that there was not much snow on the slabs. But to go farther at this late hour would be courting disaster, since they had to get back to Camp 5 before dark.

Reluctantly they turned back. This time they found an easier place to cross the couloir. They were both very tired, but Wager made a final effort to climb, and reached the summit of the ridge near the first 'step.' He is the only man who has ever looked down the terrifying ice-slopes on the southern side of Everest. When they reached Camp 6, Smythe and Shipton, who were to form the second assault-party, were already in possession. Harris and Wager passed on the information they had gained and then descended towards the North Col. When he reached a short, hump-backed ice-slope, Harris, forgetting his exhausted condition, attempted a *glissade*. A moment later, to his horror, he found himself gliding with rapid acceleration not towards the North Col, but towards a great precipice which overlooks the East Rongbuk glacier. He promptly turned over on his face and slowly twisted the pick of his ice-axe against the hard snow, until it was making a deep groove and acting as a brake. If he had executed this difficult manœuvre too quickly the axe would undoubtedly have been torn from his grasp, and then nothing could have saved him. As it was he came to rest on the very brink of the precipice, and then slowly, much shaken, he traversed to a place where Wager could help him. It had been a close shave.

A little lower down Harris had the unenviable task of escorting one of the 'tigers' who had carried loads to Camp 6, and who was so exhausted by the return-trip that for the time being his wits were bewildered, and he volubly argued that he was in fact a corpse! So convinced had he become of his recent decease that he refused to move until 'friendly compulsion' was applied in the rear. However, a few days' rest at lower levels soon proved to the eccentric old 'tiger' that he was in truth still alive—even though it were by a miracle.

Meanwhile Smythe and Shipton were making the second assault. For two nights and a day they had been blizzard-bound on their tiny sloping ledge. Then at 6.30 on the next morning they donned their numerous pairs of pull-overs, pants, stockings, and so on, and then struggled into their boots, which were frozen like solid rocks. At last all was ready, and they began the traverse. Far away, over a maze of jagged, saw-like peaks, they caught a glimpse of the towering, dun-coloured, monsoon clouds drenching the distant foothills. Shipton soon complained of stomach-trouble, and when they had passed beneath the first 'step,' he announced that he would not be able to go any farther. This was a bitter disappointment, since it was almost certain that Smythe could not reach the summit alone. Nevertheless, having seen Shipton safely started on the return-journey to camp, Smythe went on.

Having reached the great couloir he could see what he thought to be a reasonably clear route to the summit. The actual crossing of the couloir proved to be a difficult task. To enter it he first of all tried traversing along a ledge; soon the ledge began to narrow until he was only able to move along by edging sideways and clinging with outstretched arms to small bumps on the face of the cliff. Having reached a spot where an extra deep breath would have been enough to topple him off into the icy maw of the Rongbuk glacier, he decided to try another route. He found a wider snow-covered ledge, and soon reached the couloir. Here he had to cut about a dozen steps, and finally he won through to the other side.

His aim now was the subsidiary couloir, which joins the great couloir lower down the mountain, and which creates a breach in the last defences on to the face of the final pyramid. But now he found the climbing both dangerous and difficult. Newly fallen snow had filled every little hollow, and it was loose, powdery snow of the most treacherous kind. It was like climbing over a house-roof covered with snow, into which the climber sank sometimes to his thighs. An hour's hard labour earned a gain in height of fifty feet. By this time Smythe had reached approximately the same place as Harris and Wager had done, and when he had a lucky escape from falling headlong, he decided that he had reached his limit. Lack of time and the newly fallen snow had cheated him of a brilliant solo victory.

Smythe found an easier route back to Camp 6, although this involved traversing a few feet above a steep precipice. In spite of the freezing temperature Smythe dared to take off his gloves and took some photographs. Then he suddenly saw, through the mist, the camp; there he found Shipton safe, and feeling much better. Shipton soon set off for the next camp, while Smythe elected to spend another night on the ledge, as he was feeling tired. The next morning, after a sound sleep, he found it calmer and began his descent. He found that in places the slabs—dangerous enough at the best of times—were now thinly plastered with ice. With extreme caution he made his way downward and had just reached a patch of broken rocks when a sudden, violent gust almost blew him from his feet. In half a minute a terrific storm was lashing snow into his face with such venom that he was reduced to crawling along on hands and knees. Slowly he felt his limbs grow numb with the deadly frost-biting chill. Then luckily he found a sheltered spot on the lee-side of a ridge. He restored the circulation to his half-frozen legs, and after a short rest, was able to continue. Presently he saw two figures below him, and soon he reached Camp 4 and safety.

By this time most of the climbers were suffering from exhaustion and frost-bites, so a general retreat to the base-camp was ordered. They still hoped that it would be possible to return to the attack, but for the rest of the month, snow fell heavily on the mountain. It was all too clear that the monsoon had broken, and although during a lull Camp 3 was re-established, conditions above that point were so frightful that on June 21 the glacier-camps were finally evacuated, and preparations were begun for the long homeward march. Once again the ice-demons had driven the white men from the 'abode of snows.'

THE EVEREST FLIGHT

While preparations for a fourth Mount-Everest expedition were being made, the news was announced that an attempt was to be made to fly over the summit and take photographs. Air-commodore Fellowes was in command, the Marquess of

APPROACHING EVEREST AND MAKAHI FROM THE SOUTH

By courtesy of Colonel P. T. Etherton, Houston Mount Everest Flight   274

Clydesdale was chief pilot, and Colonel Blacker was to be in charge of the photography. With some difficulty the airmen obtained permission to fly over Nepal, but were ordered not to trespass over the border into Tibet.

Reconnaissance flights in a Puss Moth showed that the main flight would be exceedingly difficult. Quite apart from the difficulty of making a heavy Westland aeroplane rise to a height of over 30,000 feet, there was the grave danger from those sudden storms and violent hurricanes, which have been such an enemy to the climbing parties. It was also necessary, of course, to carry much apparatus to keep the pilots warm in such high altitudes. On a test-flight the two Westlands climbed to a height of 34,000 feet, and on April 3, 1933, two 'planes set off from Purnea on a trial trip. They flew direct for the summit, and at 19,000 feet, Mount Everest was sighted above the haze. An hour after starting, the two 'planes flew over Chamlang, at 31,000 feet; and then, when above the south peak of Everest, a dangerous down-current reduced their altitude by 1500 feet. They had only just made good this loss when the actual summit of the mountain was reached, and the aeroplanes only cleared the pyramid by a few hundred feet.

Then, strangely enough, they found better flying-conditions, and were able to circle round for fifteen minutes, taking close-range photographs at all angles. The heated clothing and the oxygen-apparatus worked so well that the photographers were able to stand up in the open for several minutes at a time. The return-flight to the aerodrome was accomplished without accident. Later a second flight was made, and further photographs were obtained. Several regions in the immediate vicinity of Mount Everest were thus added to the surveyed parts of the Himalayas, and among the interesting discoveries was a small lake high up among the highest peaks in the world.

THE 1936 EXPEDITION

In the spring of 1935 the Mount Everest Committee were given permission to launch another attempt on the mountain, and since the season was rather late, it was decided to send Eric Shipton on a reconnaissance expedition, as a preliminary to the full expedition which was to leave England in 1936. This reconnaissance party was to collect information about conditions during the monsoon-period, to try out alternative routes along the Central Rongbuk glacier and along the Western Cwm, and to investigate conditions on the North Col. A great deal of valuable information about the mountains near Mount Everest was collected, and in the course of the expedition no less than twenty-six peaks of over 20,000 feet were climbed, which was in itself a record for the Himalayas. Shipton took with him some of the famous 'tigers' who had been with him on Nanda Devi and on Everest. They found the mountain covered with monsoon snow, and when they began to climb up the East Rongbuk glacier towards the North Col, they came across the body of Maurice Wilson, who had made a journey to Everest in 1934 unaccompanied by any Europeans. Wilson had made repeated attempts to climb the North Col, but had apparently died of exposure and exhaustion.

The North Col had changed a great deal since 1933, and the old ice-wall was now a tottering jumble of seracs. A tongue of ice gave them a fairly easy route to the top of the Col, and a few days later they had established a camp at the foot of the north-east ridge. The weather was bad, and after a few days' observation it was decided to return to the glacier. They had not gone far when they made an alarming discovery. They suddenly encountered an appalling cut-off, which stretched for hundreds of yards. There had evidently been a catastrophic avalanche along the line of their ascent, and thousands of tons of ice and snow had peeled off the slope to a depth of six feet. The situation was very disturbing. They had apparently had a narrow escape from utter destruction during the ascent. After some debate it was decided to continue downward, since the avalanche must have left a temporary line of strength, which it would be safe to follow. So they safely reached the lower camps, fully convinced that to attempt a climb on Everest during the monsoon-period would be nothing short of suicide.

276

The main expedition, under Hugh Ruttledge, reached the base-camp near Rongbuk monastery towards the end of April, 1936. The mountain seemed to be in perfect condition, because although the usual wind-plume writhed away from the final pyramid, there was little snow on the ridges, and even the great couloir reached in 1933 was almost empty. This time the wireless installations had been much improved, and the expedition was kept well informed of weather-changes. This was particularly fortunate, since the weather proved to be abnormally bad. Indeed, on April 30, a sudden fall of snow covered Everest with a white blanket, and in the days which followed, there were many more snow-falls.

Nevertheless, at this early date nobody expected that monsoon-conditions would interfere with the climbing, and so the work of establishing glacier-camps went on. Camp 3 was set up near the foot of the North Col, and then began the task of transporting tents and baggage up this steep slope. A long traverse had to be made to turn a high wall of ice, and this involved a great deal of step-cutting. The weather still continued to be bad, and it was obviously now quite impossible to tackle the slabs above Camp 4. Eventually, when the top of the col was two feet deep in snow, it was decided to retreat. The long downward traverse provided some anxious moments, since there was always a chance of a disastrous avalanche.

On May 20 the whole expedition had returned for a rest to Camp 1, and there they received the unwelcome news that weather-conditions were becoming favourable for the advance of the monsoon. Four days later came news of rain at Darjeeling. Still the climbers hoped that this was only the preliminary canter of the rains, and that a period of fair weather would intervene. Therefore they returned to Camp 3, but soon found that the monsoon had really broken. There were heavy falls of snow, and once again they had to retreat. So it went on. A promising north-west wind would blow away some of the snow, and hurried preparations would be made for renewing the assault. Then down came the snow again, and Everest looked at its worst.

On June 4 a party of climbers went as far as the lower

slopes of the North Col, and reported that much of the snow had gone. Early on the next day an advance was made, two men taking it in turns to cut steps. They soon found that the snow was in bad condition and not to be trusted. In fact, after an hour's work they found themselves among the *débris* of an avalanche, which had fallen only a few days before. Nevertheless, led by Smythe and Shipton, they attempted to force a passage, and only gave up when they found they had to dig through nine inches of snow before they could cut steps in the ice. Then a dangerous warm wind sprang up, and they had to retreat, each man moving alone at hundred-yard intervals.

The next morning there was a gale blowing, and Wyn Harris and Shipton asked that they should be allowed to go up and see what effect this was having on the slopes. The two men climbed quickly through the drifting snow until they came to a crevasse at the beginning of a traverse. They were roped together, and Shipton was leading, about thirty feet ahead of Harris. Suddenly there was a horrid crunching sound, and the slope split across some 200 feet above them. Gradually tons of snow and ice began to slip downward, towards a 400-foot precipice just below. Shipton was promptly enveloped, and was carried down with only his head free. Wyn Harris happened to be close to the edge of of the avalanche, and with a great effort he stuck his ice-axe into some hard snow and whipped the rope round it. Soon, he, too, was being buffetted by ice-blocks; nevertheless, he bore down on his ice-axe and hung on. By a miracle the Alpine rope, with Shipton dangling on the end, was not cut by the ice; then quite suddenly the avalanche slowed down and stopped on the very brink of the precipice. Slowly the two men made their way back to the steps and so reached safety.

This was the last straw. Evidently Everest would defy any attempt at climbing that year. The whole expedition returned to Camp 1, and then decided to make a prospecting-trip up the main Rongbuk glacier to see if the North Col could be approached from that side. At least they might be able to gather some information, which would be useful

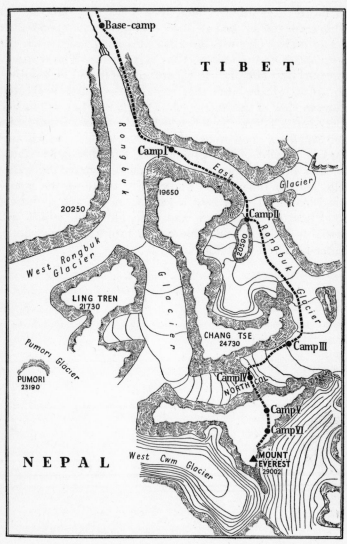

Base-camp

TIBET

Rongbuk Glacier

CampI

East Glacier

19650

20250

CampII

Rongbuk Glacier

20590

West Rongbuk Glacier

Glacier

LING TREN
21730

CHANG TSE
24730

CampIII

Pumori Glacier

PUMORI
23190

CampIV

NORTH COL

CampV

CampVI

MOUNT
EVEREST
29002

NEPAL

West Cwm Glacier

SKETCH-PLAN SHOWING THE ROUTE FOLLOWED BY THE EVEREST
EXPEDITIONS OF 1924 AND 1933

to future expeditions. Soon they were travelling up the wide main glacier, and at 18,000 feet they came upon a little grassy oasis. This was indeed a pleasant change from the grim seracs and moraines of the side-glacier. The weather-forecasts were still persistently unfavourable, but they pushed on up the glacier until they rounded the North Peak, and came in view of the North Col. They found that on this side there was a falling glacier, which did not look formidable, and finally a snow-slope of about 1000 feet, which was flanked by ribs of rock promising a fair alternative route. Further investigations were once more hindered by snow-falls, and by June 18 the whole party set off on the home-ward march. It had been a gallant failure, and at least a good deal of information had been garnered, which will probably be of considerable use to future, and, we hope, better-favoured expeditions.

INDEX

The following abbreviations have been used; c. = cape; g. = glacier; i. = island; l. = lake; mt. = mountain; mts. = mountain range; r. = river.

Abdulla, 180–182
Abruzzi, Duke of the, 84, 89, 171–175
Abu Ballas, 188–189
Abuna r., 14, 15
Acacias, 189
Adams, 129–132
Adare c., 129, 205
Aga Khan, 71
Alabama, 221, 223–224
'Aladdin's Cave,' 135, 137
Alamut, 71
Alaska, 252, 253
Alexandra Peak, 174
Alice Springs, 122, 125, 126, 127
Almásy, Ladislaus de, 186–191
Aloique, 23–27
Amadeus l., 125
Amazon r., 13–41
Amboina, 109
Amundsen, Roald, 92–98, 128, 139, 192–199, 201, 202, 203, 206, 207, 212, 214, 225–226, 246–251
Anauqua tribe, 22–27, 29
Andeason, 254
Anderson, Dr, 253–254, 257
Andes r., 13, 35, 41
Angmagssalik, 228, 229, 236
Angtharkay, 158–169
Antelope Plain, 58, 59, 60
Ariare r., 35
Arkenu, 184
Aru mts., 61
Aru Tso l., 61
Astillero, 17
Atkinson, 202
Aujela, 179
Aurora, 134, 138, 140, 150, 151
Austin, 84
Axel Heiberg g., 196, 210, 212, 213

Badrinath, 165
Baffin i., 228
Bagini g., 164
Bailey, 63
Bakairi, 20, 21, 22
Bakari tribe, 21
Baker mt., 173

Bakonjo tribe, 172, 173–174
Banaiyan, 77
Banks i., 252, 255, 256, 257, 258, 262
Bank's Land, 250
Barrow Point, 238, 240, 241, 243, 252, 253
Bartlett, Captain, 88, 89, 91, 253, 259, 260
Bass Rock, 224
Bauer, 40
Bay of Whales, 192, 193, 201, 207, 214, 217, 218
Beardmore g., 151, 193, 202, 203
Beaufort Sea, 252, 253
Bedouins, 5, 73–76, 175–185
Beechey Point, 241
Beechy i., 247
Bell, 104–108
Benghazi, 176, 177, 178
Bennett, Floyd, 100–102
Bermann, Dr, 188, 190
Bernadino, 21, 22
Bernard, Captain, 257, 258
Bernard i., 257
Berthelot i., 138
Bingham, 229, 231
Birnie, Captain, 152, 156, 267, 269
Bjaaland, 195
Blacker, Colonel, 275
Bluff Depôt, 131, 151
Boothia, 101
Borden i., 258, 262
Borup, 87, 89
Bowers, 203–204
Brahmaputra r., 42, 47, 50, 63, 64–65
Brock i., 258, 262
Brocklebank, T. A., 268
Bronlund, Jorgen, 221
Brooks, 126
Broome, 123, 125
Bruce, General, 265
Buseima, 177, 180, 181
Byrd, Commander R. E., 97, 98–102, 128, 206–218

Caird Coast, 140–141
Cairo, 188
Calamar, 38

Campbell, Commander, 205–206
Cannibals, 115–121
Carmen Land, 199
Carstensz Top, 109, 115
Caspian Sea, 70, 72
Cathay, 42, 52–56, 84
'Cathedral Grotto,' 135
Caupolican, 13, 16–19
Chala pass, 71
Chamlang, 275
Champion, 121
Changchenmo r., 57
Chang-Tang, 48
Chapman, 231, 236, 237
Charchan, 54
Charcot, Jean, 138–139
Charcot Land, 138
Chavez, 13
Chelasky c., 226
Chelyuskin, c., 225
Chiang-ssu-yeh, 53
Chunchos, 19
Clarence i., 144, 145
Clayton, P. A., 6, 186, 188, 189, 190
Clydesdale, Marquess of, 274–275
Coats Land, 140
Collinson Point, 253
Columbia c., 86, 91
Colville r., 252
Commonwealth Bay, 134, 137
Congo r., 30
Coniston, 126
Continental Shelf, 88
Cordillera mts., 17
Corumba, 15
Courtauld, 231, 232–233, 234
Courteville, 21
Crean, 146, 148, 203–206
Crozier c., 200
Cuyaba, 20, 21, 28
Cyrenaica, 177

D'AETH, 229, 231
Dainelli, 6
Dalrymple Rock, 247
Dangrayum l., 50
Danmark's Fjord, 220, 221
Danmark's Harbour, 220, 221, 223
Darfur, 184, 185
Darjeeling, 265, 268, 277
David, Professor, 132–133
Dead-horse Camp, 20, 21
Deasy, 56, 58, 59
Deasy mts., 59
De Ganahl, 208
'Devil's Ballroom,' 197, 198
'Devil's Glacier,' 197
Dhahiya, 76

Dhaoli r., 152, 159
Dhufar, 73, 74, 80
Dietrichson, 94, 97
Discovery, 129, 201
Doha, 76, 77
Dongtse, 63
'Drinking-water of the Giants' l., 61
Drygalski g., 132, 133
Durashi, 159
Duvida—see River of Doubt
Dyott, Commander, 21–28

EAGLE CITY, 251
East Kamet g., 153
East Rongbuk g., 264, 265, 272, 276
Edge i., 227
Edsel Ford mts., 213, 217, 218
Eielson, Carl, 238–246
Elburz mts., 70
El Dorado, 13, 28, 72
Elephant i., 144, 145, 148, 149
Ellesmere Land, 6, 98
Ellsworth Lincoln, 92–96, 218–219
Endurance, 139–151
Ennedi, 185
Erdi, 185
Erebus mt., 129, 201
Erichsen, Mylius, 220–223
Eskimos, 85–91, 220, 221, 228, 229,
    232, 233–234, 235, 249, 250, 252,
    254–255, 262
Etah, 85–86
Etherton, Colonel P. T., 6
Evans c., 200, 206
Evans, E. G. R., 200, 203–206
Everest mt., 42, 65, 158, 228, 263–280

FAIRBANKS, 238, 239, 245
Farewell c., 235
Farig, 179
Fawcett, Colonel, 13–30
Fawcett, Jack, 20
Fellowes, Air-commodore, 274
Finch, 265
Findlay i., 262
Fjord l., 229, 236
Fleming, Peter, 28
Fly r., 106
Forbes, Rosita, 6, 175–183
Forel mt., 233, 235
Fort Bakairi, 20, 21, 22
Fram, 192, 193, 199
'Framheim,' 193, 194, 199, 207
Franklin, 84
Franz Josef Land, 102, 171

GANGES R., 152, 156, 165
Gangotri g., 165

INDEX

Garhwal Himalaya mts., 156
Gartok, 63–66
Gartok Plain, 65–66
Garua r., 68
Gaumukh, 165
Geographical Journal, 14–15, 19, 75
Gessi mt., 173
Gilf Kebir, 186–191
Gjöa, 247–251
Gjöahavn, 247, 249
Gobi Desert, 42, 45, 55
Godhavn, 247
Godman mt., 115
Goodsell, Dr, 87
Grace McKinley mt., 217
Graham, W. W., 157–158
Graham Land, 138, 218
Grand Paititi—*see* El Dorado
Grant Land, 84, 86, 91, 243
Great Barrier, 129, 142, 207
Great Wall of China, 42
Greene, 152, 156
Greely, 84
Guarayo tribe, 16, 17–18
Gy-Parana, 31, 32

Hadley, 260
Hagen mt., 118, 119, 121
Hamilton r., 227
Hansen, 249–251
Hanssen, 195
Hargreaves, Lieutenant, 56–63
Harris, Wyn, 267, 269–272, 273, 278
Hassanein Bey, 176–185, 186
Hassel, 195
Hathi Parbat g., 164
Hawari, 177, 181
Hayward, 151
Hearst Land, 219
Heath r., 16–19
Hedin, Sven, 42–52, 53, 54
Heiberg g., 198
Heimen, 227
Helland Hansen mts., 197
Henson, 87, 89, 90
Herschel i., 252
Hides, J. G., 121
Himalaya mts., 42, 152–169, 263–280
Holdsworth, 152, 155
Hollick-Kenyon, 218–219
Holsteinborg, 233
Hopedale, 228
Hope mt., 202
Horlick mts., 218
Hsuan-Tsang, 53
Hudson Bay, 228
Humphreys, Dr Noel G., 6, 175
Huntington, Ellsworth, 53

Husainabad, 69, 70
Husvik, 148

Icana R., 37, 40
Incas, 14, 26
Indus r., 42, 51, 65
Inirida, r., 37, 40
Irvine, 266–267, 271
Italia, 97
Iversen, 221–224
Ivigtut, 233
Ivy Leases, 126
Iwaka r., 113

Jabrin, 78
'Jackies,' 123, 125
Jacob Rupert, 214–215
Jaghabub, 183
Jalo, 177, 180
James Caird, 146–147
Jedabia, 178
Jof, 181
Jones, Winton, 29
Josephine Ford, 98–102
Joshimath, 165, 169
Joyce, 151
Julio, 34
June, 211–213

Kailas Parbat Mt., 50–51, 65
Kalapalos tribe, 25, 26, 27
Kamet mt., 152–156, 164, 267
Kanakas, 117
Kanchenjunga mt., 267
Kaparé r., 110, 111, 112
Karakoram mts., 47, 155; Pass, 51
Karius, 121
Karluk, 252–253, 254, 257, 259, 262
Kash r., 53–54
Kashgar, 42, 53
Kashmir, 56
Kasim, 43–44
Kebir Kuh, 67, 68
Kedarnath, 166
Kenya mt., 268
Kerhane, 202
Kerim, Abdul, 51–52
Kesar Singh, 156
Khalik, Abdul, 56–63
Khotan, 54
Khotan Daria r., 44
Kiang Plain, 58
Kikor r., 104, 108
King and Winge, 261
King Christian Land, 262
King Edward VII Land, 129, 193, 195, 207
King George V Land, 135

King Haakon Bay, 147, 149
King Point, 250
King William Land, 247
Kirghiz, 5, 43
Kisumu, 171
Kleist, Baron, 260
Koch, Captain, 220, 221
Kubla Khan, 42
Kubor mt., 119
Kufara, 176, 177, 178, 181, 182, 183, 184, 185, 188, 189
Kuikuru tribe, 29
Kukukuka tribe, 118
Kuluene r., 23, 24, 25, 26, 27, 29
Kuluseu r., 21, 22, 24, 27
Kun Lun mts., 56
Kusang, 158–169

LAE, 118
Lander Creek, 126, 127
Lane, Captain, 259
La Paz, 17, 19
Larti, 69
Lashly, 203–206
Leahy, Michael, 115–121
Leahy, Patrick, 118–119
Leh, 47, 56, 60, 62
Lewa, 152, 154, 156
Lhasa, 42, 46, 47, 49
Lhatse, 64
Lindsay, Martin, 6
'Little America,' 206–219
Liv's g., 212
Longland, 270
Longstaff, Dr, 6, 158
Lougheed i., 262
Loulan, 45, 54
Luigi di Savoia mt., 173
Luitpold Land, 141
Luristan, 66–70

MABRUK, 179
Macaya r., 38
Mackay, 122, 132–133
Mackenzie r., 253
Mackintosh, Captain, 140, 150–151
Macmillan, 87, 88
Macquarie i., 134
Madeira r., 32, 35
Madre de Dios r., 17
Malaysia r., 30
Mallory, 265–267
Manasarovar l., 50, 52, 65
Marie Byrd Land, 213, 217, 219
Markham, 84
Markham r., 118
Marshall, 129–132
Marvin, 87, 88, 89, 91

Mary Sachs, 252, 253, 257, 258
Matto Grosso, 16, 20, 28
Maud, 225, 226
Mawson, Dr Douglas, 128, 132–138
Mazanderan, 72
McCarthy, 146
McCarthy, Patrol-officer, 118
McClintock, 258
McClure, 84
McKenna, Captain James, 250
McKinley, 212, 213
McMurdo Sound, 132, 139, 150, 151, 192
McNeish, 146, 147
Meigren i., 262
Melville Bay, 247
Melville i., 252, 258, 262
Mertz, 135–136, 137
Mikkelsen, Captain Einar, 221–224
Milam g., 164
Mimika r., 109, 110, 113
Miran, 55
Mobi r., 105
Mobuko g., 173
Mobuko r., 171
Mohammed, 178–182
Montana, 251
Morcegos, 14
Morton, 126
'Mountains of the Moon,' 5, 170–175
Mount Everest Committee, 6, 275
Mugshin, 75
Murra tribe, 76–77
Murray mt., 104
Muscat, 74
Mustaghata, 5

NANDA DEVI MT., 152, 156–169, 276
Nansen, 84, 225, 254
Nansen mt., 196, 212
Nan-Shan mts., 56
Nares, 84
New Siberian Islands, 226
Nias, 110
Nimrod, 129, 132, 133
Ninnis, 135–136
Niti, 152
Nobile, Colonel, 96–97, 98
Nome, 226, 251, 252, 262
Norge, 96–97, 98
Northern Star, 257
North-west passage, 246–251
Norton, 265–267
Nunatak, Scott's, 208

'OASIS OF THE SIRENS,' 5
Oates, Captain, 128, 203–204
Odell, 267, 271

INDEX

Omdal, 94
Ophir, 72–77, 78
Orinoco r., 36, 37

PAISHON, 34
Pamir mts., 53
Papanin expedition, 102
Papua, 104, 117, 118
Paracis Plateau, 32
Passang, 158–169
Paulet i., 142
Peary, Robert, 84–91, 192, 244, 254
Peary Land, 222
Pedro Christopherson mt., 196
Penderel, Squadron-leader, 188–189, 190
Pennell, 201
Pessione, Signor, 28
Petermann i., 139
Philby, H. St John, 77–83
Pigmies, 15, 111–112
'Pisgah,' 160, 162
Pizarro, 13
Polar Bear, 258–259
Polo, Marco, 42, 54
Ponting, 200
Port Moresby, 117
Possession Bay, 148
Poulter, Dr, 216–217
Pourquoi-Pas ? 138–139
Pratt, 104–108
Prestrud, 208
Prince Patrick i., 258
Purari r., 116, 117, 121
Pusht-I-Kuh mts., 67, 68, 70

QAZVIN, 71
Queen Maud mts., 212, 218
Quest, 229

RAHIM, ABDUL, 178
Raikana g., 153
Ram Singh, 57–63
Ramu r., 119
Ranikhet, 152, 158
Rashidi tribe, 74
Rasmussen, 6
Rattin, Stephen, 28
Raumuli r., 175
Rawling, Captain, 56–66, 109–115
Rhamani r., 160
Ribiana, 177
Rice, Dr Hamilton, 35–41
Richards, 151
Riley, 236
Rimell, Raleigh, 20
Ringnes Islands, 262

Rio Branco, 41
Rio Kermit, 34
Rio Negro, 35, 36, 37, 41
Rio Roosevelt—see River of Doubt
Rio Verde, 15–16
Rishi Ganga r., 157, 158, 159, 161, 164, 165, 166, 169
Rishi Nala r., 159
Ristvedt, 248
Risut, 74
River of Doubt, 30–35
River of Tapirs, 31
Riyadh, 77
Rockefeller mts., 208, 209, 213
Rohlfs, 176
Rondon, Colonel, 13, 31–35
Rongbuk g., 153, 266, 273, 276, 278
Rongbuk monastery, 263, 266, 268, 277
Roosevelt, 84, 86, 89, 91
Roosevelt i., 84, 86, 89, 91
Roosevelt, Kermit, 31–35
Roosevelt, Theodore, 30, 31–35
Ross, 84
Ross Barrier, 192
Ross Sea, 128, 129, 132, 134, 139, 150, 199, 207, 208, 210, 218, 228
Roth, 208
Royal Geographical Society, 6, 14, 20, 66, 109, 121, 227, 263
Rub' al Khali Desert, 72–83, 123
Rudok, 61, 62
Ruth Gade mt., 212
Ruttledge, Hugh, 267, 277
Ruwenzori, 170–175
Ryder, 63–66
Rymill, 236, 237

SA'AR TRIBE, 74–75
Sachu-Tsangpo r., 46
Sahara Desert, 5, 6, 123, 175–183
Sahma Plain, 82
Salamaua, 116
'Sanderson his Hope,' 84
São Joaquin, 36
São Manoel, 28
Sarikol, 53
Satopanth g., 166
Sayed Idris, 183
Scott, Captain, 6, 87, 128–129, 139, 140, 151, 192, 193, 199–204, 205, 208
Scott, J. M., 6, 227, 229–231, 232
Scott Land, 209
Senussi, 175–185
Sepik r., 120, 121
Shackleton, Sir Ernest, 128, 129–132, 133, 139–151, 192, 198, 203

Shaikh Salih, 74, 76
Shannon, 76
Shannon i., 221, 223
Shemen Tso l., 58
Sheridan c., 86, 91
Shigatse, 48, 49, 63–65
Shipton, Eric, 152, 158–169, 267, 268–269, 272–274, 276, 278
Simla, 66
Simpson Strait, 250
Sin-Kiang, 42
Siwa, 183
Smith, Staniforth, 103–109
Smythe, F. S., 6, 152–155, 267, 268–269, 272–274, 278
Snegamook, 228
Sollum, 183
'Solomon's Throne,' 70, 71
Somervell, 265–267
Soomjeling Plain, 57
South Victoria Land, 196
Speke mt., 173
Spencer-Smith, 151
Spitsbergen, 84, 92, 96, 97, 98, 101, 102, 238, 243, 244, 245, 246
Srinagar, 47
Stanley, Henry, 170, 171
Stanley mt., 173, 174
Stark, Freya, 66–72
Stefansson, Vilhjalmur, 251–262
Stein, Aurel, 52–56
St Elias mt., 171
Storkerson, 254, 255
St Petersburg, 259
Strickland r., 106
Sudan Desert, 184
Sulaiyil, 72, 80, 82, 83
Sutlej r., 52, 66
Suyá tribe, 23, 24, 26, 29
Sverdrup, Dr, 226

Taiserbo, 177, 180
Tai Tso, 62
Taj, 182
Takla-Makan Desert, 42, 43–44, 53
Tambopata r., 19
Tanami, 125, 126
Tarim r., 43, 45
Tashi-lhumpo monastery, 47, 48, 49
Tehran, 70
Terra Nova, 193, 199–200, 205
Terry, Michael, 122–127
Thomas, Bertram, 73–77, 80
Thorne g., 217
Thorne, Robert, 84
Thorvald Nilsen mt., 197
Tilman, H. W., 158–169

Tilmouth, 126–127
Tinkye Dzong, 268
Titicaca l., 17
Todd, 18
Tooling, 66
Trans-Himalaya mts., 48, 50, 52
Tsangpo r.—see Brahmaputra r.
Tua r.—see Purari r.
Tun-Huang, 62
Turkestan, 45, 53

Uaupes R., 35, 36–37
Ubar, 76, 78–80
Uganda, 171, 172
Upper Paraguay r., 31
Upper Watut r., 118
Utakwa r., 109
'Uweinat, 177, 184–185, 186, 190

'Valley of a Myriad Buddhas,' 56
'Valleys of the Assassins,' 70, 71
Victoria i., 262
Victoria l., 171, 175
Vincent, 146, 147

Wabar—see Ubar
Wager, 231, 269–272, 273
Wahgi r., 119–120
Wainwright, 97
Wakatimi, 110
Watkins, Gino, 226–237
Wegener, 6
Wellby, 56
Weston, S., 123
Wicuru tribe, 26–28
Wild, 129–132, 143, 149–151
Wilkins, George, 238–246
Wilkins, Sir Hubert, 218
Wilson, Dr, 203–204
Wilson, Maurice, 276
Winton, 123
Wisting, 195, 225–226
Wood, 63
Wollaston Land, 250
Worsley, 146, 148
Wrangel i., 259, 260
Wyatt Earp, 218–219
'Wyckham's Claim,' 125–126

Yanaidar, 5
Yarkand, 42
Yusuf, 178–181

Zeighen, 177
Zerzura, 185–191
Ziqirt, 80
Zouias, 177, 181